Singapore

city guide

Peter Turner

Tony Wheeler

Singapore – city guide
2nd edition

Published by
   Lonely Planet Publications
   Head Office: PO Box 617, Hawthorn, Vic 3122, Australia
   Branches: PO Box 2001A, Berkeley, CA 94702, USA
                 12 Barley Mow Passage, Chiswick,
                 London W4 4PH, UK
                 71 bis rue du Cardinal Lemoine,
                 75005 Paris, France

Printed by
   Colorcraft Ltd, Hong Kong

Photographs by
   Joe Cummings (JC), Mark Fraser (MF), Charlotte Hindle (CH),
   Jurong Bird Park (BP), Richard Nebesky (RN), Raffles Hotel (RH),
   Arasu Ramasamy (AR), Singapore Tourist Promotion Board (STPB),
   Chris Taylor (CT), Peter Turner (PT), Tony Wheeler (TW)

   Front cover: Sin Chinese Opera (Scoopix, Phillip Little)
   Front gatefold: Top: Central Singapore (PT),
   Bottom Left: Chettiar Hindu Temple (PT),
   Bottom Right: Vanda Jochim, National Flower (AR)
   Back cover: Fans, Chinatown (CT)
   Back gatefold: Top: National Museum & Art Gallery (TW),
   Middle: Hotel Lobby (PT), Bottom Left: Jurong Bird Park (AR),
   Bottom Right: Mask Seller (RN)

First Published
   June 1991

This Edition
   March 1994

Although the authors and publisher have tried to make the information as accurate as possible, they accept no responsibility for any loss, injury or inconvenience sustained by any person using this book.

National Library of Australia Cataloguing in Publication Data

Turner, Peter.
   Singapore city guide.

   2nd ed.
   Includes index.
   ISBN 0 86442 210 5.
   1. Singapore – Guidebooks. I. Wheeler, Tony, 1946- II. Title.
   (Series: Lonely Planet city guide).

   915.957045

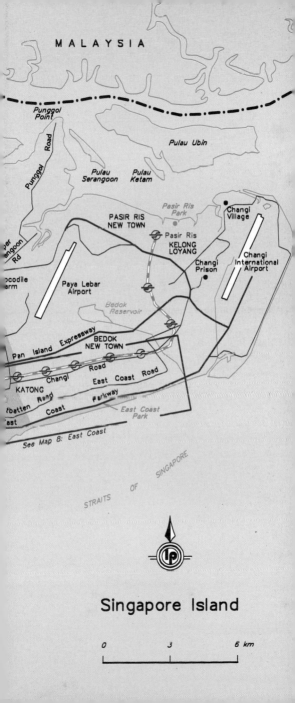

Peter Turner

Peter was born in Melbourne and studied Asian studies, politics and English at university before setting off on the Asian trail. His long-held interest in South-East Asia has seen him make numerous trips to the region, and he has also travelled further afield in Asia, the Pacific, North America and Europe. He worked with Lonely Planet as an editor from 1986 to 1993, when he became a full-time writer. Peter has also worked on Lonely Planet's guides to Malaysia, Singapore & Brunei, Indonesia, South-East Asia and Australia.

Tony Wheeler

Tony was born in England but grew up in Pakistan, the Bahamas and the USA. He returned to England to do a degree in engineering at Warwick University, worked as an automotive design engineer, returned to university to complete an MBA in London, then dropped out on the Asian overland trail with his wife Maureen. Eventually settling down in Australia, they've been travelling, writing and publishing guidebooks ever since, having set up Lonely Planet Publications in the mid-1970s. Travel for the Wheelers is considerably enlivened by their daughter Tashi and their son Kieran.

From the Author

Many Singaporeans went out of their way to provide their time, assistance and information to help enhance this book. Special thanks must go to the Singaporean Tourism Promotion Board, particularly Suzanne Parker and Lalita Kasinatan in Sydney, and in Singapore, Wong Seng Kit and Faizah Hanim Ahmad, who shared her expertise and extensive knowledge of Singapore. Thanks also to Bob and Alice for insights into living in Singapore and for some great dining recommendations, and to Hugh Finlay, colleague and nightclub hound, who proved that it is possible to party until dawn in Singapore.

From the Publisher

This edition of *Singapore – city guide* was edited by Katie Cody and Frith Pike and proofed by Vyvyan Cayley, Tom Smallman and Caroline Williamson. Chris Klep was responsible for the mapping, photograph selection and the overall design of the book.

Thanks also go to: Margaret Jung for the front cover, and Louise Keppie for artistic assistance; Sally Woodward, Valerie Tellini and Vicki Beale for artistic suggestions and guidance; and Rowan McKinnon for doing the index.

This Book

This edition of *Singapore – city guide* was updated by Peter Turner, who was jointly responsible for the first edition with Tony Wheeler.

Warning & Request

Things change – prices go up, schedules change, good places go bad and bad places go bankrupt – nothing stays the same. So if you find things better or worse, recently opened or long since closed, please write and tell us and help make the next edition better.

Your letters will be used to help update future editions and, where possible, important changes will also be included in a Stop Press section in reprints.

We greatly appreciate all information that is sent to us by travellers. Back at Lonely Planet we employ a hard-working readers' letters team to sort through the many letters we receive. The best ones will be rewarded with a free copy of the next edition or another Lonely Planet guide if you prefer. We give away lots of books, but unfortunately not every letter/postcard receives one.

Contents

PLACES TO STAY

PLACES TO EAT 178

ENTERTAINMENT 200

SHOPPING 208

EXCURSIONS 221

INDEX..239

MAPS 245

Introduction

Lying almost on the equator, Singapore is a prosperous city-state that has overcome its lack of natural resources to become one of the powerhouse economies of Asia. In less than 200 years, Singapore has been transformed from a swampy island into a modern industrial nation.

Modern Singapore is a city of concrete, glass, freeways and shopping centres. You can stay in fashionable Orchard Rd at a luxury hotel, eat Italian food, drink Californian wine, buy European designer-label clothes and never know you were in the East at all. But for those who wish to do a little exploring, Singapore offers a taste of the great Asian cultures in a small, easy-to-get-around package.

In the crowded streets of Chinatown, fortune tellers, calligraphers and temple worshippers are still a part of everyday Singapore. In Little India, you can buy the best sari material, freshly ground spices or a picture of your favourite Hindu god. In the small shops of Arab St, the cry of the imam can be heard from the nearby Sultan Mosque.

Singapore may no longer be the rough-and-ready port of rickshaws, opium dens, pearl luggers and pirates, but you can still recapture the colonial era with a gin sling under the flashing ceiling fans at Raffles Hotel. Many other fine reminders of Singapore's colonial past remain, despite Singapore's relentless development.

Perhaps Singapore's greatest treat is the variety and quality of its food. For only a dollar or two, you can have a bowl of steaming noodles, curry and rice, or delicious satay, all at the same food-stall table. Spend a little more, or a lot more, and Singapore has hundreds of restaurants serving the best of Chinese, Indian, Malay and European food.

Some visitors to Singapore see it as just another modern city specialising in instant tours and packaged delights, but a little independent exploration will still uncover enough glimpses of exotic Singapore to keep any visitor interested.

Facts about Singapore

HISTORY

Today, Singapore is one of the great modern city-states, yet in the 14th century Chinese traders described Singapore, or Temasek as it was then known, as a barren, pirate-infested island.

According to Malay legend, a Sumatran prince encountered a lion on Temasek and this good omen prompted him to found Singapura, or 'Lion City'. Although lions have never inhabited Singapore and there is little evidence of any early city, it was likely that Singapore was a small trading outpost of the powerful Sumatran Srivijaya Empire before it became a vassal state of the Javanese Majapahit Empire in the mid-13th century.

In the early 1390s, Parameswara, a prince from Palembang, threw off allegiance to the Majapahit Empire and fled to Temasek. Although Parameswara and his party were well received, they promptly murdered their host and used the island as a pirate base. In 1398, the Thais attacked Temasek, and Parameswara fled to Malacca (now called Melaka). It was a propitious move, for he went on to found one of the great trading ports of the East.

Singapore again became a quiet backwater, but during the 15th century in the nearby Straits of Malacca, the Portuguese and their cannons came to contest the Arab monopoly on the lucrative spice and China trades. The Portuguese seized Malacca in 1511 but their dominance was short-lived. The Dutch undermined their trade by founding Batavia (now Jakarta), allowing ships to use the Sunda Straits to Europe and to avoid the Straits of Malacca altogether. The Dutch then seized Malacca in 1641 and became the dominant European power in the region.

The Arrival of Raffles

The British became interested in the Straits of Malacca (now called Melaka) in the 18th century when the East India Company set out to establish a port to secure and protect its line of trade from China to the colonies in

India. In 1786, Captain Francis Light founded a settlement on Penang Island.

In 1795, Holland and her colonies were annexed by France. Britain, at war with the French, then seized all Dutch possessions in South-East Asia, including Malacca, which became the second of the Straits Settlements, and ruled them for the duration of the war.

Sir Stamford Raffles was lieutenant-governor of Java from 1811 to 1816. Raffles, a great believer in the British Empire's right to rule, was also an admirer and scholar of ways of the East. Although a far-sighted, progressive thinker, he proved to be an impractical and overzealous administrator. He was recalled to Britain in disgrace after heavy financial losses, but returned to the East in 1817 to become lieutenant-governor of Bencoolen, an insignificant British trading post in Sumatra.

With the end of the Napoleonic wars and the defeat of France, Britain returned Dutch territories. Raffles, fearing a resurgence of the Dutch trading monopoly, argued strongly for an increased British influence in the Straits of Malacca.

After petitioning the governor-general of India, Raffles set forth to establish a settlement in Riau with Colonel William Farquhar, the former Resident of Malacca. Farquhar had married a Malay woman and was well versed in local politics.

On 29 January 1819, Raffles landed on the island of Singapore. He reached agreement to found a settlement with the local ruler, the Temenggong, and with Sultan Hussein, a contender to the fragmented Malay court. Raffles promptly left Singapore to return to Bencoolen, leaving Farquhar as Resident.

The Dutch were furious at this incursion into their territory and the fledging colony lived under constant fear of attack, but the Dutch did not intervene. Farquhar quickly set about establishing a trading post. The port was declared free of tariffs and Farquhar used his influence to attract Malaccan traders.

Raffles briefly visited Singapore in May 1819 to find a thriving town, and by 1821 Singapore's population had grown to 5000, including 1000 Chinese. The Temenggong established his settlement on the Singapore River, while Sultan Hussein built his palace at Kampong Glam.

Raffles, who had little direct involvement in Singapore's early development, returned in 1822. After illness and the death of three of his children, Raffles was a broken man but the sight of his thriving colony revived his spirits. Raffles delayed his return to England and set about running Singapore.

Raffles' Statue (PT)

He moved the commercial district across the river to its present site and levelled a hill to form Raffles Place. The government area was allocated around Forbidden Hill (now Fort Canning Hill) and the east bank of the river. Chinatown was divided among the various Chinese groups, and Raffles himself moved to Forbidden Hill.

By the time Raffles left in 1823, he had laid the foundations of the city, but more importantly he had firmly established Singapore as a free port – something that Singapore traders have vehemently fought for ever since.

By 1824, the Temenggong and Sultan Hussein were living beyond their stipends and agreed to be bought out in one payment. Singapore and the surrounding islands were seceded to the British.

The Early Years

In 1826, Singapore became part of the Straits Settlements with Penang and Malacca, which had been swapped with the Dutch for Bencoolen. The Straits Settlements came under the authority of Calcutta, which allocated few funds to running these areas. While commerce boomed, the judiciary and bureaucracy were hopelessly underfunded and social services were nonexistent.

By all accounts, Singapore was a fetid, stinking, disease-ridden colony. Piracy remained a problem and was not eliminated until the 1870s. While merchants petitioned Calcutta for more services, at the same time they recoiled at any suggestion of increased taxes. Singapore's revenue was derived mostly from gambling, opium and *arak* (the local firewater).

Despite Singapore's problems, migrants came in their thousands. Singapore became the major port in the region, and its population – Bugis, Javanese, Arab, Indian and Chinese – reflected its trade. The Chinese, who were soon the largest group, were comprised mostly of immigrants from the southern provinces – Hokkien, Teochew, Cantonese and Hakka.

The hard-working, resourceful Chinese migrants formed guilds, but they also joined the Triad, a secret society dedicated to overthrowing the Manchu Dynasty in China. The Triad, and other secret societies, were responsible for much of Singapore's crime, yet, like the guilds and clan societies, they also provided the social framework that the government neglected. The societies provided housing and jobs, and settled disputes within the communities.

Singapore's trade went through boom and bust periods in the early days and depended on uncertain entrepôt trade. It was controlled by European trading houses, while the Chinese acted as intermediaries, dealing with Chinese and other Asian traders.

Early attempts at agriculture were a disaster and crops failed because of disease and poor soil. Gambier and pepper had some success, but the push to establish plantations in the island's interior exposed another threat – tigers.

Tigers killed many labourers and one village had to be abandoned. A tiger was even found in the well-to-do residential district of Orchard Rd, and this prompted the government to place a bounty on tigers. Tiger hunting became a fashionable pastime and many tigers were killed in the 1860s. The last tiger on Singapore was shot in 1904.

Laissez-faire Singapore continued to grow with little or no social, educational or medical services, but by the 1860s Calcutta began to provide more funds and many of Singapore's grand colonial buildings date from this period.

A Thriving Colony

On 1 April 1867, the Straits Settlements became a fully fledged crown colony, run from Singapore. Singapore was a key link in the chain of British ports, especially with the opening of the Suez Canal, and a full army regiment was stationed there.

Chinese migration continued and in the 1870s massive numbers came to Singapore. Many of the Chinese were now wealthy in their own right and owned trading houses. Indian migration had also increased steadily from the mid-19th century.

Trade with the Malay Peninsula had been going on for years, but Singaporean merchants pressed for a greater government presence to enforce contracts and control the autonomous sultanates. The government began to install British Residents and advisers on the peninsula.

Peninsular trade, most of which was exported through Singapore, grew dramatically at the end of the 19th century. Tin mines dotted Malaya and in 1877, rubber seeds, originally smuggled out of Brazil, were sent to Singapore. A year later, the pneumatic tyre was invented and the rubber trade boomed.

All the while, Singapore came to take on the appearance of a cosmopolitan city. Tennis was played on the Padang, and in the evening it was a favourite strolling ground for British gentlefolk. The manually drawn rickshaw was imported into Singapore during 1880, the first car arrived in 1896 and the main building of Raffles Hotel was opened in 1899.

The government also registered the Chinese organisations and attempted to control the secret societies. Opium addiction was rife and in an attempt to control it, the government manufactured and sold opium in 1910, which provided almost half of the government's revenue.

Singapore was also a centre for South-East studies and thought. Muslim thought and literature blossomed, and Singapore was a major staging point for the Hajj, or pilgrimage to Mecca. The Arab St area was, and still is, a popular place for pilgrims to stay.

The 1920s witnessed another boom, despite a massive fall in rubber prices in 1920, and immigration soared. Millionaires, including a number of Chinese migrants such as Aw Boon Haw, the 'Tiger Balm King', were made overnight.

The Chinese were by far the greatest immigrant group and Chinese immigration peaked in 1930 when 250,000 Chinese came to Singapore. The upheavals in China were played out in Singapore with the establishment of the Kuomintang party, which had a very active communist faction.

The Chinese secret societies were allied with political factions, and gunmen and street gangs made headlines. The colonial government attempted to control the

Chinese community, but it was mainland politics which provided the greatest sway and inspiration.

The communists played a dominant role in the trade unions and the mainland-controlled parties fostered anticolonial sentiments. In 1929, the government was faced with the twin problems of controlling subversive forces and shoring up an economy battered by the great depression.

Its answers lay in banning the Kuomintang, censoring the Chinese press, withdrawing funds for Chinese education and establishing strict immigration quotas. Chinese immigration was cut to a tenth of its previous levels, and Singapore would never again witness the massive migration that had played such a large part in its development. Yet by the 1930s, Singapore was undeniably and irrevocably a Chinese city.

Singapore's inexorable economic growth continued after the depression, and the well-to-do prospered. The 1930s were a time of greater public works and social amenities. Though the Malayan Communist Party was well established and the seeds of independence grew in the community, the colonial government was firmly ensconced, convinced of its right to rule and looking forward to a long and prosperous reign.

The Japanese Invasion

The Japanese brutally destroyed the complacency of British rule and forever laid to rest notions of European superiority and British military might.

On 7 December 1941, the Japanese bombed Pearl Harbor and invaded the Malay Peninsula. In less than two months, they routed ill-prepared British and Commonwealth forces and stormed down the peninsula, conquering all before them. By 31 January, they were in Johor Bahru, massing in preparation for an assault on Singapore.

The Japanese commander, General Yamashita, was already a national hero but his rapid successes had left his supply lines overextended, and his troops were outnumbered. Nonetheless, he decided to attack before the retreating forces regrouped and reinforcements could arrive.

The Japanese invaded Singapore from the north-west on 8 February 1941. They met fierce resistance but over the next week they slowly advanced towards the city. Churchill sent word to hold Singapore at all cost but the pessimistic military command led by Lieutenant-General Arthur Percival feared a bloodbath of Singapore's citizens.

On 15 February, with the city in range of Japanese artillery, Percival called upon the Japanese to discuss peace terms.

Yamashita was stunned. With only a few days of ammunition and supplies left, he had feared that continued resistance would force him to call off the attack. Percival, unaware of the Japanese position, saw no way out and surrendered unconditionally.

It was one of the worst defeats in the history of the British Empire. The European population was herded onto the Padang and then marched away for internment, many of them at the infamous Changi Prison.

Singapore was renamed Syonan (Light of the South) and the Japanese quickly set about establishing control. Anti-Chinese sentiment was unleashed and Japanese troops started a massacre. Communists and intellectuals were singled out, but there was no method in the ensuing slaughter. In one week, thousands were executed and the Japanese lost any chance to gain the respect and cooperation of the people.

Though the Japanese ruled harshly, life in Singapore was tolerable while the war went well for Japan. As the war progressed, however, inflation skyrocketed and food, medicines and other essentials were in short supply.

Conditions were appalling during the last phase of the war, and many people died of malnutrition and disease. The war ended suddenly with Japan's surrender, and Singapore was spared the agony of recapture.

Post War & the Road to Independence

After the suffering experienced under the Japanese, the British were welcomed back to Singapore but their right to rule was now in question. Plans for limited self-government and a Malayan Union were drawn up, uniting the Malay states of the peninsula with British possessions in Borneo. Singapore was excluded, largely because of Malay fears of Chinese Singapore's dominance.

Singapore was run-down and its services neglected after the war. Poverty, unemployment and shortages provided fuel for the Malayan Communist Party, whose freedom fighters had emerged as the heroes of the war. The General Labour Union, the communist labour organisation, had a huge following and in 1946 and 1947 Singapore was crippled by strikes.

Meanwhile, new political opportunities in Malaya saw the rapid development of Malay nationalism. The United Malays National Organisation (UMNO) was the dominant Malay party and presented strong opposition to the Malay Union. UMNO argued for a federation, based on the Malay sultanates, and opposed citizenship laws which gave equal rights to all races, thereby undermining the special status of Malays.

Singapore moved slowly to self-government. The socialist Malayan Democratic Union was the first real political party, but it became increasingly radical and boycotted the first elections in 1947, leaving the conservative Progressive Party as the only party to contest the election.

After early successes, the communists realised that they were not going to gain power under the colonial government's political agenda and they began a campaign of armed struggle in Malaya. In 1948, the Emergency was declared. The communists were outlawed and a guerrilla war was waged on the peninsula for 12 years. There was no fighting in Singapore but left-wing politics languished under the political repression of Emergency regulations.

The Rise of the PAP & Lee Kuan Yew

By the early 1950s, the communist threat waned and left-wing activity again surfaced into the open. The centre-left Labour Front was active, and student and union movements were at the forefront of communist and socialist activity.

One of the rising stars of this era was Lee Kuan Yew, a third generation Straits-born Chinese who had studied law at Cambridge. Lee Kuan Yew had good contacts with the elite and British-educated intellectuals. He became involved with the Progressive Party, but grew dissatisfied with its conservative politics. Lee then became a legal adviser to several unions where he became acquainted with the left and the power of union politics. Most importantly, he realised the need to be aligned with the forces that appealed to the Chinese-educated majority.

The People's Action Party (PAP) was founded in 1954 with Lee Kuan Yew as secretary-general. The PAP was an uneasy alliance – Lee Kuan Yew led the noncommunist faction, but the party's main power base was communist. Lee, always a pragmatic and shrewd politician, realised that power in Singapore was impossible without communist support.

With the easing of the Emergency and the 1955 elections, Singaporean politics came of age. A spirited campaign saw the right-wing parties trounced and David Marshall's Labour Front form a coalition government. The PAP was vocal in opposition, competing with the Labour Front for the left position.

PAP's influence continued to grow; although a non-communal party, it appealed to the majority Chinese and attracted the strong left-wing vote. The PAP contested all seats in the 1959 elections and it was swept to power with an overwhelming majority. Lee Kuan Yew became prime minister.

The establishment was shocked. The PAP's left-wing image sent a wave of fear through the business community. Foreign companies moved their headquarters and there was a flight of capital from Singapore. The government embarked on an anti-Western campaign, but it was anticolonial rather than anticapitalist.

The radical PAP leadership had, in fact, been replaced by moderates after the Internal Security Council, comprised of British, Singaporean and Malaysian representatives, had ordered the arrest of the extreme left of the party in a communist crackdown in 1958. The PAP found votes in fiery speeches but its socialist policies were in fact quite temperate.

The Federation of Malaya had already achieved independence in 1957, and the PAP's aim was for full independence and union with the federation. The British agreed, but Malaya had no desire for union with a left-wing Singapore. The PAP government took a strongly pro-Malay stance to appease Malaya, and introduced Malay as the national language. It tried to woo foreign capital to bolster the ailing economy, much to the disgust of the extreme-left faction.

A split was inevitable. In 1961, the PAP was torn asunder by the wholesale defection of the left to form the Barisan Sosialis.

The PAP was one seat short of a majority in parliament and it held precariously onto power with the help of the right-wing Alliance party. The position of the PAP strengthened after February 1963 when 100 left-wing leaders, including half of the Barisan Sosialis leadership, were arrested under Operation Cold Store for supporting a rebellion in Brunei.

Independence

Full independence and union with Malaya was now firmly back on the agenda. Thinking in Malaya had also turned around, with Malaya preferring to have a moderate Singapore within a union rather than a communist Singapore outside it. The Federation of Malaysia came into being in September 1963, and at the same time Lee Kuan Yew held a snap election.

The government campaigned on its already impressive list of achievements – increases in public housing,
health standards and education spending were dramatic. Crime was down and the government used its
powers under the Emergency to arrest secret-society
members. The PAP won 37 of the 51 seats, while the
Barisan Sosialis won 13.

The Malaysian union was never going to be easy and
the PAP made a grave mistake in contesting the 1964
federal elections, even though it had earlier promised
not to stand. Its social democrat platform was soundly
rejected by the conservative Malaysian electorate, and
its campaign had only aroused suspicions of a Singaporean takeover.

Tension mounted when Singapore refused to extend
the privileged position held by Malays in Malaya to the
Malays in Singapore. Communal violence broke out in
the Malay Geylang district of Singapore in 1964 and
more than 20 people were killed. To add to these problems, Indonesia embarked on a campaign of
confrontation against Malaysia, and Singapore became
a target of Indonesian bombings.

By 1965, Singapore was expelled and the union was
over. A tearful Lee Kuan Yew likened Singapore to a
head without a body, and feared that Singapore, with no
natural resources, would not survive.

The Republic of Singapore

Singapore became independent on 9 August 1965. Lee's
fears proved to be unfounded, and Singapore boomed
and became the economic success story of the region.
Rapid industrialisation and large foreign investment
helped give Singapore full employment and a rising
standard of living. In 1968, the PAP won every parliamentary seat after the Barisan Sosialis boycotted the
election.

Gross domestic product expanded at nearly 10% per
year and Singapore, through a programme of govern-
ment-planned economic expansion, rapidly developed
its industry and became a centre of Asian finance. Stable
government, industrial calm and previously unknown
political quiet prompted further foreign investment. Lee
Kuan Yew presided over an economic miracle and
Singapore's international standing grew.

The face of Singapore changed dramatically with
modernisation. Slum clearance and new building pro-
jects were the order in Singapore's brave new world, and
many old buildings fell to the wreckers. The Housing

Development Board's new estates were a huge success as more and more Singaporeans acquired decent housing.

Singapore's government was talented, relatively free of corruption and enjoyed popular support. However, opposition to the Government was dealt with harshly. The media was the instrument of government campaigns and national objectives; in 1971 the government closed the *Nanyang Siang Pau* after its criticism of government education policy, and attacked the *Eastern Sun* and the *Singapore Herald*. Further laws to control the media were introduced in 1974 and 1977. Government control over student groups and labour organisations also increased.

The PAP believed its benign dictatorship was the only way to secure peace and prosperity for Singapore, and Lee Kuan Yew remains staunchly unrepentant, convinced that his tough measures were necessary to develop Singapore. By the 1970s, Singapore was the wealthiest country in Asia behind Japan.

The PAP won every seat in each election held until 1981 when J B Jeyaretnam of the Workers' Party won a seat at a by-election. The government was shocked, undertook even greater control of the press and Lee Kuan Yew mounted a vitriolic campaign against Jeyaretnam, who was convicted of failing to correctly declare party funds in 1986, resulting in his being barred from parliament for five years.

A second opposition member was elected in the 1984 elections, and the government decided that if the electorate wanted an opposition voice then the government would supply it. The government instituted a system whereby it could appoint its own nonelected opposition members. The 1984 election also saw the election of Lee Hsien Loong, Lee Kuan Yew's son, who rapidly became a rising star in cabinet and was widely touted as a future leader.

By the 1980s, the second tier of PAP leaders came to the fore and Lee Kuan Yew handed over greater responsibility to his juniors. Goh Chok Tong became deputy prime minister and Lee Kuan Yew's designated successor. Singapore's economic miracle continued, despite a hiccup in the mid-80s, and the country possessed a diversified economic base and a literate, skilled population.

Lee Kuan Yew resigned as prime minister in November 1990 and Goh Chok Tong took over. Many commentators saw Goh Chok Tong as a seat-warmer for Lee Hsien Loong, but Lee the younger's political career has been on hold since the shock announcement that he was undergoing chemotherapy in a battle against cancer.

Lee's resignation coincided with the completion of the Mass Rapid Transit (MRT) subway system, an impressive testament to Singapore's modernisation and technological achievements. Though Lee has detractors, especially in the Western media, his achievements are undeniable. He transformed Singapore from a poverty-stricken, run-down city with no natural resources and an uncertain future, to a great city-state where its citizens enjoy a safe and prosperous existence. A shrewd politician, brilliant orator and astute leader, he remains the father of modern Singapore and his popularity is as high as ever.

Lee Kuan Yew is now Special Minister, and he remains a powerful influence in cabinet and in the public arena. The largely ceremonial president's role has been given wider powers, and many speculate that Lee will become president in the future, ensuring that Singapore will not depart from the course he has steered since 1959. In fact, Lee has even promised to return from the grave if things go wrong in Singapore.

Yet Singaporeans are demanding change. The new generation, which has not lived through the hardships of the past, are seeking liberalisation and increased freedom. There are calls for the repeal of the Internal Security Act, which was used to detain church activists without trial in 1987.

Goh Chok Tong has shown a desire to create a kinder, gentler government, more inclined to consultation and liberal values. Goh's social reforms have seen a relaxation of censorship laws, greater personal freedoms, a flourishing in the arts and a greater awareness of the quality-of-life issues that concern most modern, industrialised nations. Politically, the new government showed signs of change by allowing political exiles to return to Singapore, but despite a change in style away from Lee Kuan Yew's aggressively paternalistic rule, few real steps have been made towards democratisation.

Goh Chok Tong called a snap election in August 1991 to legitimise his rule and reforms. The opposition increased its vote to nearly 40% and four opposition MPs were elected. The result shocked the government, and PAP hardliners, including Lee Kuan Yew, questioned Goh's reforms and the direction of the party. In December 1992, Goh Chok Tong placed his position on the line by calling a by-election in his own electorate, Singapore's safest, but an election that Goh had to win convincingly. The PAP won with a resounding 72.9% of the vote, strengthening Goh's position.

ORIENTATION

Singapore is a city, an island and a country. While there are built-up, high-density areas all around the island, the main city area is in the south.

Raffles founded Singapore on the Singapore River, and this is still the centre of the city. To the south of the river at its mouth is the Central Business District, centred around Raffles Place.

To the south-west, Chinatown adjoins the Central Business District, further inland from Robinson Rd. South Bridge Rd runs through the centre of Chinatown, while New Bridge Rd further west is the main shopping area.

To the north of the Singapore River is the colonial district, which has many reminders of British rule, as well as a number of top-end hotels and shopping centres. Raffles Hotel is on the corner of Bras Basah and Beach Rds. Between Bras Basah and Rochor Rds further north is the main budget accommodation area, centred on Beach Rd and Bencoolen St.

Further north-east of Rochor Canal Rd are Little India, centred on Serangoon Rd, and Arab St. Both these areas are interesting, traditional areas that have escaped wholesale demolition and development.

From the colonial district, Bras Basah Rd heads north-west to become Orchard Rd, Singapore's main tourist area, with dozens of luxury hotels, shopping complexes, restaurants and bars. South of Orchard Rd and west of Chinatown, Havelock Rd is a quieter and much smaller hotel enclave.

To the west of the island, Jurong is an industrial area, but it also contains a number of tourist attractions. The east coast has some older suburbs and a major beach park, and at the far east of the island is Changi airport. The eastern and north-eastern parts of the island are home to some huge housing developments. The central north of the island has much of Singapore's undeveloped land and most of the remaining forest. Points of interest include the zoo and a number of parks. The north-west is less developed, especially along the coast, which is a live firing area containing many reservoirs.

Singapore Island is crisscrossed by a typically efficient expressway system. The Pan Island Expressway runs from Changi airport inland right across to Jurong in the west. The East Coast Parkway runs from Changi airport to the central city via the east coast, and meets the Ayer Rajah Expressway, which runs along the west coast. The Central Expressway meets the Ayer Rajah Expressway in the south, running though and under the central city area, then crosses the Pan Island Expressway and continues north. The Bukit Timah Expressway runs from the Causeway at Woodlands and meets the Pan Island Expressway in the centre of the island.

Singapore Addresses

Unlike many Asian cities, Singapore is well laid out with signposted streets and logically numbered buildings. As many of the shops, businesses and residences are located in high-rise buildings, addresses are often preceded by the number of the floor and then the shop or apartment number. Addresses do not quote the district or suburb, but rely on post code for identification. For example, 03-12, Far East Plaza, Scotts Rd, S0922 is shop No 12 on the 3rd floor of the Far East Plaza in the 9th district (S0922 shows the district, which in this case covers most of Orchard Rd).

GEOGRAPHY

Singapore consists of the main, low-lying Singapore Island and 58 much smaller islands within its territorial waters. It is situated just above 1° N in latitude, a mere 137 km north of the equator. Singapore Island is 42 km in length and 23 km in breadth, and together with the other islands, the republic has a total land mass of 626 sq km (and growing through land reclamation). The other main islands are Pulau Tekong (17.9 sq km), which is gazetted as a military area but planned to be semi-residential eventually; Pulau Ubin (10.2 sq km), which is a rural haven from downtown Singapore; and Sentosa (3.3 sq km), Singapore's fun park. Built-up urban areas comprise around 50% of the land area, while parkland, reservoirs, plantations and open military areas occupy 40%. Remaining forest accounts for only 4%.

Bukit Timah (Hill of Tin), in the central hills, is the highest point on Singapore Island at an altitude of 162 metres. The central area of the island is an igneous outcrop, containing most of Singapore's remaining forest and open areas. The western part of the island is a sedimentary area of low-lying hills and valleys, while the south-east is mostly flat and sandy.

Singapore is connected with Peninsular Malaysia by a km-long causeway. To relieve congestion, a second causeway is planned for the west of the island. Under current plans, further land reclamation and housing developments will dramatically change Singapore's geography. The MRT will be extended to the north and east, where new housing developments will occur, and

Top: Central Singapore (PT)
Bottom: Cavenagh Bridge (PT)

massive land reclamation will create new islands along
the south-east coast.

CLIMATE

Singapore has a typically tropical climate. It's hot and
humid year round, and initially it can be very uncomfortable. Once you are used to the tropics, however, it
never strikes you as too uncomfortable. The temperature
almost never drops below 20°C (68°F), even at night, and
usually climbs to 30°C (86°F) or more during the day.
Humidity tends to hover around the 75% mark.

Rain, when it comes, tends to be short and sharp. You
may be unlucky and strike rain on every day of your
visit, but don't believe local legend about it raining every
day for months on end. Only about half the days of the
year receive rain. Singapore is at its wettest from
November to January, and at its driest from May to July,
but the difference between these two periods is not
dramatic and Singapore gets an abundance of rainfall in
every month.

Being almost right on the equator, Singapore receives
a steady supply of 12 hours daylight every day. The sun
shines for about half of the day on average (less from
November to January). Much of the sunshine is filtered
through thin cloud but can be intense, nonetheless.

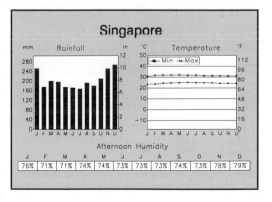

GOVERNMENT

Singapore's government is based on the Westminster
system. The unicameral parliament has 81 elected

members representing 52 electoral divisions: 42 single-member constituencies and 13 GRCs (group representation constituencies), such as Prime Minister Goh's own four-member Marine Parade GRC. In GRCs, one of the team must be from a minority group. Voting is compulsory, and governments are elected for five years, but a ruling government can dissolve parliament and call for an election at any time.

As well as elected members the government has instituted a system that allows it to appoint an opposition. NCMPs are 'nonconstituency members of parliament', who have failed to win enough votes but are appointed to parliament as runners up, if less than four opposition members are elected. NMPs are 'nominated MPs', comprising six prominent citizens that are appointed to give nonpartisan views. NCMPs and NMPs are not allowed to vote on financial and constitutional bills, although they can participate in parliamentary debate.

Singapore also has a president who is elected to the position. The position is largely ceremonial, and real power lies with the prime minister and his government, though recent legislation increased the president's power of veto over financial bills and government appointments. Ong Teng Cheong, a former PAP deputy prime minister, was elected president on 29 August 1993. The other candidate admitted during the campaign that he was only standing to give the public a choice and stated that Mr Ong was the best candidate. Nonetheless 41.3% voted against Ong. Two opposition party candidates who applied to stand for the presidency were rejected as unsuitable.

The legal system is also based on the English system. The Supreme Court is the ultimate arbitrator and consists of the High Court, the Court of Appeal and the Court of Criminal Appeal. Most cases are heard by the District Courts and Magistrates Courts except for the most serious criminal or civil hearings.

So in theory Singapore has a democratically elected government and political system similar to many Western democracies. The political practice is somewhat different.

The judiciary's independence is enshrined in the constitution, but many judges are appointed on short tenure and their renewal is subject to party approval. Rulings that have gone against the government have seen new laws quickly enacted by parliament to ensure government victory. The old communist bogey is used to justify Singapore's Internal Security Act, which is still used to detain outspoken critics. Singapore's Internal Security Department has sophisticated databanks with detailed information on Singapore's citizens, and there is widespread fear of losing jobs, promotional opportunities or contracts through criticism of the government. There is little freedom of the press and a tight lid is held on government criticism.

The PAP is becoming increasingly concerned that it may lose power, though to the credit of Goh Chok Tong and his supporters, the government is trying to address, even if in a superficial way, some of the electoral concerns that have seen a decline in PAP support. Rather than repress opposition, there is seen to be a need to listen to it.

The main opposition party is the SDP (Singapore Democratic Party), which has taken over the mantle from the Workers' Party. The PAP has seen the opposition vote of 39% in 1991 as mainly nontraditional Chinese, ie Malay, Indian and the English-educated Chinese middle class. However, the evidence and size of the vote also shows that the Chinese-educated Chinese working class, traditionally the backbone of PAP support, is also turning away.

However, the chances of the opposition gaining power are very remote. The PAP undeniably has popular support, and as long as the government can keep the economy and personal wealth growing, the opposition is unlikely to gain the huge increase in its vote required to attain government. Hip pocket issues, like taxation or state housing waiting lists, are of prime political importance and only economic disaster or a major government scandal is likely to shake the PAP's political dominance.

ECONOMY

Singapore is one of Asia's four 'dragons' – the Asian economic boom countries of Taiwan, Korea, Hong Kong and Singapore. For over 20 years Singapore has recorded phenomenal growth rates, and even in the recession-hit '90s Singapore's growth has hardly faltered. Singapore has a large current account surplus, it is a net creditor, inflation is low and unemployment is virtually nonexistent.

Singapore's economy is based on trade, shipping, banking and tourism, with a growing programme of light industrialisation. It also has a major oil refining business producing much of the petroleum for the South-East Asian region. Other important industries include ship building and maintenance, and electronics. Singapore's port vies with Hong Kong to be the busiest in the world.

For many Western countries with mounting foreign debt, declining exports and increasing imports, Singapore is seen as a model free-market economy. A model economy it may be, but its approach is not free market.

While tariffs are low or nonexistent and foreign capital is encouraged with minimal restrictions, Singapore is very definitely a managed economy in the Japanese mould. It is the government that provides direction by targeting industries for development and offering tax incentives, or by simply telling them what to do. Unions and the labour market are controlled by the government, and there is tough legislation against strikes.

While the government promotes free trade, it always reserves the right to intervene, as it did in 1985 when it closed the stock exchange for three days after a major Singaporean company, Pan Electric Industries, went into receivership.

The Monetary Authority of Singapore (MAS) is a good example of government involvement in the economy. It acts as a central bank and powerful financial market regulator to promote sustained economic growth and provide stability in the financial services sector. Singapore's finance market is one of the largest in Asia and provides 25% of the country's income – to a large degree this is because of the investment stability provided by the MAS.

Singapore does have its share of free marketeers though, and many in the business community want less government involvement in the economy. Singapore wants to assume the role of Asia's finance centre, especially with Hong Kong's changeover to the mainland in 1997, but investors in 'anything goes' Hong Kong are wary of more regulated Singaporean markets. Singapore's restrictive society is also a problem, and Singapore suffers from a brain drain that sees it lose many of its skilled professionals.

Singapore guarantees its citizens decent housing, health care, high standards of education and superannuation, making it a welfare state in comparison to its Asian neighbours. There are no unemployment payments or programmes, but unemployment is negligible and the government insists that anyone who wants work can find it. In fact, Singapore has to import workers from neighbouring countries, particularly to do the hard, dirty work which Singaporeans no longer want any part of.

All workers and their employers make sizeable contributions to the Central Provident Fund (CPF), a form of superannuation that is returned on retirement. Some

CPF savings, however, can be used in the purchase of government housing.

POPULATION

Singapore's polyglot population numbers 2.7 million. It's made up of 77.7% Chinese, 14.1% Malay, 7.1% Indian and 1.1% from a variety of races.

Singapore's population density is high but the government waged a particularly successful birth control campaign in the 1970s and early 1980s. In fact, it was so successful that the birth rate dropped off alarmingly, especially in the Chinese community. To reverse the trend and further the government's genetic engineering programme, tax incentives were introduced for university-educated women who had children, although at the same time rewards of S$10,000 were offered to those willing to undergo sterilisation.

Later policies offered tax rebates of up to S$20,000 for couples who have a third and fourth child. In another move, government-sponsored marriage brokers are teaching social skills to hard-working Singaporeans who are so dedicated to their work that they don't know how to woo the opposite sex. Government-sponsored 'love boats' cruise the harbour with potential breeding stock.

PEOPLE

Singapore's character, and the main interest for the visitor, lies in the diversity of its population. Chinatown

Residents of Singapore (STPB)

still has some of the sights, sounds and rituals of a
Chinese city, Little India is a microcosm of the subconti-
nent, and in Arab St the muezzin's call from the mosque
still dominates the lives of its inhabitants. But modern
Singapore is essentially a Chinese city with strong
Western influences.

English is the principal language of education, and
growing prosperity sees Singaporeans consuming
Western values along with Western goods. For the government, this divergence from traditional values
threatens to undermine the spirit – essentially the work-
oriented Chinese spirit – that built Singapore. In an
attempt to reverse the new ways of the young, the government runs campaigns to develop awareness of
traditional culture and values. These include cultural
exhibitions and the compulsory study of the mother
tongue in schools.

Government policy has always been to promote
Singapore as a multicultural nation where the three
main racial groups can live in equality and harmony,
while still maintaining their own cultural identities. The
government strives hard to unite Singaporeans and
promote equality, though there are imbalances in the
distribution of wealth and power amongst the racial
groups. For the most part, the government is successful
in promoting racial harmony, a not-always-easy task in
multiracial Singapore.

Chinese

The Chinese first settled in the Nanyang, as South-East
Asia is known in China, as far back as the 14th century.
In the 19th and 20th centuries, waves of Chinese
migrants in search of a better life poured into Singapore
and provided the labour that ran the colony.

The migrants came mostly from the southern provinces: Hokkien Chinese from the vicinity of Amoy in
Fukien province; the Teochew from Swatow in eastern
Kwangtung; Hakka from Kwangtung and Fukien; and
Cantonese from Canton. Hokkiens and Teochews
enjoyed an affinity in dialect and customs, but the Cantonese and Hakkas may as well have come from
opposite ends of the earth. The Chinese settlers soon
established their own areas in Singapore, and the divisions along dialect lines still exist to some extent in the
older areas of town.

Settlement for the immigrants was made easier by
Chinese organisations based on clan, dialect and occupation. Upon arrival, immigrants were taken in by the
various communities and given work and housing. The

secret societies were particularly prevalent in Singapore in the 19th century; they provided many useful social functions and were more powerful than the colonial government in the life of the Chinese. However, they eventually declined and became nothing more than criminal gangs.

Nowadays, most Chinese are Singaporean born. The campaign to speak Mandarin has given the Chinese a common dialect, but English is also a unifying tongue. Increasing Westernisation and English education for the most part have not undermined traditional Chinese customs and beliefs.

Malays

The Malays are the original inhabitants of Singapore. They are the main racial group throughout the region stretching from the Malay Peninsula across Indonesia to the Philippines. Many Malays migrated to Singapore from the peninsula, and large numbers of Javanese and Bugis (from Riau and Sulawesi) also settled in Singapore.

Malays in Singapore are Muslim. Islam provides the major influence in everyday life and is the rallying point of Malay society. The month of Ramadan, when Muslims fast from sunrise to sunset, is the most important month of the Islamic year. Hari Raya Puasa, the end of the fast, is the major Malay celebration.

Islam was brought to the region by Arab and Indian traders and adopted in the 15th century, but traditional Malay culture still shows influences of pre-Islamic Hindu and animist beliefs. For example, *wayang kulit*, the Malay shadow puppet play, portrays tales from the Hindu epics of the *Ramayana* and *Mahabharata*.

Malays have a strong sense of community and hospitality, and the *kampong*, or village, is at the centre of Malay life. The majority of Malays live in high-rise districts such as Geylang, but in fast-diminishing rural Singapore and the islands to the north, a few Malay kampongs still exist.

Indians

Indian migration dates mostly from the middle of the 19th century when the British recruited labour for the plantations of Malaya. While many Indians arrived in Singapore, most passed through and eventually settled in Malaya.

In Singapore, approximately 60% of the Indian population are Tamil and a further 20% are Malayalis from the southern Indian state of Kerala. The rest come from all over India and include Bengalis, Punjabis and Kashmiris. The majority of Indians are Hindu, but a large number are Muslim and there are also Sikhs, Parsis, Christians and Buddhists.

Major Indian celebrations are Thaipusam and Deepavali.

ARTS

Singapore is a country that is normally associated with business and technology and the arts have tended to take a back seat to economic development. In the liberalised environment under Goh Chok Tong Singapore contemporary arts are starting to flourish, and the more traditional forms of music and dance can still be seen in Singapore.

Chinese Opera

Chinese drama is a mixture of dialogue, music, song and dance. It is an ancient form of theatre but reached its peak during the Ming Dynasty from the 14th to 17th centuries. It went through a decline in the 19th century but its highest form survived in the Beijing Opera, which has enjoyed a comeback in China after the Cultural Revolution. Chinese opera, or *wayang*, in Singapore and Malaysia has come from the Cantonese variety, which is seen as a more music hall, gaudy variety.

What it lacks in literary nuance is made up for by the glaring costumes and crashing music that follows the action. Performances can go for an entire evening, and it is usually easy enough for the uninitiated to follow the gist of the action. The acting is heavy and stylised, and the music can be searing to Western ears, but a performance is well worthwhile if you should chance upon one. Street performances are held during important festivals such as Chinese New Year, Festival of the Hungry Ghosts or the Festival of the Nine Emperor Gods.

The band that accompanies the action is usually composed of fiddles, reed pipes, lutes, and drums, bells and cymbals that are most noticeable when the action hots up. The scenery is virtually nonexistent and props rarely consist of more than a table and chairs, but it is the action that is important.

The four main roles are the *sheng, dan, jing* and *chou*. The sheng are the leading male actors and they play scholars, officials, warriors etc. The *laosheng* wear beards and represent old men, while the *wusheng* play soldiers and warriors and acrobatics may be included in the performance. The dan are the female roles: the *laodan* are the elderly, dignified ladies, the brightly costumed *huadan* are the maids and the *caidan* are the female comedians. Traditionally female roles were played by men.

The jing are the painted-face roles and they represent warriors, heroes, statesmen, adventurers and demons.

Their counterparts are the *fujing*, ridiculous figures who are anything but heroic. The chou is basically the clown.

Lion Dance

This dance is accompanied by musicians who bash cymbals and drums to invoke the spirits. The intricate papier-mâché lion's head is worn by the lead performer while another dancer takes the part of the body. At its best it is a spectacular, acrobatic dance with the 'head' jumping on the shoulders of the 'body', climbing poles and performing acrobatic tumbling. The lion may also be accompanied by two clowns who attend it.

The dance is usually performed during Chinese festivals to gain the blessings of the gods, and traditionally a dance troupe would be paid with *ang pow* (red packets of money) held up high to be retrieved with acrobatics. The dragon dance is a variation on the same theme.

Other Performing Arts

Malay and Indian dances sometimes can be seen. *Bangsawan* or 'Malay Opera' was introduced from Persia and is a popular drama form still performed in Singapore.

Singapore's theatre scene is becoming more active and more local plays are being produced. The Substation is an alternative venue, while the Drama Centre, the Victoria Theatre and Kallang Theatre stage local and overseas productions.

The Victoria Concert Hall is the home of the Singapore Symphony Orchestra and concerts of classical Chinese music are performed by the Singapore Broadcasting Corporation's Chinese Orchestra.

The Singapore Festival of Arts, which features many drama performances, is held every second year around June. Music, art and dance are also represented at the festival, which includes a Fringe Festival featuring plenty of street performances.

Art Galleries

There are a number of art galleries and displays apart from the major National Museum Art Gallery. On Clemenceau Ave, the National Theatre also has a gallery with paintings and ceramics. Exhibitions are listed in the newspapers. Some of the better known galleries featuring local artists and arts from South-East Asia include: Art Base, Art Focus, Clifford Gallery and Collector's Gallery.

CULTURE

Growing Westernisation and the pace of modern life has seen a change in the traditional customs among the various ethnic groups in Singapore. While some traditional customs are given less importance or have been streamlined, the strength of traditional religious values and the practice of time-honoured ways remains.

Chinese Customs

The moment of birth is most important for the Chinese and strictly recorded; it is essential for horoscopes and astrological consultations that are important in later life. Traditionally, only close relatives come to visit after the third day and the household has to undergo purification rites after one month. At this time the child is named, but the name may be changed if it is not deemed to be a prosperous one.

Every family wants at least one boy, as only males can carry out the necessary rituals associated with the worship of the ancestors and the passing of the parents. In the Confucian tradition, children are taught to have great respect for their parents and education is stressed.

Marriages were traditionally arranged and the astrologer consulted to see if the would-be couple were compatible. While the astrologer might still be consulted for an auspicious day, marriages are rarely arranged these days and the Chinese wedding ceremony shows much less tradition. The western tradition of a white wedding is popular and religion is not really part of the wedding ceremony. In keeping with the Singaporean love of food, wedding receptions are often held at restaurants where guests are treated to a banquet.

Funerals on the other hand are much more traditional, elaborate affairs. The Chinese funeral is an important event and one of the most colourful and expensive ceremonies. At a traditional funeral, paper houses, cars, television sets and even paper servants are offered and

Kiasu or What?

One of the buzz words of the '90s in Singapore is *kiasu*. In a recent courtesy campaign, a yearly event to increase social awareness and good manners among Singaporeans, the overseas *kiasu* Singaporean tourist was targeted. There have been reports of *kiasu* Singaporeans on holiday piling their plates to overflowing at buffets, and then being unable to finish and sneaking out the leftovers. Then there was the excitement among a *kiasu* tour group when one of its members found a phone that allowed overseas calls at the local rate and the entire group rushed off the magic booth and spent the rest of the day on the phone. Throw in queue jumping, noisy antics in hotels and desperate attempts to avoid entrance fees, and the government decided it was time to do something about *kiasu* Singaporeans.

So what is *kiasu*? It is best summed up by Mr Kiasu, a Singaporean cartoon hero, whose philosophy from A to Z includes: Always must win, Everything also must grab, Jump queue, Keep coming back for more, Look for discounts, Never mind what they think, Rushing and pushing wins the race, and Winner takes it all! all! all!

And are Singaporeans kiasu? At the risk of generalising, it's true that Singaporeans are competitive and a bargain will never pass a Singaporean by, but would Singapore's economy be so dynamic if Singaporeans were otherwise? It can sometimes be frustrating trying to get out of a lift or MRT train as fellow passengers push to get off while boarding passengers rush to get in, but it is better than trying to board the subway in New York or Tokyo. Singaporeans haven't inherited the British love of queues, and as in most Asian countries, don't have much time for the deferential excesses of continually saying 'please', 'thank you' and 'sorry', but in a world of plastic smiles and 'have a nice day' the no-nonsense Singaporean approach has something going for it.

Singaporeans have taken the *kiasu* tag in good humour, as shown by the popularity of Mr Kiasu, and fast-food outlets even offer *kiasu* burgers. So, when in Singapore, hunt out those bargains, don't pay unless you have to, over-indulge at buffets, and have a *kiasu* good time. ∎

burnt so that the deceased can enjoy all these material benefits in the next life. The body is dressed in best clothes and sealed in the coffin along with a few valuables. The coffin is placed in front of the ancestral altar in the house and joss sticks and candles are burnt. Mourning and prayers may go on for three days before the funeral, which is an expensive affair involving the hire of professional mourners and musicians who clash symbols and gongs to drive away the evil spirits. Food and drink is provided to all those who visit the house to pay their respects.

Traditionally children would mourn the death of a father for three years and white would be worn, but modern life has seen the mourning period greatly reduced. Whatever changes in tradition have occurred, the importance of the grave and it upkeep remains and most Chinese will pay their respects to the elders on All Souls' Day.

Chinese New Year is the major festival, and even Chinese who profess no religion will celebrate it with gusto. It is a time for clearing out the old and bringing in the new. The house is given a spring clean and all business affairs and debts bought up to date before the new year. It is a time for family, friends and feasting and ang pow (red packets of money) are given to children. Chap Goh Meh is the last day of the Chinese New Year and is the peak of celebrations.

Malay Customs

Adat or customary law guides the important ceremonies and events in life such as birth, circumcision and marriage. When Islam came to South-East Asia it supplanted existing spiritual beliefs and systems of social law, but conversion to Islam did not mean a total abolition of existing customs and beliefs, and many aspects of adat exhibit Hindu and even pre-Hindu influences.

At a birth, evil spirits must be kept at bay, and traditionally rituals are undertaken to nullify the spirits. Traditionally in a birth attended by the midwife, the baby is spat on to protect it from the spirits of disease, and the Muslim call to prayer is whispered in the baby's ear. On the seventh day the baby's first hair-cutting *(bercukur)* is performed and the baby is named. If it is later decided that the name does not suit the baby or is hampering its development, then the name can be changed.

The circumcision of boys *(bersunat)* is a major event and usually occurs around the ages of eight to 12 years. The boy will be dressed in finery and seated on a dais. After feasting, passages from the Koran are read and the boy will repeat verses read by the imam. The circumcision occurs the next morning when the boy sits astride a banana trunk and the *mudin* or circumciser performs the operation.

The Malay wedding tradition is quite involved and there are a number of rituals which must be observed.

The prospective husband despatches an uncle or aunt to his wife-to-be's house to get the family's permission to marry *(hantar tanda)*. Once this is given, the couple are engaged *(bertunang)*, and then the actual ceremony *(akad nikah)* takes place.

The bride and groom, dressed in traditional *kain songket* – silk with gold thread – have henna applied to their palms and fingertips *(berinai)*, and then in a ceremony with significant Hindu influence *(bersanding)*, they 'sit in state' on a dais and are surrounded by both modern gifts and traditional offerings, such as folded paper flowers in a vase of bath towels, ringed by quail eggs in satin ribbons.

The couple are showered with *bunga rampai* (flower petals and thinly shredded pandan leaves) and sprinkled with *air mawar* (rose water).

Important ceremonies in family life are accompanied by a feast known as *kenduri*. Guests can number in the hundreds and preparations take days as many traditional dishes, such as *nasi minyak* (spicy rice) and *pulut kuning* (sticky saffron rice) have to be prepared.

The most important festival is Hari Raya Puasa, the end of the fasting month. This is the equivalent of the Malay new year and new clothes are bought, families are reunited and, of course, there is much feasting.

Indian Customs

Most Singaporean Indians come from southern India and so the customs and festivals that are more important in the south, especially in Madras, are the most popular in Singapore.

Traditionally, after the birth of a baby the *namakarana* or name-giving ceremony is held about 10 days after the birth. An astrologer will be called upon to give an auspicious name, often the name of a god. Boys are very much favoured, as only males can perform certain family rituals and the dowry system in India that requires large dowries to be paid on the marriage of a daughter can mean financial ruin for a family with too many daughters.

One of the major ceremonies in the life of a boy of higher caste is the initiation involving receiving the sacred threads, though this ceremony is generally restricted to the Brahman caste and not widely practised in Singapore. The boy is bathed, blessed by priests and showered with rice by guests. Then three strands of thread, representing Brahma, Vishnu and Shiva, are draped around the boy's left shoulder and knotted underneath the right arm, thus officially initiating the boy into his caste.

Arranged marriages are still common, though the bride and groom have an increasing say in the choice of their intended partner. The day, hour and minute of the wedding are also the preserve of the astrologer. The marriage is usually held at the house of the bride's family and the couple will be seated on a dais and a sacred flame is placed in the centre of the room. The final ceremony involves the bridegroom placing the *thali* necklace around the bride's neck and then the couple proceed around the fire seven times.

Deepavali or the Festival of Lights is the major Indian festival in Singapore and homes are decorated with oil lamps to signify the victory of light over darkness. The spectacular Thaipusam is the most exciting festival.

RELIGION

The variety of religions found in Singapore is a direct reflection of the diversity of races living there. The Chinese are predominantly followers of Buddhism and Shenism (or deity worship), though some are Christians. Malays are overwhelmingly Muslim, and most of Singapore's Indians are Hindus from south India, though a sizeable proportion are Muslim and some are Sikhs.

Despite increasing Westernisation and secularism, traditional religious beliefs are still held by the large majority of Singaporeans. Singaporeans overwhelming celebrate the major festivals associated with their religions, though religious worship has declined among the young and the higher educated, particularly the English-educated. In the Chinese community, for example, almost everyone will celebrate Chinese New Year, while the figure for those that profess Chinese religion is around 70%. An interesting reversal of the trend away from religion is the increase in Christianity, primarily among the English-educated Chinese elite, and the charismatic movements in particular are finding converts.

The government is wary of religion, and has abolished religious instruction in schools with the stated aim of avoiding religious intolerance and hatred, but it is also interesting to note that religious groups have been at the forefront of political opposition. The government's stated philosophy is Confucian, which is not a religion as such but a moral and social model. Its ideal society is based on the Confucian values of devotion to parents and family, loyalty to friends, and the emphasis is on education, justice and good government. It is a secular, pragmatic society instilled with a healthy dose of materialism.

Chinese Religion

The Chinese religion is a mix of Taoism, Confucianism and Buddhism. Taoism combines with old animistic beliefs to teach people how to maintain harmony with the universe. Confucianism takes care of the political and moral aspects of life. Buddhism takes care of the afterlife. But to say that the Chinese have three religions – Taoism, Buddhism and Confucianism – is too simple a view of their traditional religious life. At the first level Chinese religion is animistic, with a belief in the innate vital energy in rocks, trees, rivers and springs. At the second level people from the distant past, both real and mythological, are worshipped as gods. Overlaid on these beliefs are popular Taoism, Mahayana Buddhism and Confucianism.

On a day-to-day level the Chinese are much less concerned with the high-minded philosophies and asceticism of Buddha, Confucius or Lao Zi than they are with the pursuit of worldly success, the appeasement of the dead and the spirits, and the seeking of hidden knowledge about the future. Chinese religion incorporates what the West regards as superstition; if you want your fortune told, for instance, you go to a temple. The other important thing to remember is that Chinese religion is polytheistic. Apart from Buddha, Lao Zi and Confucius there are many divinities such as house gods and gods and goddesses for particular professions, and the worship of these gods is the most common form of religious practice in Singapore.

The most popular gods and local deities or *shen* in Singapore are Kuan Yin, the goddess of mercy, and Toh Peh Kong, a local deity representing the spirit of the pioneers and found only outside China. Kuan Ti, the god of war, is also very popular and is nowadays regarded as the god of wealth. Offerings of joss sticks and fruit are made at temples but most households also have their own altars.

Integral parts of Chinese religion are death, the afterlife and ancestor-worship. At least as far back as China's Shang Dynasty there were lavish funeral ceremonies involving the interment of horses, carriages, wives and slaves. The more important the person the more possessions and people had to be buried with them since they would require them in the next world. The deceased had to be kept happy because people's powers to inflict punishments or to grant favours greatly increased after their death. Even today, a traditional Chinese funeral can be an extremely extravagant event (see Chinese Customs earlier).

While ancestor worship plays an important role, it is not as extensive as in China where many generations of ancestors may be worshipped. Singaporean Chinese generally only honour the ancestors of two or three generations, ie going as far back as their immigrant forefathers.

The most important word in the Chinese popular religious vocabulary is *joss* (luck), and the Chinese are too astute not to utilise it. Gods have to be appeased, bad spirits blown away and sleeping dragons soothed to keep joss on one's side. *Feng-shui* (literally wind-water) is the Chinese technique of manipulating or judging the environment. Feng-shui uses unseen currents that swirl around the surface of the earth and are caused by dragons which sleep beneath the ground.

If you want to build a house, HDB estate, high-rise hotel or find a suitable site for a grave then you call in a feng-shui expert; the wrath of a dragon which wakes to find a house on his tail can easily be imagined! It is said that Lee Kuan Yew when in power regularly consulted feng-shui experts, and his luck declined when he insisted on continuing with badly sited land reclamation.

Incense and Lanterns, Thian Hock Keng Temple (CT)

Islam

In the early 7th century in Mecca, Mohammed received the word of Allah (God) and called on the people to turn away from pagan worship and submit to the one true God. His teachings appealed to the poorer levels of society and angered the wealthy merchant class. By 622 life had become sufficiently unpleasant to force Mohammed and his followers to migrate to Medina, an oasis town some 300 km to the north. This migration – the *hijrah* – marks the beginning of the Islamic calendar, year 1 AH or 622 AD. By 630 Mohammed had gained a sufficient following to return and take Mecca.

With boundless zeal the followers of Mohammed spread the word, using force where necessary, and by 644 the Islamic state covered Syria, Persia, Mesopotamia, Egypt and North Africa; in following decades its influence would extend from the Atlantic to the Indian Ocean.

Islam is the Arabic word for submission, and the duty of every Muslim is to submit themselves to Allah. This profession of faith (the *Shahada*) is the first of the Five Pillars of Islam, the five tenets in the Koran which guide Muslims in their daily life:

Shahada 'There is no God but Allah and Mohammed is his prophet' – this profession of faith is the fundamental tenet of Islam. It is to Islam what The Lord's Prayer is to Christianity, and it is often quoted (eg to greet the newborn and farewell the dead).

Salah The call to prayer. Five times a day – at dawn, midday, mid-afternoon, sunset and nightfall – Muslims must face Mecca and recite the prescribed prayer.

Zakat It was originally the act of giving alms to the poor and needy and the amount was fixed at 5% of one's income. It has been developed by some modern states into an obligatory land tax which goes to help the poor.

Ramadan This is the ninth month of the Muslim calendar when all Muslims must abstain from eating, drinking, smoking and sex from dawn to dusk. It commemorates the month when Mohammed had the Koran revealed to him; the purpose of the physical deprivation is to strengthen the will and forfeit the body to the spirit.

Hajj The pilgrimage to Mecca, the holiest place in Islam. It is the duty of every Muslim who is fit and can afford it to make the pilgrimage at least once in their life. On the pilgrimage, the pilgrim *(haji)* wears two plain white sheets and walks around the *kabbah*, the black stone in the centre of the mosque, seven times. Other ceremonies such as sacrificing an animal and shaving the pilgrim's head also take place.

According to Muslim belief, Allah is the same as the God worshipped by Christians and Jews. Adam, Abraham, Noah, Moses, David, Jacob, Joseph, Job and Jesus are all recognised as prophets by Islam. Jesus is not, however, recognised as the son of God. According to Islam, all these prophets partly received the word of God but only Mohammed received the complete revelation.

In its early days Islam suffered a major schism that divided the faith into two streams: the Sunnis (or Sunnites) and the Shi'ites. The prophet's son-in-law, Ali, became the fourth caliph following the murder of Mohammed's third successor, and he in turn was assassinated in 661 by the governor of Syria, who set himself up as caliph. The Sunnis, who comprise the majority of Muslims today, including the Malays, are followers of the succession from this caliph, while the Shi'ites follow the descendants of Ali. The Shi'ites are mostly distributed in Iran, Iraq, Syria, India and Yemen.

Islam came to South-East Asia with the Indian traders from south India and was not of the more orthodox Islamic tradition of Arabia. Islam was adopted peacefully by the coastal trading ports of Malaysia and Indonesia, and Islam absorbed, rather than conquered, existing beliefs.

Islamic sultanates replaced Hindu kingdoms, though the Hindu idea of kings remained. The traditions of adat (customary law) continued, but Islamic law dominated, while the caste system, never as entrenched as in India, had no place in the more egalitarian Islamic society. Women exerted a great deal of influence in pre-Islamic Malay society, but Islam weakened their position. Nonetheless, women were not cloistered or forced to wear full purdah as in the Middle East, and Malay women today enjoy more freedom than women do in many other Muslim societies.

Malay ceremonies and beliefs still exhibit pre-Islamic traditions, but most Malays are ardent Muslims and to suggest otherwise to a Malay would cause great offence. The Koran is the main source of religious law for Malays and, though few are proficient in Arabic, Malay children are sent to learn to read the Koran. However, the main medium of religious instruction is *Jawi*, the Malay language written in the Arabic script.

Hinduism

On first appearances Hinduism is a complex religion, but basically it postulates that we all go through a series of rebirths and reincarnations that eventually lead to *moksha*, the spiritual salvation which frees one from the cycle of rebirths. With each rebirth you can move closer to or further from eventual moksha; the deciding factor is your karma, which is literally a law of cause and effect. Bad actions during your life result in bad karma, which ends in lower reincarnation. Conversely, if your deeds and actions have been good you will reincarnate on a higher level and be a step closer to eventual freedom from rebirth. Dharma, or the natural law, defines the total social, ethical and spiritual harmony of your life.

Hinduism has three basic practices: *puja*, or worship; the cremation of the dead; and the rules and regulations of the caste system. Although still very strong in India, the caste system was never significant in Malaysia chiefly because the labourers who were brought here from India were mainly from the lower classes.

Westerners often have trouble understanding Hinduism, principally because of its vast pantheon of gods. In fact you can look upon all these different gods simply as pictorial representations of the many attributes of a god. The one omnipresent god usually has three physical representations: Brahma, the creator; Vishnu, the preserver; and Shiva, the destroyer or reproducer. All three gods are usually shown with four arms, but Brahma has the added advantage of four heads to represent his all-seeing presence. The four *Vedas*, the books of 'divine knowledge' which are the foundation of Hindu philosophy, are supposed to have emanated from his mouths.

Hinduism is not a proselytising religion since you cannot be converted. You're either born a Hindu or you are not; you can never become one.

Hinduism in South-East Asia dates back 2000 years or more and there are Hindu influences in cultural traditions, such as the wayang kulit and the bersanding wedding ceremony. However, it is only in the last 100 or so years, following the influx of Indian contract labourers and settlers, that it has again become widely practised.

LANGUAGE

The four official languages of Singapore are Mandarin, Malay, Tamil and English. Chinese dialects are still widely spoken, especially amongst the older Chinese. The most common dialects are Hokkien, Teochew, Cantonese, Hainanese and Hakka. The government's long-standing campaign to promote Mandarin, the main nondialectal Chinese language, has been very successful and increasing numbers of Chinese now speak Mandarin at home.

Malay is the national language. It was adopted when Singapore was part of Malaysia, but its use is mostly restricted to the Malay community.

Tamil is the main Indian language; others include Malayalam and Hindi.

English is becoming even more wide spread. After independence, the government had a bi-lingual education policy that attempted to develop the vernacular languages and lessen the use of English. However, Chinese graduates found that they had fewer opportunities for higher education and greater difficulties in finding a job. English was the language of business and united the various ethnic groups, and the government eventually had to give it more priority. It officially became the first language of instruction in schools in 1987. The only communication problems you may have are with older Singaporeans who did not learn English at school.

All children are also taught their mother tongue (which in the case of the Chinese is Mandarin) at school. This policy is largely designed to unite the various Chinese groups and to make sure Chinese Singaporeans don't lose contact with their traditions.

Singapore has developed its own brand of English, humorously referred to as Singlish. While irate Singaporeans write to the *Straits Times* and complain about the decline in the use of the queen's English, many Singaporeans revel in their own unique patois. It contains borrowed words from Hokkien and Malay, such as *shiok* (delicious) and *kasar* (rough), and is often a clipped form of English, dropping unnecessary prepositions and pronouns. The ever-present 'lah' is an all-purpose word that can be added to the end of sentences for emphasis.

Facts for the Visitor

VISAS & EMBASSIES

Most nationalities do not require a visa to visit Singapore. Citizens of Australia, Canada, the Republic of Ireland, Malaysia, Netherlands, New Zealand, Switzerland, UK and USA do not require visas for any number of visits. Citizens of Austria, Belgium, Denmark, Finland, France, Germany, Italy, Japan, Korea, Luxembourg, Norway, Pakistan, Spain and Sweden do not require visas for social purposes for stays of up to 90 days.

Upon arrival a 14-day stay permit is normally issued, but a month permit is usually no problem if you ask for it. You can easily extend a 14-day stay permit for another two weeks but you may be asked to show an air ticket out of Singapore and/or sufficient funds to stay. Further extensions are more difficult but in theory most nationalities can extend for up to 90 days. The Immigration Department (☎ 532 2877) is in the Pidemco Centre, 95 South Bridge Rd, on the corner of Pickering St.

Citizens of Israel, South Africa and Taiwan do not need visas for stays of up to 14 days, while most other nationalities from communist or socialist countries require a visa.

Singaporean Embassies

Some Singaporean embassies and high commissions overseas include:

Australia
    17 Forster Crescent, Yarralumla, Canberra ACT 2600 (☎ (06) 273 3944)
Germany
    Substrasse 133, 5300 Bonn 2 (☎ (0228) 31-20-07)
Hong Kong
    17th Floor, United Centre, 95 Queensway (☎ (5) 27 2212)
India
    E6 Chandragupta Marg, Chanakyapuri, New Delhi 110021 (☎ 60 4162)
Indonesia
    Jalan H R Rasuna Said, Kuningan, Jakarta 12950 (☎ (21) 52 1489)

Japan
12-3 Roppongi, 5 Chome, Minato-ku, Tokyo (☎ 3585 9111)
Malaysia
290 Jalan Tun Razak, 50400 Kuala Lumpur (☎ (03) 261 6404)
New Zealand
17 Kabul St, Khandallah, Wellington (☎ 79 2076)
Philippines
6th Floor, ODC International Plaza, 217-219 Salcedo St, Legaspi Village, Makati, Metro Manila (☎ 816 1764)
Thailand
129 Sathorn Tai Rd, Bangkok (☎ (2) 286 2111)
UK
2 Wilton Crescent, London SW1X 8RW (☎ (071) 235 8135)
USA
1824 R St NW, Washington DC 20009-1691 (☎ (202) 667 7555)

Consulates & Embassies in Singapore

Many foreign consulates and embassies are conveniently located around Orchard Rd. Addresses for some of them include:

Australia
25 Napier Rd (☎ 737 9311)
Austria
22-04, Shaw Centre, 1 Scotts Rd (☎ 235 4088)
Belgium
09-24 International Plaza, 10 Anson Rd (☎ 220 7677)
Brunei
325 Tanglin Rd (☎ 733 9055)
Canada
14-00 IBM Towers, 80 Anson Rd (☎ 225 6363)
Denmark
13-01 United Square, 101 Thomson Rd (☎ 250 3383)
France
5 Gallop Rd (☎ 466 4866)
Germany
14-00 Far East Shopping Centre, 545 Orchard Rd (☎ 737 1355)
India
31 Grange Rd (☎ 737 6777)
Indonesia
7 Chatsworth Rd (☎ 737 7422)
Ireland
08-02 Liat Towers, 541 Orchard Rd (☎ 732 3430)
Italy
27-02 United Square, 101 Thomson Rd (☎ 250 6022)
Japan
16 Nassim Rd (☎ 235 8855)
Republic of Korea
10-03 United Square, 101 Thomson Rd (☎ 256 1188)

Malaysia
    301 Jervois Rd (☎ 235 0111)
Myanmar (Burma)
    15 St Martin's Drive (☎ 737 8566)
Netherlands
    13-01 Liat Towers, 541 Orchard Rd (☎ 737 1155)
New Zealand
    13 Nassim Rd (☎ 235 9966)
Norway
    44-01 Hong Leong Building, 16 Raffles Quay (☎ 220 7122)
Pakistan
    20A Nassim Rd (☎ 737 6988)
Philippines
    20 Nassim Rd (☎ 737 3977)
Russia
    51 Nassim Rd (☎ 235 1834)
Sri Lanka
    Goldhill Plaza, 51 Newton Rd (☎ 254 4595)
Sweden
    PUB Building, 111 Somerset Rd (☎ 734 2771)
Thailand
    370 Orchard Rd (☎ 737 2644)
UK
    Tanglin Rd (☎ 473 9333)
USA
    30 Hill St (☎ 338 0251)

CUSTOMS

Visitors to Singapore are allowed to bring in one litre of
wine, beer or spirits duty free. Electronic goods, cosmet-
ics, watches, cameras, jewellery (but not imitation
jewellery), footwear, toys, arts and crafts are not duti-
able, and for other items such as clothes the usual
duty-free concession for personal effects applies. Singapore no longer allows duty-free concessions for
cigarettes and tobacco, though this is not advertised by
airlines or Singaporean customs. Importing of chewing
gum is banned, but you are most unlikely to have your
gum confiscated if it is for personal use.

Duty-free concessions are not available if you come
from Malaysia or if you leave Singapore for less than 48
hours (ie you can no longer stock up on duty-free goods
on a day trip to Batam in Indonesia).

Drugs, fire crackers, toy coins and currency, obscene
or seditious material, gun-shaped cigarette lighters,
endangered species of wildlife or their by-products,
pirated recordings and publications are prohibited. *The
importation of illegal drugs carries the death penalty* for more
than 15 grams of heroin, 30 grams of morphine, 500
grams of cannabis or 200 grams of cannabis resin, or 1.2
kg opium. Trafficking in lesser amounts ranges from a

minimum of two years jail and two strokes of the rotan to 30 years and 15 stokes of the rotan. If you bring in prescription drugs you should have a doctor's letter or prescription confirming that they are necessary.

There is no restriction on the importation of currency.

MONEY

Singapore uses 1c, 5c, 10c, 20c, 50c and S$1 coins, while notes are in denominations of S$1, S$2, S$5, S$10, S$50, S$100, S$500 and S$1000; Singapore also has a S$10,000 note – not that you'll see too many. Brunei notes are interchangeable with Singapore notes, but Malaysian notes are no longer interchangeable.

A$1	=	S$1.04
C$1	=	S$1.21
HK$1	=	S$0.21
NZ$1	=	S$0.85
RM 1 (Malaysia)	=	S$0.62
Rp 1000 (Indonesia)	=	S$0.76
UK£1	=	S$2.37
US$1	=	S$1.59
Y100	=	S$1.50

Credit Cards & ATMs

All major credit cards are widely accepted, although you're not going to make yourself too popular after a hard bargaining session for a new camera if you then try to pay for it with your Visa card. The authorities suggest that if shops insist on adding a surcharge you contact the relevant credit company in Singapore.

If your credit card has a personal identification number (PIN) attached, you can make cash withdrawals at most automatic teller machines (ATMs). If you are in Singapore for only a short time, a credit card is an easier way to carry your money than travellers' cheques. Of course, you will be charged interest unless you make sure your account is in the black before you leave. It is still a good idea to have some back up cash, travellers' cheques or another credit card or two, in case something goes wrong with your main credit card account.

Many banks are now connected to international networks, allowing you to withdraw funds from your savings account if you have a card with a PIN attached, eg Singapore banks are networked to the US Plus and Star systems. Check with your bank at home before you leave.

Banks & Moneychangers

Most of the major banks are in the Central Business District, although there are also a number of banks along Orchard Rd and local banks all over the city. Exchange rates tend to vary from bank to bank and some even have a service charge on each exchange transaction – this is usually S$2 to S$3, so ask first. Banks are open from 10 am to 3 pm weekdays and from 11 am to 1 pm on Saturdays.

Moneychangers do not charge fees, so you will often get a better overall exchange rate for cash and travellers' cheques than at the banks. You will find moneychangers in just about every shopping centre in Singapore. Indeed, most of the shops will accept foreign cash and travellers' cheques at a slightly lower rate than you'd get from a moneychanger.

Apart from changing other currencies to Singapore dollars, moneychangers also offer a wide variety of other currencies for sale and will do amazing multiple currency transactions in the blink of an eye. You can even get good rates for some restricted currencies.

Costs

Singapore is much more expensive than other South-East Asian countries and the strength of the Singapore dollar against most currencies has seen a substantial rise in costs for most visitors.

If you are travelling on a shoestring budget, prices will come as a shock but you can still stay in Singapore without spending too much money. The great temptation is to run amok in the shops and blow your budget on electrical goods or indulge in all the luxuries you may have craved for while travelling in less-developed Asian countries.

Expect to pay US$4 per night or more for a dorm bed and from US$15 to US$35 for a double room in a cheap hotel or guesthouse. You can eat well in Singapore for a reasonable price. A good meal at a food centre can cost less than US$3. Transport is cheap in Singapore and many of the island's attractions are free. So it is possible to stay in Singapore for under US$15 per day, though US$20 is a more realistic minimum. You should be prepared to spend a lot more if you want to eat in some restaurants, check out the nightlife or visit a lot of the attractions.

If you have more to spend, then most of your cash will be absorbed in hotel bills and restaurants. Mid-range, second-string hotels cost from US$35 to US$60, though hotels at the top of this range are of a pretty good standard. International-standard hotels cost from US$70 and go way up. Depending on discounts available, top-end hotels can offer good value for the facilities on offer. Restaurants cost US$10 or less for a good meal in an old-style coffee shop or a meal in a fast-food restaurant. For US$10 to US$20 you can eat at a fancier restaurant, and you can dine in top restaurants in this range if set meals, buffets or cheaper lunch menus are on offer. Above US$20 should get you high standards of food and service, though you will generally have to spend US$30 or much more to dine at Singapore's best restaurants. Taxis are quite cheap in Singapore, as are many other nonessentials.

Tipping

Tipping is not usual in Singapore. The most expensive hotels and restaurants have a 10% service charge – if the charge is paid, tipping is actually prohibited. Don't tip at hawkers' stalls, though the more expensive coffee shops and restaurants that do not add a service charge may expect a tip. Taxi drivers do not expect a tip and may actually round a fare down if it is 10c or 20c above an even dollar, though they may expect you similarly to round it up. Staff in the international hotels, such as the room staff or the doorman who hails your taxis, may expect a tip when you leave if they have provided good service.

Taxes & Service Charges

A 10% service charge and 4% 'cess' (government entertainment tax) is added to the more expensive hotel and restaurant bills, as well as at most nightspots and bars. This is the 'plus-plus' that follows quoted prices, eg S$120++, while some of the cheaper establishments don't have a service charge and absorb the tax into the quoted price. This is 'nett' price, eg S$70 nett.

Singapore's new 3% goods and services tax (GST) comes into force on 1 April 1994. This across-the-board tax is fixed for five years and rebates for tourists will not apply. There has been talk of reducing the 4% cess but whether this happens remains to be seen.

TOURIST OFFICES

The Singapore Tourist Promotion Board has two Tourist Information Centres. The first is upstairs in the Raffles Hotel shopping arcade in the colonial district, 02-34

Raffles Hotel Arcade (☎ 1-800-334 1335). It is open daily from 9 am to 8 pm. The other office is in the Orchard Rd area at 02-02 Scotts Shopping Centre (☎ 738 3778) on Scotts Rd and is open from 9.30 am to 9.30 pm. They can answer most of your queries and have a good selection of hand-outs. These offices may change when the new STPB offices are completed, on the corner of Tanglin and Napier Rds near the Marco Polo Hotel. The big hotels and Changi airport also stock a range of tourist leaflets and free tourist maps.

Pick up a copy of the *Singapore Official Guide*, which is updated monthly and has the latest opening hours, prices and bus routes. The STPB also produces other excellent publications, such as food and shopping guides.

Singapore Tourist Promotion Board

The Singapore Tourist Promotion Board offices in Singapore and overseas include:

Australia
> Suite 1604, Level 16, Westpac Plaza, 60 Margaret St, Sydney 2000 (☎ (02) 241 3771)
> 8th Floor, St George's Court, 16 St George's Terrace, Perth 6000 (☎ (06) 221 3864)

Canada
> Suite 1112, North Tower, Toronto, Ontario M4W 3R8

France
> Centre d'Affaires Le Louvre, 2 Place du Palais Royal, 75044 Paris Cedex 01 (☎ (01) 42 97 16 16)

Germany
> Poststrasse 2-4, D-6000 Frankfurt/Main (☎ (069) 23 1456)

Hong Kong
> 1-3, D'Aguilar St, Central, Hong Kong (☎ (5) 22 4052)

New Zealand
> c/o Walshes World, 2nd Floor, Dingwall Building, 87 Queen St, Auckland 1 (☎ (9) 79 3708)

Singapore
> Head office: 36-04 Raffles City Tower, 250 North Bridge Rd, Singapore 0617 (☎ 339 6622)

UK
> 1st Floor, Carrington House, 126-130 Regent St, London W1R 5FE (☎ (071) 437 0033)

USA
> NBR 12th Floor, 590 Fifth Ave, New York, NY 10036 (☎ (212) 302 4861)
> Suite 510, 8484 Wilshire Blvd, Beverly Hills, CA 90211 (☎ (213) 852 1901)

USEFUL ORGANISATIONS

Disabled Travel

Access Singapore is a guidebook to Singapore for the disabled produced by the Singapore Council of Social Services. It is available from the Singapore Tourist Promotion Board offices in Singapore or overseas, or contact:

Singapore Council of Social Services
    11 Penang Rd
    Singapore 0923
    (☎ 336 1544, fax 337 3175)

Places of Worship

Singapore has no shortage of churches, and of course mosques and Chinese and Hindu temples are everywhere.

Anglican
    St Andrew's Cathedral
    Coleman St (☎ 337 6104)
Buddhist
    Temple of 1000 Lights
    366 Race Course Rd (☎ 294 0714)
Catholic
    Cathedral of the Good Shepherd
    4 Queen St (☎ 337 0236)
Hindu
    Sri Mariamman Temple
    244 South Bridge Rd (☎ 223 4064)
Jewish
    Magain Aboth Synagogue
    Waterloo St (☎ 336 0692)
Methodist
    Wesley Methodist Church
    5 Fort Canning Rd (☎ 336 1433)
Muslim
    Sultan Mosque
    North Bridge Rd (☎ 293 4405)
Presbyterian
    Orchard Rd Presbyterian Church
    3 Orchard Rd (☎ 337 6681)
Taoist
    Tian Fu Gong Temple
    158 Telok Ayer St (☎ 222 2651)

Cultural & Social Clubs

Alliance Française
    4 Draycott Park (☎ 737 8422)

American Association
    21 Scotts Rd (☎ 734 4811)
Australian & New Zealand Association
    PO Box 426, Tanglin Post Office (☎ 734 4902)
British Council
    30 Napier Rd (☎ 473 1111)
German Club
    12 First Ave (☎ 466 3156)
Goethe Institute
    Singapore Shopping Centre (☎ 337 5111)
Hollandse Club
    22 Camden Park (☎ 469 5211)
Swiss Club
    36 Swiss Club Rd (☎ 466 3270)

BUSINESS HOURS & HOLIDAYS

In Singapore, government offices are usually open from
Monday to Friday and Saturday mornings. Hours vary,
starting around 7.30 to 9.30 am and closing between 4
and 6 pm. On Saturdays, closing time is between 11.30
am and 1 pm. Shop hours are also variable, although
Monday to Saturday from 9 or 10 am to 8 or 9 pm is a
good rule of thumb.

    The following days are public holidays in Singapore.
For those days not based on the Western calendar, the
months they are likely to fall in are given:

1 January
    New Year's Day
January or February
    Chinese New Year
February or March
    Hari Raya Puasa
April
    Good Friday
April or May
    Vesak Day
1 May
    Labour Day
May or June
    Hari Raya Haji
9 August
    National Day
November
    Deepavali
25 December
    Christmas Day

CULTURAL EVENTS

With so many cultures and religions, there is an amazing number of celebrations in Singapore. Although some of them have fixed dates, the Hindus, Muslims and Chinese follow a lunar calendar which varies annually. In particular, the Muslim festivals vary enormously. The tourist office puts out a *Calendar of Festivals & Events* leaflet with dates and venues of festivals and events.

January-March

Ponggal – Ponggal is a harvest festival and the time for thanksgiving. Celebrated by south Indians, they offer rice, vegetables, sugar cane and spices to the gods. It is celebrated at the Sri Srinivasa Perumal Temple on Serangoon Rd.

Chinese New Year – Dragon dances and pedestrian parades mark the start of the new year. Families hold open house, unmarried relatives (especially children) receive ang pows (money in red packets), businesses traditionally clear their debts and everybody wishes you a *Kong Hee Fatt Choy* (a happy and prosperous new year). Chinatown is lit up, especially along Eu Tong Sen St and New Bridge Rd, and the *Singapore River Hong Bao Special* features *pasar malam* (night market) stalls, variety shows and fireworks.

Chingay – Processions of Chinese flag bearers down Orchard Rd, balancing bamboo flag poles six to 12-metres long, can be seen on the 22nd day after the Chinese New Year.

Thaipusam – One of the most dramatic Hindu festivals in which devotees honour Lord Subramaniam with acts of amazing masochism. In Singapore, they march in a procession from the Sri Srinivasa Perumal Temple on Serangoon Rd to the Chettiar Hindu Temple on Tank Rd carrying *kavadis*, heavy metal frames decorated with peacock feathers, fruit and flowers. The kavadis are hung from their bodies with metal hooks and spikes driven into the flesh. Other devotees pierce their cheeks and tongues with metal skewers or walk on sandals of nails. Along the procession route, the kavadi carriers dance to the drum beat while spectators urge them on with shouts of *Vel, Vel.* In the evening, the procession continues with an image of Subramaniam in a temple car. This festival is now officially banned in India.

Hari Raya Puasa – The major Muslim events are connected with Ramadan, the month during which Muslims cannot eat or drink from sunrise to sunset. In the evenings food stalls are set up in the Arab St district near the Sultan Mosque. Hari Raya Puasa marks the end of the month-long fast with three days of celebration; in the Malay areas, Geylang Serai is draped in lights for the occasion. In 1995 Ramadan begins on 1 February and Hari Raya Puasa begins on 4 March; and in 1996 the dates are 22 January and 22 February.

March-April

Cheng Beng – On All Souls' Day, Chinese traditionally visit the tombs of their ancestors to clean and repair them and make offerings.

Birthday of the Monkey God – The birthday of T'se Tien Tai Seng Yeh is celebrated twice a year at the Monkey God Temple in Seng Poh Rd opposite the Tiong Bahru Market. Mediums pierce their cheeks and tongues with skewers and go into a trance during which they write special charms in blood.

April-May

Vesak Day – Buddha's birth, enlightenment and death are celebrated by various events, including the release of caged birds to symbolise the setting free of captive souls. Temples such as Thian Hock Keng Temple on Telok Ayer St and the Temple of 1000 Lights on Serangoon Rd are thronged with worshippers.

May-June

Birthday of the Third Prince – The child-god is honoured with processions, and devotees go into a trance and spear themselves with spikes and swords. Celebrations, if you can call them that, are held at various temples and in Queen St, near Bencoolen St.

Dragon Boat Festival – Commemorating the death of a Chinese saint who drowned himself as protest against government corruption, this festival is celebrated with boat races across Marina Bay.

Singapore Festival of Arts – A biennial event held every even year, this festival has a world-class programme of art, dance, drama and music. The innovative Fringe Festival puts on free performances.

June-September

Singapore National Day – On 9 August, a series of military and civilian processions and an evening firework display celebrate Singapore's independence in 1965.

Festival of the Hungry Ghosts – The souls of the dead are released for one day of feasting and entertainment on earth. Chinese operas and other events are laid on for them and food is put out, which the ghosts eat the spirit of but thoughtfully leave the substance for mortal celebrants.

September-October

Thimithi (Fire Walking Ceremony) – Hindu devotees prove their faith by walking across glowing coals at the Sri Mariamman Temple.

Temple Door, Thian Hock Keng Temple (TW)

Moon Cake Festival – The overthrow of the Mongol warlords in ancient China is celebrated by eating moon cakes and lighting colourful paper lanterns. Moon cakes are made with bean paste, lotus seeds and sometimes a duck egg.

Navarathri – In the Tamil month of Purattasi, the Hindu festival of 'Nine Nights' is dedicated to the wives of Shiva, Vishnu and Brahma. Young girls are dressed as the goddess Kali and this is a good opportunity to see traditional Indian dancing and singing. The Chettiar, Sri Mariamman and Sri Srinivasa Perumal temples are centres of activity.

Temple Door, Chettiar Hindu Temple (PT)

October-November

Pilgrimage to Kusu Island – Tua Pek Kong, the God of Prosperity, is honoured by Taoists in Singapore by making a
pilgrimage to the shrine on Kusu Island.

Deepavali – Rama's victory over the demon King Ravana is
celebrated with the 'Festival of Lights', with tiny oil lamps
outside Hindu homes, and lights all over Hindu temples.

Festival of the Nine Emperor Gods – Nine days of Chinese operas,
processions and other events honour the nine emperor
gods.

December

Christmas – Orchard Rd celebrates Christmas with shopfront displays and the Christmas light-up, another of the illuminations that Singapore is so fond of.

POST & TELECOMMUNICATIONS

Post

The GPO on Fullerton Rd, close to the Singapore River, is open 24 hours for basic postal services. The efficient poste restante service is only open normal business hours. The Comcentre, 31 Exeter Rd, very near the Somerset MRT station on Orchard Rd, is also open 24 hours, as are three of the four post offices at Changi airport.

An airmail letter to most Asia-Pacific countries costs 35c for the first 10 grams and 25c for each additional 10 grams; to Europe and the Americas costs 75c for the first 10 grams and 55c for each additional 10 grams. An aerogramme costs 30c.

Telephone

From telephone booths, the cost of a call is 10c for three minutes. Calls from Changi airport are free. A few hotels have free local calls, though most charge around 50c per call, and some charge by the minute. The going surcharge on international calls is 25%.

Overseas telephone calls can be made 24 hours a day and the service is very efficient. As well as at hotels, you can make international phone calls at a Telecom centre like the ones at 15 Hill St or 71 Robinson Rd, or selected post offices such as the GPO.

The easiest way to make international phone calls is to dial them yourself from public pay phones but you'll need a phonecard and to use one of the phones which accept these cards (many pay phones will now only operate with phonecards – not coins). Phonecards, which cost from S$2, are available at Telecom centres, and a number of retail outlets such as newsagents and some supermarkets.

Credit-card phones are available (just swipe your Amex, Diners, MasterCard or Visa card through the slot). At the phone centres, there are also Home Country Direct phones – press a country button to contact the operator, then reverse the charges or have it charged to your international telephone card acceptable in your country. The Home Country Direct service is available from any phone by dialling the appropriate code, listed in the front pages of the phone book.

For directory information call 03; the police emergency number is 999.

TIME

Singapore is eight hours ahead of Greenwich Mean Time (GMT/UTC) (London), two hours behind Australian Eastern Standard Time (Sydney and Melbourne), 13 hours ahead of American Eastern Standard Time (New York) and 16 hours ahead of American Western Standard Time (San Francisco and Los Angeles). Thus, when it is noon in Singapore, it is 2 pm in Sydney, 4 am in London, and 11 pm in New York and 8 pm in Los Angeles the previous day.

ELECTRICITY

Electricity supplies are dependable and run at 220-240 V and 50 cycles. Plugs are of the three, square-pin type as used in the UK.

LAUNDRY

Singapore has plenty of laundries, such as the Wishy Washy chain (check the phone book). There is a Wishy Washy laundromat on the 1st floor of Orchard Plaza, 150 Orchard Rd, next to the Meridien Hotel. A large load, including drying and folding, costs S$9. All major hotels offer a laundry service, which can set you back a small fortune, and even most cheap hotels do laundry at more moderate rates.

WEIGHTS & MEASURES

Singapore uses the metric system, though you may occasionally come across references to odd measurements such as the *thola*, an Indian weight, or *batu*, the Malay word for mile (literally meaning stone).

BOOKS & MAPS

History

There are a great number of books dealing with various events in Singapore's history.

A History of Singapore by C M Turnbull is the best choice for a detailed overview of Singapore's history from prehistory to the present. It is an excellent scholarly work which is also very readable and a mine of interesting information. The author has also written *A Short History of Malaysia, Singapore & Brunei*.

Singapore: Its Past, Present and Future by Alex Josey deals mostly with Singapore's later history and is very pro-People's Action Party (PAP).

Raffles by Maurice Collins is the straightforward story of the man who founded Singapore. *The Duke of Puddle Dock* by Nigel Barley is a recent travelogue about this English author's journey in the region, mostly Indonesia, as he follows in the footsteps of Raffles. This sympathetic account of Raffles' life and achievements portrays Raffles as the ideal colonist and visionary, often comparing Raffles to Sukarno as a nation-builder. Though the book is often a celebration of English influence in the region, the author is at his best when observing the societies around him.

The fall of Singapore, and the subsequent Japanese occupation is a well-covered subject. *Sinister Twilight – The Fall of Singapore* by Noel Barber recounts the bunglings, underestimations and final heroics that culminated in the rapid collapse of Singapore. *Out in the Midday Sun* by Kate Caffrey tells of the hardships of those who were captured and spent the rest of the war years in prison camps like the notorious Changi camp.

Politics

Lee Kuan Yew – The Struggle for Singapore by Alex Josey covers all the twists and turns of Lee Kuan Yew's rise to power and the successful path along which his People's Action Party has piloted Singapore.

Governing Singapore by Raj Vasil is widely available in Singapore and is as close as you'll get to the official PAP line. It includes interviews with Lee Kuan Yew and Goh Chok Tong.

No Man is an Island by James Minchin is hard to find in Singapore. For an insight into both sides of the PAP story, this warts-and-all portrait of Lee Kuan Yew is one of the best. A boots-and-all portrait of the authoritarian nature of Singapore's government is *Obstacles to Democratization in Singapore* by E C Paul. This academic paper is a fascinating, often frightening but sometimes overstated look at the government's machinations and repression of opposition. Surprisingly, this paper is on sale at Singapore's better independent book stores.

A lighter look at politics is *Hello Chok Tong, Goodbye Kuan Yew*, a cartoon book that has a good-humoured dig at Singapore's leaders. It is hardly biting satire, but it is evidence of publishing liberalisation as this book would not have been tolerated a few years ago.

People & Society

Tales of Chinatown by Sit Yin Fong is a readable and informative piece on Chinese life. Fong was a journalist in Singapore for many years and writes anecdotal short stories about Chinese customs and beliefs.

Son of Singapore by Tan Kok Seng is the fascinating autobiography of a labourer who grew up in Singapore in the 1950s.

Culture Shock! (Singapore & Malaysia) by Jo Ann Craig, one of a popular series, explains the customs, cultures and lifestyles of Singapore's polyglot population to expatriates working there.

Tiger Balm King by Sam King is an insider's view of Aw Boon Haw, one of the most famous Asian tycoons and founder of Haw Par Brothers, makers of Tiger Balm. This rags-to-riches story is more concerned with examining the Aw household than business exploits.

Fiction

Singapore and Malaysia have always provided a fertile setting for novelists, and Joseph Conrad's *The Shadow Line* and *Lord Jim* both use the region as a backdrop. Somerset Maugham spent time in Singapore writing his classic short stories, many of which were set in Malaya – look for the *Borneo Stories*.

WW II has spawned a number of novels. *Saint Jack* by Paul Theroux is the story of an American pimp in Singapore, and *King Rat* by James Clavell is based on the experiences of POWs in Changi Prison. *The Singapore Grip* by J G Farrell was a local bestseller and provides an almost surreal view of life in Singapore, which was 'fiddling while Rome burned' as the Japanese stormed down the peninsula in WW II.

For a view from the other side, Jiro Osaragi's *Homecoming* is a Japanese novel about a Japanese naval officer who goes to Singapore to escape scandal. Much of it is set in Malacca and Singapore in the 1940s. *Southward lies the Fortress* by Lim Thean Soo is about the siege of Singapore as seen through a Singaporean's eyes. Also worth reading is Lim's collection of short stories, *The Parting Gift and Other Stories*.

Singapore has recently experienced a literary boom and many young novelists are hard at work, writing in English about Singapore. Of the old guard, Goh Sin Tub is a respected writer who has written many books. *Goh's 12 Best Singapore Stories* is widely available. *Juniper Loa* by Lin Yutang is set mostly in the 1920s, and is typical of earlier literature looking back at the mother land and the immigrant experience. It is about a young man who leaves China for Singapore and Juniper Loa is the woman he leaves behind.

Of the recent novelists, Philip Jeyaretnem is one of the leading lights and his *Raffles Place Ragtime* is a Singaporean bestseller. *A Candle or the Sun* by Gopal Baratham was published in 1991, after years of rejection by skittish Singaporean publishers. It is about a Christian group that runs foul of the authorities by questioning the government's authoritarianism. *Fistful of Colours* by Suchen Christine Lim, a winner of the Singapore Literature Prize, contrasts the difference and tensions between the modern and traditional, the old and the young in Singapore's ethnic communities. Catherine Lim is another highly regarded woman writer. Her books, such as *Little Ironies – Stories of Singapore*, are mostly about relationships with Singapore as a backdrop.

The real boom in Singaporean publishing has been in popular fiction. Ghost and horror stories abound in Singapore's bookshops and slightly risqué novels are walking out the door as Singapore discovers, after Goh Chok Tong's relaxation of censorship, that sex sells.

Travel Guides

Streets of Old Chinatown by Sumiko Tan is a street-by-street look at Chinatown's buildings, attractions and history, with maps, interesting photographs and some restaurant and hotel recommendations. Even though it was only published in 1990, many of the streetscapes have changed dramatically, but it will always be a good read.

Living in Singapore by the American Association of Singapore is handy for Westerners planning to set up house in Singapore. This is a useful introduction to life in the tropical city-state.

1907 Handbook to Singapore by G M Reith is a reprint by the Oxford University Press of a British colonial guide that describes the sights of old Singapore. It concentrates on the public buildings, gardens and clubs, many of which have hardly changed. It comes with the attitudes of the times, eg Malay is called a 'primitive language', but largely avoids reference to Asian cultures. It is a good insight into the interests of the British colonial, and the photographs, old map and advertisements are interesting.

South-East Asia on a shoestring (Lonely Planet) is our overall guidebook to the region. If you're travelling further afield, there are individual Lonely Planet guides to all South-East and North-East Asian countries.

General

Singapore: a Guide to Buildings, Streets, Places by Norman Edwards & Peter Keys is a wonderful architectural guide to Singapore. It has photographs and discussions of Singapore's major buildings and streetscapes, but it also includes a number of interesting titbits on Singapore's history and culture. *A History of Singapore Architecture* by Jane Beamish and Jane Ferguson is another good publication.

The *Mr Kiasu* comic books portrays the 'kiasu' (ie selfish, pushy, always-on-the-lookout-for-a-bargain) Singaporean. The Singlish-speaking, nonconformist, 'everything also must grab' Mr Kiasu has reached celebrity status in Singapore. These original and distinctly Singaporean cartoons are proof that Singaporeans can laugh at themselves.

Bookshops

Singapore's main bookshop chains are MPH and Times. In the Orchard Rd area, Centrepoint and Plaza Singapura shopping centres have a good selection of bookshops.

MPH's main shop at 71-77 Stamford Rd has been extensively renovated and is probably the best general bookshop in the region. It is also the most salubrious, and has a coffee shop and a record store. MPH also has other stores on the 4th floor of Centrepoint on Orchard Rd, Robinson Rd, at Changi airport, at Dhoby Ghaut and Orchard MRT stations.

Times also has a large bookstore on the 4th level of Centrepoint in Orchard Rd. Other Times bookshops include those at Lucky Plaza and Plaza Singapura on Orchard Rd, Holland Village, Changi airport, the World Trade Centre and a large store at Raffles City.

The Bras Basah Complex on North Bridge Rd in the colonial district specialises in textbooks and stationery, but has a few good general bookshops. Popular Book occupies four floors and is one of Singapore's largest bookstores, with a good collection of computer books, and books about the region. Skoob Books on the 4th Floor has a varied collection of academic books and is good for browsing.

Select Books on the 3rd floor of the Tanglin Shopping Centre, 19 Tanglin Rd, specialises in general and academic books on Asia and is the best in Singapore for books on South-East Asia.

Kinokuniya, the Japanese chain, has some interesting collections and good books on the region. Their main shop is in the Shaw Centre on the corner of Scotts and Orchard Rds, and features a large collection of books in Japanese. There are also book and magazine stalls in many of the larger hotels.

Maps

The American Express/STPB *Map of Singapore* is an excellent free map; it is available at the airport on arrival, at most middle and top-end hotels and at some shopping centres. Other giveaway maps, many in Japanese as well as English, are available.

Of the commercial maps, *Nelles* and *Periplus* are the best. The best reference of all if you plan on spending any length of time in Singapore or want to rent a car is the *Singapore Street Directory*, a bargain at S$8 and available at most bookshops. It includes a good fold out map of Singapore Island and Central Singapore.

MEDIA

Newspapers & Magazines

Singapore has three Chinese daily newspapers with a combined circulation of over 350,000 and three English newspapers with a similar circulation. There is also a Malay daily and an Indian daily. The major newspapers come under the umbrella of the gigantic Singapore Press Holdings.

The English daily newspapers are the establishment *Straits Times* and the *Business Times*, and the *New Paper*, an evening tabloid. The *Straits Times* has good regional and foreign news and some good feature articles. The best independent views on Singaporean politics are found in the readers' letters.

The *New Paper* is a long way behind the *Straits Times* in circulation, and is seen as the fun alternative. It is a more staid version of an English tabloid and comes up with some amazingly trite, attention-grabbing headlines. It contains very little news.

The press in Singapore knows its limits and you will find very little criticism of the government. The foreign media sometimes doesn't know its limits, and the government has been known to bring pressure to bear on those that do not report to its liking, as the *Far Eastern Economic Review* found out. A few newsstands in Singapore still stock the Review, under the counter with all advertising missing. *Times, Newsweek* and many other foreign magazines are readily available, though the government has the power to impose circulation quotas.

Radio & TV

The government-run Singapore Broadcasting Corporation controls broadcasting.

Singapore has six radio stations transmitting in four languages – Malay, Mandarin, Tamil and English – on the AM, FM and short-wave bands. The BBC transmits in Singapore on 889 FM. Two pirate stations transmit from Batam Island in the Riau Archipelago on 100.7 and 101.6.

Singapore has three TV channels: 5 and 12, which transmit mostly in English, and 8 which transmits mostly in Mandarin, though all stations carry programmes in Mandarin, English, Malay or Tamil. Singaporeans can also pick up Malaysian television – TV1 and TV2.

Television censorship is fairly strict. *Beverley Hills 90210* was very popular in Singapore until it was abruptly taken off the air because its morals and attitudes were deemed unsuitable role models for Singaporean youth.

FILM & PHOTOGRAPHY

It is, of course, polite to ask permission before photographing people or taking pictures in mosques or temples. There is usually no objection to taking photographs in places of worship; in Chinese temples virtually anything goes.

The usual rules for tropical photography apply: try to take photographs early in the morning or late in the afternoon. By 10 am the sun will already be high in the sky and colours are easily washed out. A polarising filter can help to keep down the tropical haze. Try to keep your camera and film in a happy environment – don't leave them out in direct sunlight, try to keep film as cool as possible and have it developed as soon as possible after use. Colour film can be developed quickly, cheaply and competently, but Kodachrome colour slides are usually sent to Australia for developing.

Film is cheap and readily available in Singapore. Processing is also reasonably priced.

HEALTH

In Singapore, you can eat virtually anywhere and not worry, and the tap water is safe to drink. Vaccinations are required only if you come from a yellow fever area, and Singapore is not a malarial area. The main health concern is the heat; it is important to avoid dehydration by drinking plenty of fluids.

Dehydration or salt deficiency can cause heat exhaustion. Take time to acclimatise to high temperatures and make sure you get sufficient liquids. Salt deficiency is characterised by fatigue, lethargy, headaches, giddiness and muscle cramps, and in this case salt tablets may help.

Medical facilities are of a high standard, readily available and reasonably priced. In fact, if you need dental work done, Singapore is a root-canal discount centre compared to most Western countries.

A visit to a general practitioner costs around S$30. Singapore's public hospitals will accept self-referred patients. Singapore General Hospital (☎ 222 3322) is on Outram Rd, near Chinatown and the Outram Park MRT station.

Health Insurance

A travel insurance policy to cover theft, loss and medical problems is a wise idea. There are a wide variety of policies and your travel agent will have recommendations. Check the small print: some policies specifically exclude 'dangerous activities' such as scuba diving; you may prefer a policy which pays doctors or hospitals direct rather than you having to pay on the spot and claim later; and check if the policy covers ambulances or an emergency flight home.

WOMEN TRAVELLERS

Singapore is probably the safest Asian country to travel in and sexual harassment is very rare. Women are not cloistered in Singaporean society and enjoy much more freedom and equality than in the rest of Asia. Government policy favours sexual equality, and abortion is available on request but not for 'foreign' pregnancies.

DANGERS & ANNOYANCES

Singapore is a very safe country with low crime rates. The usual precautions apply and pickpockets are not unknown, but in general crime is not a problem. This is

Fines

'Singapore is a fine country,' said the taxi driver. 'In Singapore we have fines for everything.'

Singapore has a number of frowned-upon activities, and the sometimes Draconian methods of dealing with minor transgressions has caused both mirth and dread amongst visitors. The famous anti-long-hair campaign is a thing of the past, but it wasn't that long ago that immigration inspections included looking at hair length, and long-haired men were turned away on arrival or given a short back and sides on the spot.

Singapore remains tough on a number of other minor issues, however, and the standard way of stamping out un-Singaporean activities is to slap a S$1000 fine on any offender. Actually, it is very rare that anybody does get fined that amount, but the severity of the fines is enough to ensure compliance.

Smoking in a public place – buses, lifts, cinemas, restaurants, air-conditioned shopping centres and government offices – is hit with a S$500 fine. You can smoke at food stalls and on the street (as long as you dispose of your butt, of course). The move to ban smoking in private cars was eventually quashed because of the difficulty in enforcing it. A few years ago it was the fashion among Singapore subversives was to urinate in elevators, but a successful campaign of heavy fines and security cameras has stamped that one out.

Jaywalking is a relatively minor crime – walk across the road within 50 metres of a designated crossing and it could cost you S$50. The successful antilittering campaign continues – up to S$1000 fine for dropping even a cigarette butt on the street – and, not surprisingly, Singapore is amazingly clean.

The MRT, Singapore's pride and joy, attracts some particularly heavy fines. Eating, drinking and smoking are forbidden, and if you use the MRT toilet and don't flush it – watch out. In fact, the 'flush or fine' campaign applies all over Singapore and has prompted apocryphal reports of flush sensors in the toilets to detect offenders.

The latest frowned upon activity in Singapore is gum chewing. Anti-social elements were leaving their gum deposits on the doors of the MRT, causing disruptions to the underground rail services. The sale and importation of chewing gum is now banned and subject to heavy fines, though individual 'possession' is not an offence. ■

not surprising given the harsh penalties meted out to offenders and the fact that 1000 suspected criminals are held in jail without trial because the government does not have enough evidence to ensure conviction!

The importation of drugs carries the death penalty and, quite simply, drugs in Singapore should be avoided at all costs, not that you are likely to come across them. In case you think the government is bluffing, the tally of executions for drug convictions stands at 37 so far, an astonishing number given the size of Singapore's population.

WORK

Work opportunities for foreigners are limited in Singapore, and while Singapore does have a fairly large expatriate European community, this is a reflection of the large representation of overseas companies rather than a shortage of skills in the Singaporean labour market.

In the great majority of cases, foreign workers obtain employment before they come to Singapore. One of the main reasons for this is the high cost of accommodation and car ownership, which overseas companies normally cover. There is a slight demand in some professions but Singapore is attempting to fill labour shortages by attracting Hong Kong professionals wanting out before 1997. The overwhelming majority of jobs are for domestic servants (newspapers are full of agencies advertising Filipino house maids) and unskilled labourers.

Some foreigners arrive in Singapore and find work. Business experience and economic training are a bonus, or those with easily marketable job skills can do the rounds of the companies that might be interested. It has become fashionable for some of the restaurants serving Western food to employ Westerners, and some travellers have picked up temporary work as waiters.

FOOD

While travelling around some parts of Asia is as good as a session with weight watchers, Singapore is quite the opposite. The food is simply terrific, the variety unbeatable and the costs pleasantly low. Whether you're looking for Chinese food, Malay food, Indian food, Indonesian food or even a Big Mac, you'll find happiness!

Chinese Food

In Singapore, you'll find a variety of Chinese food to send any epicure into raptures.

Cantonese When people in the West speak of Chinese food, they usually mean Cantonese food. It's the best known and most popular variety of Chinese cooking even in Singapore where the majority of Chinese are not Cantonese, as they are in Hong Kong. Cantonese food is noted for the variety and freshness of its ingredients. The food is usually stir-fried with just a touch of oil to ensure that the result is crisp and fresh. All those best known 'Western' Chinese dishes fit into this category – sweet & sour dishes, won ton soup, chow mein and spring rolls.

With Cantonese food, the more people you can muster for a meal the better as dishes are traditionally shared so that everyone manages to sample the greatest variety. A corollary of this is that Cantonese food should be balanced; traditionally all foods are said to be *ying* ('cooling' – like vegetables, most fruits and clear soups) or *yang* ('heaty' – starchy foods and meat). A 'cooling' dish should be balanced by a 'heaty' dish; too much of one or the other is not good for you.

Another Cantonese speciality is *dim sum*, or 'little heart'. Dim sum (often spelt tim sum, or called *din xiang*) is usually eaten at breakfast or lunchtime or as a Sunday brunch. Dim sum restaurants are usually large, noisy affairs and the dim sum, little snacks, are whisked around the tables on individual trolleys or carts. As they come by you, simply ask for a plate of this or a bowl of that. At the end of the meal, your bill is totted up from the number of empty containers on your table. Eating dim sum is fun as well as tasty.

Cantonese cuisine can also offer real extremes – shark's fin soup or bird's nest soup are expensive delicacies from one end of the scale; *mee* (noodles) or *congee* (rice porridge) are cheap basics from the other end.

North & West China Far less familiar than the dishes of Canton are the cuisines from the north and west of China – Szechuan, Shanghai and Beijing. Szechuan (or Sichuan) food is the fiery food of China – where the peppers really get into the act. Whereas the tastes of Cantonese food are delicate and understated, in Sichuan food the flavours are strong and dramatic – garlic and chillies play their part in dishes like diced chicken or sour & hot soup.

Beijing food is, of course, best known for the famous Peking duck, where the specially fattened ducks are basted in syrup and roasted on a revolving spit. The duck skin is served as a separate first course. Like the other northern cuisines, Beijing food is less subtle and more direct than Cantonese food. Although Beijing food is usually eaten with noodles or steamed buns in China, because rice doesn't grow in the cold northern Beijing region, in Singapore it's equally likely to come with rice.

Food from Shanghai is to some extent a cross between northern and Cantonese cuisines – combining the strong flavours of the north with the ingredients of Canton. It is not easy to find, however, in Singapore.

South China Cantonese is, of course, the best known southern Chinese cuisine but it is quite easy to find a number of other regional styles in Singapore, particularly since so many of the region's Chinese are Hokkiens or Hakkas.

One of the best known of these southern dishes comes from the island of Hainan. Throughout Singapore and Malaysia, one of the most widespread and economical meals you can find is Hainanese chicken rice. It's one of those dishes whose very simplicity ensures its quality. Chicken rice is simply steamed chicken, rice boiled or steamed in the chicken stock, a clear soup and slices of cucumber. Flavour this delicate dish with soy or chilli sauce and you've got a delicious meal for S$2.50 to S$3.50.

The Hainanese also produce steamboat, a sort of oriental variation on a Swiss fondue where you have a boiling stockpot in the middle of the table into which you dip pieces of meat, seafood or vegetables.

The Hokkiens come from Fukien province and make up the largest dialect group in Singapore. Although Hokkien food is rated way down the Chinese gastronomic scale, they have provided the unofficial national dish of Singapore – Hokkien fried mee. It's made of thick egg noodles cooked with pork, seafood and vegetables in a rich sauce. Hokkien popiah spring rolls are also delicious.

Teochew food, from the area around Swatow, is another style noted for its delicacy and natural flavour. Teochew food is also famous for seafood, and *char kway teow* (broad noodles, clams and eggs fried in chilli and black bean sauce) is a popular food-centre dish. Hakka food is noted for its simple ingredients and the best known Hakka dish, again easily found in food centres, is *yong tau foo* (bean curd stuffed with minced meat).

Taiwanese food includes rice porridge, a healthy and economical meal often with small side dishes of oysters, mussels or pork stewed in a rich sauce.

Indian Food

Indian food is one of the region's greatest delights, indeed it's easier to find really good Indian food in Singapore than in India! You can approximately divide Indian food into southern, Muslim and northern categories. Food from the south tends to be hotter and vegetarian food is well represented. Muslim food, something of a hybrid unique to Singapore and Malaysia, is based on north Indian dishes. It is subtle in its spicing and uses more meat. The rich curries and breads of north India are not as common in Singapore, and they are found in more expensive restaurants.

South Indian The typical south Indian dish is a *thali*, or rice plate. If you ask for one in a vegetarian restaurant you won't get a plate but a large banana leaf. On this leaf, a large mound of rice is placed with scoops of a variety of vegetable curries and a couple of papadams tossed in for good measure. With your right hand, for south Indian vegetarian food is never eaten with utensils, you then knead the curries into the rice and eat away.

When your banana leaf starts to get empty, you'll suddenly find it refilled – for rice plate is always an 'as much as you can eat' meal. When you've finished, fold the banana leaf in two with the fold towards you to indicate that you've had enough.

Other vegetarian dishes include the popular *masala dosa*. A dosa is a thin pancake which is rolled around the masala (spiced vegetables) with some *rasam* (spicy sauce) on the side. It provides about the cheapest light meal you could ask for.

Muslim Indian A favourite Muslim Indian dish, and one which is easy to find at low cost and of excellent standard, is *biryani*. Served with a chicken or mutton curry, the dish takes its name from the saffron-coloured rice it is served with. Other classics are *murtabak*, made from a paper thin dough which is then folded around egg and minced mutton and lightly grilled with oil. Or a *roti chanai* – simply a chopped up paratha (see under North Indian) which you dip into a bowl of dhal or curry sauce. This is a very popular and filling breakfast throughout the region. Or perhaps a *samosa* – a small triangular pastry containing meat or spiced vegetables.

Muslim Indian food is found all over Singapore in coffee shops, restaurants and food stalls.

North Indian A favourite in the north of India is *tandoori* food which takes its name from the clay tandoor oven in which meat is cooked after an overnight marinade in a complex yoghurt and spice mixture. Tandoori chicken is the best known tandoori dish. Although rice is also eaten in the north, it is not so much the ever present staple it is in the south. North Indian food makes wide use of the delicious Indian breads like *chapatti*, *paratha* and *naan*.

Malay, Indonesian & Nonya Food

Surprisingly, Malay food is not all that easily found in Singapore, although some Malay dishes, like *satay*, are everywhere. Satay is delicious tiny kebabs of chicken, mutton or beef dipped in a spicy peanut sauce. Some Malay dishes you may have a chance to try include *tahu goreng* – fried soy bean curd and bean sprouts in a peanut sauce; *ikan bilis* – tiny fish fried whole; *ikan assam* – fried fish in a sour tamarind curry; and *sambal udang* – fiery curry prawns. *Ayam goreng* is fried chicken and *rendang* is a sort of spiced curried beef in coconut marinade. *Nasi goreng* (or fried rice – *nasi* is rice and *goreng* is fried) is widely available but it is as much a Chinese and Indian dish as Malay, and each style has its own flavours.

Malay food is very similar to Indonesian food, and you'll find a few Indonesian restaurants in Singapore and Indonesian dishes on the menu in larger restaurants. *Gado gado* is an Indonesian salad dressed with a peanut sauce. In Sumatra, the Indonesian food leans much more towards curries and chillies. The popular Sumatran fare is *nasi padang*. In a nasi padang restaurant, all the different dishes are on display in the window and you select as many as you want to share amongst your group.

Nonya cooking is a local variation on Chinese and Malay food – it uses Chinese ingredients but with local spices like lemon grass and coconut cream. Nonya cooking is essentially a home skill, rather than a restaurant one, but Singapore has a number of Nonya restaurants. *Laksa*, a spicy coconut-based soup, is a classic Nonya dish.

Other Cuisine

Western fast-food addicts will find that Ronald McDonald, the Colonel from Kentucky and A&W have all made inroads into the regional eating scene. At big hotels, you can find all the usual Western dishes. In Singapore, you will also find Japanese, Korean and other regional restaurants. There are also modern air-conditioned supermarkets where you can find anything from yoghurt to packaged muesli.

Tropical Fruit

Once you've tried rambutans, mangosteens, jackfruit and durians, how can you ever go back to boring old apples and oranges? If you're already addicted to tropical fruit, Singapore is a great place to indulge the passion. If you've not yet been initiated, then there could hardly be a better place in the world to develop a taste for exotic flavours. In Singapore, the places to go for an easy introduction are the fruit stalls which you'll find in food centres or sometimes on the streets.

Slices of a whole variety of fruits (including those dull old apples and oranges) are laid out on ice in a colourful and mouth-watering display from which you can make a selection for just 30c and up. You can also have a fruit salad made up on the spot from as many fruits as you care to choose. Some tastes to sample include:

Rambutan In Malay, the name means 'spiny' and that's just what they are. Rambutans are the size of a large walnut or small tangerine and they're covered in soft red spines. You peel the skin away to reveal a very close cousin to the lychee with cool and mouth-watering flesh around a central stone.

Pineapple Probably the most popular tropical fruit, a slice of pineapple is always a delicious thirst quencher.

Fruit Stall (STPB)

You've not really tasted pineapple until you're handed a whole one, skin sliced away and with the central stem to hold it by while the juice runs down your arm!

Mangosteen One of the finest tropical fruits, the mangosteen is about the size of a small orange or apple. The dark purple outer skin breaks open to reveal pure white segments shaped like orange segments – but with a sweet-sour flavour which has been compared to a combination of strawberries and grapes. Queen Victoria, so the story goes, offered a considerable prize to anybody able to bring a mangosteen back intact from the East for her to try.

Durian The region's most infamous fruit, the durian is a large oval fruit about 25 to 30 cm long, although it may often grow larger. The durian is renowned for its phenomenal smell, a stink so powerful that first timers are often forced to hold their noses while they taste.

When the hardy, spiny shell is cracked open, pale white-green segments are revealed with a taste as distinctive as their smell. Durians are so highly esteemed that great care is taken over their selection and you'll see gourmets feeling them carefully, sniffing them reverently and finally demanding a preliminary taste before purchasing.

Durians are also expensive, and unlike other fruits which are generally ying (cooling), durians are yang (or heaty). So much so that the durian is said to be a powerful aphrodisiac. It's no wonder that durians are reputed to be the only fruit which a tiger craves!

Jackfruit or Nangka This enormous watermelon-size fruit hangs from trees and when opened breaks up into a large number of bright orange-yellow segments with a slightly rubbery texture. Externally, the nangka is covered by a green pimply skin, but it's too big and too messy to clean to make buying a whole one worthwhile. From fruit stalls, you can sometimes buy several nangka segments skewered on a stick.

Papaya The papaya, or pawpaw, originated in Central America but is now quite common throughout South-East Asia. It is very popular at breakfast time when, served with a dash of lemon juice, a slice of papaya is the perfect way to start the day. The papaya is about 30 cm or so in length and the bright orange flesh is somewhat similar in texture and appearance to pumpkin but related in taste to a melon. The numerous black seeds in the centre of a papaya are said to have a contraceptive effect if eaten by women.

Pomelo This large grapefruit-cross is the most common citrus fruit in South-East Asia. It has a thick, yellowish skin and a pink flesh that is sweeter than grapefruit.

Starfruit Known in Malaysia as *blimbing*, the starfruit takes its name from the fruit's cross-sectional star shape. A translucent green-yellow in colour, starfruit has a crisp, cool and watery taste.

Zirzat Sometimes known as soursop or white mango, the zirzat has a warty green outer covering and is ripe and ready to eat when it begins to look slightly off – the fresh green skin begins to look blackish and the feel becomes slightly squishy. Inside, the creamy white flesh has a deliciously thirst-quenching flavour with a hint of lemon in it. This is another fruit you can often find at fruit stalls.

Other Fruit Then there are coconuts, mangoes, lychees, bananas, jambu (guava), buah duku, chiku, jeruk and even strawberries. Plus all the temperate-climate fruits which are imported from Australia, New Zealand and further afield.

Desserts

Although desserts are not a really big deal in the region, you can find some interesting after-dinner snacks like *pisang goreng* (banana fritters), *ah balling* (Teochew rice balls stuffed with a sweet paste and served in syrup) or even *bo-bo cha-cha*, which is similar to ais kacang and chendol (refer to the following Drinks section). Ice-cream addicts will be relieved to hear that they can find good ice cream in Singapore, including soft-serve, multi-flavour gelati-style or packaged ice cream on a stick.

DRINKS

Life can be thirsty in Singapore, so you'll be relieved to hear that drinks are excellent, economical and readily available.

There are a wide variety of soft drinks from Coca-Cola, Pepsi, 7- Up and Fanta to a variety of F&N flavours including sarsaparilla (for root-beer fans). Soft drinks generally cost around S$1.

You can also find those fruit-juice-in-a-box drinks all over the region with both normal fruit flavours and oddities like chrysanthemum tea.

Beer drinkers will probably find Anchor Beer or Tiger Beer to their taste, although the minimum price for a small bottle of beer is now at least S$3. Travelling Irish may be surprised to find that Guinness has a considerable following – in part because the Chinese believe it has a strong medicinal value, and in part because it has a higher alcohol content than beer. ABC Stout is a cheaper priced local equivalent of the dark brew.

Sipping coffee or tea in a Chinese cafe is a time-honoured pursuit at any time of the day or night. If you want your tea, which the Chinese and Malays make very well, without the added thickening of condensed milk, then ask for *teh-o*. Shout it – as it's another of those words which cannot be said quietly. If you also don't want sugar, you have to ask for *teh-o kosong*, but you're unlikely to get it as they simply cannot believe anyone would drink tea that way!

Fruit juices are popular and very good. With the aid of a blender and crushed ice, delicious concoctions like watermelon juice can be whipped up in seconds. Old fashioned sugar-cane crushers, which look like grandma's old washing mangle, can still be seen in operation. Most food centres have a fruit stall, which will whip up a juice served in a glass, or in a plastic bag for take aways.

Halfway between a drink and a dessert are *chendol* and *ais kacang*. An ais (ice) kacang is rather like an old fashioned snow cone but the shaved ice is topped with syrups and condensed milk, and it's all piled on top of a foundation of beans and jellies. It tastes terrific! Chendol is somewhat similar.

Other oddities? Well, the milky white drink in clear plastic bins at drink sellers is soy bean milk which is also available in soft-drink bottles. Medicinal teas are popular with the health-minded Chinese.

Getting There & Away

AIR

To/From the USA

Asian airlines now offer a lot of discount fares from the US west coast to Asia. It's possible to find tickets from the US west coast to Singapore for around US$400 one-way or US$750 return. Scan the Sunday travel section of west coast newspapers like the *LA Times* or the *San Francisco Examiner* for agents handling discount tickets. Some cheap fares include a stopover in Hong Kong. There are also budget and super Apex fares available from the US west coast. Similar deals from the US east coast can be found in the Sunday newspapers there.

To/From Europe

Discount tickets to Singapore are available at London travel agents from as low as £230 one-way and £400 return. It's also possible to get flights from London to Sydney with stopovers in Singapore from around £650 to £800 return, depending on the season of travel. A ticket from London to Auckland with a Singapore stopover costs around £400 one-way. For more information, check the travel-ad pages in the weekly London 'what's on' magazine *Time Out*, daily newspapers or the various giveaway papers. Two good agents for cheap airline tickets are Trailfinders (☎ (071) 938 3444) at 46 Earls Court Rd and 194 Kensington High St, London W8, and STA Travel (☎ (071) 937 9962) at 74 Old Brompton Rd, London SW7.

To/From Australia

Advance purchase return fares from the Australian east coast to Singapore vary from around A$650 to A$1050 return, depending on the season of travel and the length of stay. From Perth fares are around A$500 to A$850. The 30-day or 45-day excursion fares are the cheapest, while the most expensive is a return ticket valid for over 60 days in the high season, generally from 15 November to 31 January.

Many of the airlines that fly from Australia to Asia, the Middle East and Europe stopover in Singapore. Currently one of the cheapest is Gulf Air, which offers good service but no alcohol. Singapore Airlines and Qantas Airways are the main carriers. Both have cheap package tours, and good stopover accommodation deals, as does Malaysian Airline System (MAS). MAS has cheap flights to Singapore, but they go via Kuala Lumpur.

For cheap tickets, STA have competitive prices for Asian airfares, as does the Flight Centre, another Australia-wide chain which can also offer good accommodation discounts, but shop around.

To/From New Zealand

A number of airlines fly from Auckland to Singapore. If you shop around, you can get discount fares between Auckland and Singapore. Some fares will allow you to stopover in Australia on the way. The standard one-way economy fare in high season is NZ$1400.

To/From Malaysia

The shuttle service operated by MAS and SIA has frequent flights between Kuala Lumpur and Singapore for RM119 (S$111 from Singapore); seats are available on a first-come, first-served basis. Booked seats cost RM159 (S$147). MAS also connects Singapore to Kuantan (RM146, S$136), Langkawi (RM218, S$204) and Penang (RM182, S$170) in Peninsular Malaysia, and Kuching (RM205, S$193) and Kota Kinabalu (RM418, S$391) in East Malaysia. First class fares are around 40% extra.

Pelangi Air has daily direct flights from Singapore's Changi airport to Melaka (RM110, S$110) and Ipoh (RM209, S$190); from Seletar airport, Pelangi has daily flights to/from Tioman Island (RM132, S$99) and Pangkor Island (RM209, S$190).

Silk Air also has daily flights to/from Tioman (RM132, S$99), flights on Thursdays and Saturdays to/from Kuantan (RM146, S$136), and flights on Mondays, Wednesdays and Saturdays to Langkawi (RM$180, S$170).

Return fares are double the single fares quoted here. Fares from Singapore to Malaysia are almost the same price as Malaysia to Singapore, but in Singapore dollars not Malaysian ringgit. With the considerable difference in the exchange rate it is much cheaper to buy fares in Malaysia, eg rather than a return fare to Kuala Lumpur from Singapore, buy a one-way ticket and the return leg in Kuala Lumpur.

Going to Malaysia, you can save quite a few dollars if you fly from Johor Bahru (JB) rather than Singapore. For example, to Kota Kinabalu the fares are RM418 from JB but S$391 from Singapore. To persuade travellers to take advantage of these lower fares, MAS offers a bus service directly from the Novotel Orchid, 214 Dunearn Rd, to the JB airport. It costs S$10 and takes about two hours. In Singapore, tickets for internal flights originating in Malaysia are only sold by the MAS office in the Singapore Shopping Centre.

To/From Indonesia

A number of airlines fly from Singapore to Jakarta for as low as S$120 one-way and around S$200 return. To Bali costs around S$300 one-way and S$500 to S$600 return. Garuda is the main carrier, though Air France has been offering the lowest prices. Garuda also has direct flights between Singapore and Medan, Padang, Palembang, Pekanbaru, Pontianak and Surabaya.

Internal flights are cheaper if tickets are bought in Indonesia. For Pontianak in Kalimantan and some destinations in Sumatra, such as Pekanbaru, it is cheaper to take the ferry to Batam and then an internal flight from there. Garuda offers an internal air pass costing US$300 for three flights and US$100 for each additional flight, but this is only economical for very long distances.

From Jakarta to Singapore, flights cost from US$80 (with Sempati). *Seabreeze Travel* (☎ 32 6675), 43 Jalan Jaksa, in the budget accommodation area, is one of the cheapest travel agents in Jakarta; also worth trying are Travel International (☎ 33 0103) in the President Hotel on Jalan Thamrin and, next door, Vayatour (☎ 310 0720).

Airline Offices

Singapore is a major international crossroad and a great number of airlines fly there. Offices of some of the airlines include:

Aeroflot
    01-02 Tan Cheong Tower, 15 Queen St (☎ 336 1757)
Air India
    17-01 UIC Building, 5 Shenton Way (☎ 225 9411)
Air Lanka
    02-00/B PIL Building, 140 Cecil St (☎ 223 6026)
Air Mauritius
    04-02 LKN Building, 135 Cecil St (☎ 222 3033)
Air New Zealand
    24-08 Ocean Building, 10 Collyer Quay (☎ 535 8266)

Alitalia
  20-02 Wisma Atria, 435 Orchard Rd (☎ 737 3166)
British Airways
  01-56 United Square, 101 Thomson Rd (☎ 253 8444)
Cathay Pacific
  16-01 Ocean Building, 10 Collyer Quay (☎ 533 1333)
China Airlines
  08-02 Orchard Towers, 400 Orchard Rd (☎ 737 2211)
Garuda
  01-57 United Square, 101 Thomson Rd (☎ 250 2888)
Indian Airlines
  01-03 Marina House, 70 Shenton Way (☎ 225 4949)
Japan Airlines
  01-01 Hong Leong Building, 16 Raffles Quay (☎ 221 0522)
KLM
  01-02 Mandarin Hotel, 333 Orchard Rd (☎ 737 7622)
Korean Air Lines
  07-08 Ocean Building, 10 Collyer Quay (☎ 534 2111)
Lufthansa
  05-01 Palais Renaissance, 390 Orchard Rd (☎ 737 9222)
MAS
  02-09 Singapore Shopping Centre, 190 Clemenceau Ave
  (☎ 336 6777)
Northwest Airlines
  08-06 Odeon Towers, 331 North Bridge Rd (☎ 336 3371)
Olympic Airways
  08-21 Parkmall, 9 Penang Rd (☎ 336 6061)
Pakistan International Airlines
  01-01 United Square, 101 Thomson Rd (☎ 251 2322)
Philippine Airlines
  01-10 Parklane Shopping Mall, 35 Selegie Rd (☎ 336 1611)
Qantas Airways
  04-02 The Promenade, 300 Orchard Rd (☎ 737 3744)
Royal Brunei Airlines
  01-4/5 Royal Holiday Inn Crowne Plaza, 25 Scotts Rd
  (☎ 235 4672)
Royal Nepal Airlines
  03-07 Peninsula Shopping Centre, 3 Coleman St (☎ 339
  5535)
Scandinavian Airlines System
  23-01 Gateway East, 152 Beach Rd (☎ 294 1611)
Sempati
  02-43 Meridien Shopping Centre, 100 Orchard Rd (☎ 734
  5077)
Silk Air
  SIA Building 77 Robinson Rd (☎ 223 8888)
Singapore Airlines
  SIA Building 77 Robinson Rd (☎ 223 8888)
Swiss Air
  18-01 Wisma Atria, 435 Orchard Rd (☎ 737 8133)
Thai International
  02-00 The Globe, 100 Cecil St (☎ 224 9977)
United Airlines
  44-02 Hong Leong Building, 16 Raffles Quay (☎ 220 0711)

Arriving in Singapore

Singapore's ultramodern Changi International Airport is another of those miracles that Singapore specialises in. It's vast, efficient, organised and was built in record time. It has banking and moneychanging facilities, a post office and telephone facilities (open 24 hours), free hotel reservation counters from 7 am to 11.30 pm, left luggage facilities (S\$3 per bag for the 1st day and S\$2 per day thereafter), nearly 100 shops, restaurants, day rooms, a fitness centre and a business centre. There are free films, audio/visual shows, bars with entertainment, hairdressers, medical facilities, a mini Science Discovery Museum (in Terminal 2), etc, etc. In fact, Changi has just about everything, so you can book into a hotel room in the terminal, pig out on Singapore's food, take a free city tour and you've done Singapore!

Changi is not really one airport but two – Terminal 1 and the newer, even more impressive Terminal 2 – each in themselves international airports to match the world's best. They are connected by the Changi Skytrain, a monorail that shuttles between the two. Terminal 2 is expected to handle Singapore's increasing air traffic well into the 21st century but Terminal 1 still handles most of the airlines. The following airlines use Terminal 2: Air France, Finnair, MAS, Myanma Airways, Philippine Airlines, Royal Brunei Airlines, Silk Air, Singapore Airlines and Swiss Air. All other airlines use Terminal 1.

On your way through the arrivals concourse, pick up the free booklets, maps and other guides available from stands. They give you a lot of useful information and good-quality colour maps of Singapore island and the city centre. There's even a free booklet listing all flights to and from Singapore, guides to the airport and the glossy monthly travel rag *Changi*.

Well-appointed day rooms cost from S\$22 to S\$35 per six hours. They are on the departure side of immigration and you must stay at the terminal you depart from. Or, if you just need a shower, you can have one for S\$5, including towel and soap.

If you are one of the millions of air travellers fed up with overpriced and terrible food at airports, then Changi airport has a variety of restaurants serving a whole range of cuisines at normal prices. Terminal 2 just pips Terminal 1 for the silver fork award in dining excellence. To find even cheaper food, just take the elevator beside McDonald's on the arrival level in Terminal 1 to the basement 1 'Food Centre', where you'll find a typical Singapore hawkers' food centre! It's the staff cafeteria but the public can eat there.

Changi airport continues to poll in the various travel-trade magazines as the best airport in the world. You'll understand why when you arrive and are whisked through immigration to find your bags waiting on the other side.

The airport tax (Passenger Service Charge) from Changi is S$15, payable at check-in or you can purchase PSC coupons in advance at airline offices, travel agencies and major hotels.

Singapore does have another 'international' airport – forgotten Seletar which handles a few services for the smaller regional airlines. It is in the north of the island, and the easiest way to get there is to take a taxi; the nearest MRT station is Yio Chu Kang. The airport tax from Seletar is only S$10.

To/From the Airport Singapore's Changi International Airport is at the extreme eastern end of the island, about 20 km from the city centre. The public buses (catch them in the basement), taxis or the more expensive limousine services run along the expressway into the city centre.

For visitors the most convenient bus service is No 390, which operates every eight to 12 minutes from 6 am to midnight daily, and takes about half an hour to reach the city. It costs S$1.20 but bus drivers don't give change so make sure you get some coins when you change money. As this bus approaches the city, it comes off the flyover into Raffles Blvd and then Stamford Rd. For Beach Rd, get off when you see the round towers of the Raffles City skyscraper on your right, just past the open playing fields of the Padang on your left. A half km further along is the National Museum and the stop for Bencoolen St. The bus then continues up Penang Rd, Somerset Rd and Orchard Blvd (which all run parallel to Orchard Rd) and then comes back along Tanglin and Orchard Rds. When heading out to the airport, catch bus No 390 on Orchard or Bras Basah Rds.

An alternative is to take the No 27 bus (80c, 20 minutes) to the Tampines Interchange, then hop on the MRT. From Tampines to City Hall costs $1.20 and takes 20 minutes.

Taxis from the airport are subject to a S$3 supplementary charge on top of the meter fare, which will probably be from S$12 to S$15 to most places. This supplementary charge only applies to taxis from the airport, not from the city.

LAND

To/From Malaysia

Bus For Johor Bahru, SBS bus No 170 leaves from the Ban San terminal on the corner of Queen and Arab Sts and costs 90c; the Bugis MRT is within walking distance. You can also catch the bus on Rochor Rd, Rochor Canal Rd or Bukit Timah Rd. For S$1.80, you can take the express bus to Johor Bahru operated by Singapore-Johor Express Ltd (☎ 292 8149) which departs every 10 minutes, also from the Ban San terminal.

The bus stops at the Singapore checkpoint, but don't worry if it leaves while you clear immigration – keep your ticket and you can just hop on the next one that comes along. The bus then stops at Malaysian immigration and customs at the other end of the Causeway, one km away. After clearing the Malaysian checkpoint, you can then catch the bus again (your ticket is still valid) to the Johor Bahru bus terminus, or you can walk to town. Moneychangers, whose first offer will usually be less than the going rate, will approach you or there are plenty of banks and official moneychangers in Johor Bahru.

If you are travelling beyond Johor Bahru, it is easier to catch a long-distance bus straight from Singapore, but there is a greater variety of bus services from Johor Bahru and the fares are cheaper.

In Singapore, most of the long-distance buses to Malaysia leave from and arrive at the bus terminal on the corner of Lavender St and Kallang Bahru, opposite the large Kallang Bahru complex. It is to the north-east of Bencoolen St, near the top end of Jalan Besar. Take the MRT to Lavender station then bus No 5 or 61, otherwise it's a half-km walk. However, current plans are to move the Malaysia bus terminal to Beach Rd, near Arab St.

Pan Malaysia Express (☎ 294 7034) has buses to Kuala Lumpur (S$17.80) at 9 am and 9 pm, Mersing (S$11.10) at 8, 9, 10 am and 10 pm, Kuantan (S$16.50) at 9 and 10 am and 10 pm, and Kota Bharu (S$30.10) at 7.30 pm. Also at the bus station, Hasry-Ekoba (☎ 292 6243) has buses to Kuala Lumpur (S$17), Ipoh (S$24) and Taiping (S$26) at 7.30 and 9.30 pm, Penang (S$30) at 6.30, 7.30 and 8 pm, and Melaka at 8 am and 2.30 pm. Melacca Singapore Express (☎ 293 5915) has buses to Melaka at 8, 9, 10, 11 am and 1, 2, 3 and 4 pm. The fare is S$11 for an air-con bus and the trip takes six hours. Many travel agents also sell bus tickets to Malaysia.

Morning Star Travel (☎ 299 2221) is another agent right at the Lavender MRT station. They have buses to Kuala Lumpur (S$17) at 9.30 am and 9.30 pm, Penang

(S$35) at 8 pm, Alor Setar (S$36) at 6 pm and Melaka (S$11) at 8.30 am. All buses leave from next to the MRT station, except for the Melaka bus which leaves from the Kallang Bharu terminal.

You can also catch buses to Kuala Lumpur from the Ban San terminal on the corner of Queen and Arab Sts. Kuala Lumpur-Singapore Express (☎ 292 8254) has buses to Kuala Lumpur at 9 am and 10 pm for S$17.30.

Most of the buses are new and in immaculate condition with mod-cons such as radio, TV, toilet and freezing air-conditioning. To Kuala Lumpur takes about eight hours; the road is very busy in both directions. There's also a lunch and snack break on the way. Hitchhikers to Malaysia should go to Johor Bahru before starting.

Train Singapore is the southern termination point for the Malaysian railway system. Malaysia has two main rail lines: the primary line going from Singapore to Kuala Lumpur, Butterworth, Alor Star and then into Thailand; and a second line branching off at Gemas and going right up through the centre of the country to Tumpat, near Kota Bharu on the east coast.

The Singapore Railway Station (☎ 222 5165 for fare and schedule information) is on Keppel Rd, south-west of Chinatown, about one km from the Tanjong Pagar MRT station.

Five trains go every day to Kuala Lumpur. The Ekspres Rakyat leaves at 7.30 am (arrives 2.50 pm), the mail train at 8.30 am (arrives 7.05 pm), the Ekspres Sinaran Pagi at 1.30 pm (arrives 9.10 pm), a limited express train at 8 pm (arrives 6.15 am) and the Sinandung Malam at 11 pm (arrives 7.10 am).

All trains are efficient, well-maintained and comfortable, but ordinary and mail trains stop at all stations and are slow. The express trains are well worth the extra money, and the Ekspres Rakyat continues on to Butterworth, arriving at 10.20 pm. There is also a train to Tumpat (in the very north-east of Malaysia) at 8.10 pm, which passes Jerantut and Kuala Lipis for Taman Negara National Park in the afternoon. Train fares from Singapore to Malaysia include:

Destination	Fare 1st	2nd	3rd
Johor Bahru	S$4.20	S$1.90	S$1.10
Kuala Lumpur	S$60	S$26	S$14.80
Ipoh	S$91.50	S$39.70	S$22.60
Butterworth	S$118.50	S$51.40	S$29.20
Kuala Lipis	S$67.50	S$29.30	S$16.70
Wakaf Bahru	S$111	S$48.10	S$27.40

Express train fares from Singapore include:

Destination	Fare 1st	2nd	3rd
Johor Bahru	S$13	S$10	S$6
Kuala Lumpur	S$68	S$34	S$19
Ipoh	S$100	S$48	S$27
Butterworth	S$127	S$60	S$34
Kuala Lipis	S$76	S$38	S$21
Wakaf Bahru	S$119	S$57	S$32

While there is a noticeable jump in comfort from 3rd to 2nd class, 1st class is not much better than 2nd class and considerably more expensive.

You can buy a 30-day rail pass allowing unlimited travel in Malaysia for RM175, or a 10-day pass for RM85. The pass entitles you to travel on any class of train, but does not include sleeping berth charges. Rail passes are only available to foreign tourists and can be purchased at a number of main railway stations.

From Singapore, there is also a *relbas* service to Kulai, just past Johor Bahru. This train is a different way to get to Johor Bahru, but you should allow up to an hour to buy your ticket and clear customs. Trains leave at 10 and 11.20 am and 12.30, 4 and 6 pm.

Taxi Malaysia has a cheap, well-developed, long-distance taxi system that makes Malaysian travel a real breeze. A long-distance taxi plies between set destinations, and as soon as a full complement of four passengers turns up, off you go. From Singapore, the best bet is to go to Johor Bahru and then take a taxi from there – it's cheaper and there are many more services – but Singapore also has such taxis to destinations in Malaysia.

For Johor Bahru, taxis leave from the Ban San terminal on the corner of Queen and Arab Sts. They cost S$6 per person, and an extra S$1 if there are long delays at the causeway. Foreigners are likely to have to pay more or hire a whole taxi for S$24 since they take longer to clear the border than Singaporeans or Malaysians, or so the taxi drivers claim. Another company is the Kuala Lumpur Taxi Service (☎ 223 1889), 191 New Bridge Rd, opposite the Majesty Theatre, which costs S$40 to Kuala Lumpur.

Crossing the Causeway The Causeway is that one-km link between Singapore and the mainland. An impressive piece of engineering in its day, it has difficulty coping with the amount of traffic on weekends and especially on long weekends and public holidays. If you're travelling by private vehicle or taxi, try to avoid these times. Take a bus, as buses sail on past in the express lane while the cars are stuck in the interminable queues.

Singapore has all sorts of future plans for improving cross-border traffic to Malaysia. A new bridge is planned between Geylang Patah in Malaysia and Tuas on the western side of Singapore Island. The MRT is being extended out to Woodlands and a new checkpoint will be built.

To/From Thailand

If you want to go direct from Singapore to Thailand overland, the quickest and cheapest way is by bus. You must have a visa to enter Thailand overland.

Bus The main terminal for buses to and from Thailand is at the Golden Mile Complex, 5001 Beach Rd. It's at the north-eastern end of Beach Rd, where it meets Crawford St; the Lavender MRT station is within walking distance. A number of travel agents specialising in buses and tours to Thailand operate from there. We Travel (☎ 293 6233) has buses to Hat Yai at 2 pm for S$32 and S$35. Grassland Express (☎ 292 1166) has a bus at 2.30 pm to Hat Yai for $45. Singapore Comfort Travel (☎ 297 2910) has a 1 pm bus to Hat Yai for S$23 and another at 2.30 pm for S$32. The difference in the fares reflects the difference in the buses, though all buses are air-con. The S$45 VIP coaches have videos and include a free meal. Most of these buses also stop in Butterworth.

Morning Star Travel (☎ 299 2221) at the Lavender MRT station also has a bus to Hat Yai at 2.30 pm for S$39. Hasry-Ekoba (☎ 292 6243) at the Malaysia bus station, on the corner of Lavender St and Kallang Bharu, has VIP coaches to Haty Yai at 2.30 and 3.30 pm.

Train The rail route into Thailand is on the Butterworth-Alor Setar-Hat Yai route which crosses into Thailand at Padang Besar. From Butterworth trains go to/from Singapore. You can take the *International Express* from Butterworth in Malaysia all the way to Bangkok with connections from Singapore. The *International Express* leaves Butterworth at 1.30 pm, arrives in Hat Yai at 4.40

pm and in Bangkok at 8.35 am the following morning. From Singapore to Bangkok costs S$91.70 (2nd class).

A variation on the *International Express* is the *Eastern & Oriental Express*, which runs once a week and caters to the well-heeled. The train is done out in antique opulence, and is South-East Asia's answer to the *Oriental Express*. It takes 42 hours to do the 2000-km journey from Singapore to Bangkok. Don your linen suit, sip a gin and tonic and dig deep for the fare – around US$1200.

SEA

To/From Malaysia

A ferry operates from north Changi to Tanjung Belungkor, east of Johor Bahru. It primarily serves as a service for Singaporeans going to Desaru in Malaysia, but hasn't proved to be a great success since its opening in mid-1993. The 11-km journey takes 45 minutes and costs S$15/24 (RM15/27) one-way/return for adults and S$9/15 (RM9/16) for children aged under 12 years. Cars cost S$20/32 (RM20/36), motorbikes S$7/12 (RM7/12) and bicycles $S4/7 (RM4/7), while checked luggage costs S$1 per piece. Ferries leave Singapore at 9 am, 12 noon and 4.15 pm and from Tanjung Belungkor departures are at 10.30 am and 1.30 and 5.45 pm. From the Tanjung Belungkor jetty two bus services operate to Desaru, and a Kota Tinggi service is planned. To get to north Changi, take bus No 2 to Changi Village and then a taxi.

From Changi Village, ferries also go to Pengerang across the strait in Malaysia. This is an interesting backdoor route into Malaysia. Ferries don't have a fixed schedule, which is most unlike Singapore, and leave throughout the day when a full quota of 12 people is reached. The cost is S$5 per person or S$60 for the whole boat. The best time to catch one is early in the morning before 8 am. Clear Singapore immigration at the small post on the Changi River dock.

To Tioman Island, Resort Cruises Pty Ltd (☎ 278 4677), 02-03 Shing Loong Building, 337 Telok Blangah Rd, is the agent for the high-speed catamaran that does the trip in 4½ hours. Departures are at 7.50 am from the World Trade Centre. To get to the World Trade Centre, take the MRT to Tanjong Pagar then bus No 10, 97, 100 or 131. Buses Nos 65, 143 and 167 go from Orchard Rd to the WTC, or buses Nos 97 and 100 go from the colonial district.

Top: Raffles City (CT)
Middle: Rickshaw Driver takes a Break (CT)
Bottom: Central Singapore (MF)

To/From Indonesia

Curiously, there is no direct shipping service between the main ports in Indonesia and near neighbour Singapore but it is possible to travel between the two nations via the islands of the Riau Archipelago. Most nationalities are issued a tourist pass, valid for two months, upon arrival in Indonesia but only at major air and sea ports. At other ports, visas are required.

The Riau Archipelago is the cluster of Indonesian islands immediately south of Singapore. The two most visited islands are Batam and Bintan, both of which can be reached by ferry services from Singapore. The ferries are modern, fast, air-conditioned and show movies. From Tanjung Pinang on Bintan, you can catch boats to Java and Sumatra.

Batam Island is a resort and industrial park. From Singapore it only takes half an hour to reach Sekupang or 45 minutes to Batu Ampar, both on Batam Island. Direct ferries from Singapore to Tanjung Pinang on Bintan Island take 2½ hours.

Departures are from the World Trade Centre. The World Trade Centre is a mini Changi airport with duty free and other shops, and a departure area where you can buy tickets from the various agents. The 2nd floor is full of travel agents which also handle bookings for the boats and resorts. You can usually buy tickets on the day of departure, but it may be wise to book on public holidays (ring the agents).

The main agents to Batam are Dino Shipping (☎ 270 0311), Indo Falcon Shipping & Travel (☎ 270 6778), Sing-Batam Ferries (☎ 734 1866) and Star Ferry Services (☎ 278 2788). Between them they have more than 100 departures per day to Batam, from 7.50 am to 8.40 pm. The going-rate is S$16 one-way and S$26 return.

For Bintan, Dino Shipping has boats to Tanjung Pinang at 10 am and 3 pm, and Indo Falcon Shipping has a 9 am departure on Saturdays. A one-way ticket is S$51 or S$81 return. Dino Shipping also has a boat to Tanjung Balai on Karimun Island at 1.30 pm for S$36 one-way or S$61 return.

Once you get to Batam and Bintan, there is a variety of ways of continuing to other parts of Indonesia. The most popular travellers' route is from Batam to Pekanbaru in Sumatra. The easiest way is to fly. Merpati has direct flights between Batam and Jakarta, Jambi, Medan, Padang, Palembang, Pekanbaru and Pontianak. Tanjung Pinang's airport is smaller and there are only a few direct flights to Jakarta and Pekanbaru.

From Batam boats go to most of the Riau islands to the west, from where it is possible to get connections to the Sumatra mainland. The easiest way to get to the mainland is the speedboat from Sepukang (Batam) to Pekanbaru which leaves at 10.30 am and costs 35,000 rp. There are other boats to Selat Panjang and then either fast or slow boats to Pekanbaru. Boats go to Tembilahan (four hours, 40,000 rp) in Sumatra and to Kuala Tungkal (six hours, 50,000 rp), from where buses go to Jambi for 7,500 rp.

From Bintan boats go to Singkep and Lingga islands to the south. Pelni's KM *Lawit* stops at Tanjung Pinang every second week on its way to either Jakarta or Sumatra. The fare to Jakarta costs 34,500 rp economy, 134,000 rp 1st class, but check with travel agents in Singapore to book a passage on this boat – otherwise you could miss it and have to wait a month.

To/From the Rest of the World

If you have ever wanted to jump ship and see the world, some cargo ships have passenger services, and of course many of them stop in Singapore. Don't expect it to be cheap – it can be many times more expensive than flying – but here are some suggestions:

ABC Containers
  The Strand Cruise & Travel Centre
  Charing Cross Shopping Concourse, The Strand, London WC2N 4HZ, UK (☎ (071) 836 6363, fax (071) 497 0078). This company has ships sailing via Europe, Israel and the Suez canal to Singapore and then Australia.
Bankline
  Andrew Wier & Co, Dexter House, 2 Royal Mint Court, London EC3N 4XX, UK (☎ (071) 265 0808, fax (071) 481 4784). This company has ships from Antwerp to French Polynesia, Fiji and Papua New Guinea before reaching Singapore and returning to Rotterdam.
Laeisz Line
  Freighter World Cruises Inc, 180 South Lake Ave, Suite 335, Pasadena, CA 91101, USA (☎ (818) 449 3106, fax (818) 449 9573). Operates from Long Beach via Oakland, Japan, Korea and Hong Kong to Singapore, before returning via Europe.
Leonhardt & Blumburg
  Hamburg-Sud Reiseagentur GmbH, Ost-West Strasse 59, 2000, Hamburg, Germany (☎ (040) 370 5593, fax (040) 370 5420). Sailing on one of the most direct routes from Europe, ships leave from Hamburg and stop in European ports then Saudi Arabia before reaching Singapore.

NSB Frachtstiff-Touristik
Niederlassung Bremen, Violenstrasse 22, 2800 Bremen, Germany (☎ (0421) 321668, fax (0421) 324089). This company is the main operator with ships out of Bremerhaven stopping in Felixstowe, Rotterdam, Antwerp, Le Havre and other European ports then sailing via Saudi Arabia before reaching Singapore. Other routes are via Australia, Japan, New Zealand, the South Pacific and the USA.

Cruises There is no shortage of cruises operating from Singapore or including Singapore in their itineraries. Plenty of cruises around Asia depart from Singapore (especially to Indonesia, Malaysia and Thailand), to/from Australia, India, Kenya, Europe and other destinations. One of the major operators is Pearl Cruises, but plenty of other companies such as P&O, Seven Seas, CTC, Winstar, etc operate services. It is best to book these through a travel agent.

LEAVING SINGAPORE

Departure Tax

From Singapore, the departure tax is S$15 from Changi airport and S$10 from Seletar.

Travel Agents/Airline Tickets

Singapore is also a good place to look for cheap plane tickets, and it competes with Bangkok and Penang to be the discount flight centre of the region. For good travel agents, Airpower Travel (☎ 294 5664), 26 Sultan Gate, near Arab St, is recommended by many travellers. Airmaster Travel (☎ 338 3942) on Bencoolen St is another long-running, reliable agent. STA Travel (☎ 734 5681) in the Orchard Parade Hotel is also worth trying. Many others advertise in the *Straits Times'* classified columns.

Fares vary with when you want to fly and with whom you want to fly. The cheapest fares are likely to be with the least loved airlines (various Eastern European ones, Bangladesh Biman etc), via inconvenient routes (you're forced to make stopovers on the way) at awkward times (they only fly every other Tuesday at 3 am).

Some typical rock-bottom discount fares being quoted in Singapore include South-East Asian destinations like Bangkok from S$180 one-way, Denpasar from S$320 one-way or S$550 excursion return, Jakarta S$120 one-way or S$200 return. To the subcontinent, you can fly to Delhi for S$430 one-way or S$860 return and Kathmandu for S$410 or S$740 return.

Fares to Australia include Sydney or Melbourne for S$540 one-way or Perth S$620 return. London, or other European destinations, costs from S$590 one-way with the Eastern European airlines and from S$700 one-way with the better airlines.

One-way fares to the US west coast are around S$900 direct or with a stop in Manila.

There are always some special multistop deals on offer such as Singapore-Jakarta-Sydney-Noumea-Auckland-Papeete-Los Angeles for S$1550 with Air France.

Getting Around

Bus

Singapore has an extremely frequent and comprehensive bus network. While the Mass Rapid Transit (MRT) subway system is easy and convenient to use, for door-to-door public transport it is hard to beat the buses. You rarely have to wait more than a few minutes for a bus and they will get you almost anywhere you want to go. The *Singapore Official Guide*, available free from the tourist office, lists Singapore's major attractions and the buses that go to them. An update list of buses is very handy because the bus route numbers change frequently.

If you intend to do a lot of travelling by bus in Singapore, a copy of the *Transitlink Guide*, the combined bus and MRT guide, is a worthwhile investment. It costs S$1 at bookshops and MRT stations. The guide lists all bus routes in a convenient pocket-size format, and has a street index that gives the numbers of all buses going to each of the listed streets.

Bus fares start from 50c (60c for air-con buses) for the first 3.2 km and go up in 10c increments for every 2.4 km to a maximum of 90c (S$1.20 air-con) for distances over 10.4 km. There are also a few flat-rate buses, usually charging 25c or 90c. When you board the bus drop the exact fare into the change box. No change is given.

The Transitlink farecard is a stored-value card that can be used on the MRT and on buses that have validator ticket machines. Put the card in the validator and select the correct fare. Farecards can be bought at MRT stations and bus interchanges for S$12 – S$2 deposit and S$10 of value – and are valid for six months.

Singapore Explorer tickets cost S$5 for one day and S$12 for three days of unlimited travel on the buses. A map of the major tourist attractions is included. These maps are available from many hotels, including the YMCAs, and travel agents, or phone 287 2727 for more details.

The Singapore Trolley is a grotesque bus made to look like an old-fashioned tram and it plies the Orchard Rd area, the colonial district, Central Business District and Chinatown, stopping at the major hotels and points of interest. It is a very handy route and the bus is certainly distinctive and easy to find. All-day (from 9 am to 9 pm) tickets cost S$9 for adults and S$7 for children, and this includes discounts to some attractions. A second route connects the Havelock Rd hotels to Orchard Rd. Some of the hotels offer complimentary tickets for guests.

Mass Rapid Transit (MRT)

Singapore's ultramodern Mass Rapid Transit (MRT) is the easiest, quickest and most comfortable way of getting around Singapore, and it can transport you across town in air- conditioned comfort in minutes.

The MRT was primarily designed to provide a cheap, reliable rail service from the housing estates to the city and industrial estates. Most of the 44 km of underground track is in the inner-city area, but out towards the housing estates the MRT runs above ground. Not content with this most impressive system, the government has new lines planned and work is well underway on a line linking Choa Chu Kang and Yishun, via Woodlands near the Causeway. Another line is planned to eventually run to Punggol in the north-east.

The Orchard Rd area is well serviced by the Somerset, Orchard and Newton MRT stations. In the colonial district, Dhoby Ghaut is close to Bencoolen St, while the Beach Rd accommodation area is between City Hall and Bugis stations. Raffles Place MRT station is right in the heart of the Central Business District and Outram Park and Tanjong Pagar are on the edge of Chinatown.

The excellent *Transitlink Guide* lists places of interest, government offices and shows the nearest MRT station and connecting bus services if they are needed. Maps show the surrounding areas for all stations, including bus stops.

Using the subway system is extremely simple. You check the map showing fares from your station, put money in the slot and press the button for the fare you want. You can get a single-trip ticket or a stored-value card that is valid until you've used up the value of the ticket. You insert the ticket into the entry gate to enter and on departure the ticket is retained by the exit gate unless it still has 'stored value'.

Single-trip tickets cost from 60c to S$1.50. Ticket machines take 10c, 20c, 50c and S$1 coins; they also give change. Note-changing machines change S$1 notes to coins, and some S$2 machines can be found. Stored-value farecards cost S$10 (plus S$2 deposit) and are purchased from the Transitlink sales offices found at MRT stations.

The trains run from around 6 am to midnight. At peak times, trains run every four to five minutes, and at off-peak periods every six to eight minutes.

Taxis

Singapore has a good supply of taxis – over 10,000 of them – and it's usually not too difficult to find one. The exceptions may include rush hours or at meal times (Singaporeans are not at all enthusiastic about missing a meal).

It is quite easy to recognise Singapore taxis although they come in several varieties – most common being black with a yellow roof or pale blue. Taxis are all metered and they are used – unlike some Asian countries where the meters always seem to be 'broken'. Flagfall is S$2.20 for the first 1.5 km then 10c for each additional 250 metres.

From midnight to 6 am, there is a 50% surcharge over the meter fare. From the airport, there is a surcharge of S$3 for each journey – but not to the airport. Radio bookings cost an additional S$2, or S$3 if booked 30 minutes or more in advance. There is also a S$1 surcharge on all trips from the Central Business District between 4 and 7 pm on weekdays and from noon to 3 pm on Saturdays. You may also have to pay the S$3 restricted area licence (see the following Restricted Zone & Car Parking section) if you are the first passenger of the day to take the taxi into the Central Business District during restricted hours.

Singapore taxi drivers are generally refreshingly courteous and efficient, plus the cars themselves are super-clean since drivers can be fined for driving a dirty cab. Some taxis also accept Visa cards. There are many taxi companies; for radio bookings 24 hours, NTUC (☎ 452 5555) is one of the biggest companies.

Trishaws

Singapore's bicycle rickshaws are fast disappearing, although you'll find a few still operating in Chinatown and off Serangoon Rd. Trishaws had their peak just after WW II when motorised transport was almost non-existent and trishaw riders could make a very healthy income. Today, they are mainly used for local shopping trips or to transport articles too heavy to carry. They rarely venture on to Singapore's heavily trafficked main streets.

There are, however, trishaws at many tourist centres in case you want to try one out. Always agree on the fare beforehand. On the street, a very short ride is S$2 and the price goes up from there.

Trishaw tours of Chinatown and Little India are operated from a number of the larger hotels.

Rickshaws (RN)

Car

Singaporeans drive on the left-hand side of the road and the wearing of seat belts is compulsory. Unlike in most Asian countries, traffic is orderly, but the profusion of one-way streets and streets that change names can make driving difficult for the uninitiated. The *Singapore Street Directory* is essential for negotiating Singapore's streets.

Rent-a-Car Singapore has branches of the three major regional rent-a-car operators – Sintat, Hertz and Avis. There are also a large number of small, local operators. If you want a car just for local driving, many of the smaller operators quote rental rates that are slightly cheaper than the major companies. Rental rates are more expensive than in Malaysia and there are expensive surcharges to take a Singapore rent-a-car into Malaysia. If you intend renting a car to drive in Malaysia for any length of time, then it is much better to rent a car in Johor Bahru or elsewhere in Malaysia.

Rates start from S$90 a day, including insurance, for a small car such as a Laser or Sunny, though the main operators charge around S$120 a day without insurance. There are hire booths at Changi airport and in the city; addresses of some of the main operators are:

Avis
    200 Orchard Blvd (☎ 737 1668)
Hertz Rent-a-Car
    19 Tanglin Rd (☎ 734 4646)

Bum Boat Tour, Singapore River (PT)

Ken-Air Rent-a-Car
01-41 Specialists Centre, Orchard Rd (☎ 737 8282)
Sintat Rent-a-Car
320 Orchard Rd (☎ 235 5855)

Restricted Zone & Car Parking From 7.30 to 10.15 am from Monday to Saturday, or 4.30 to 6.30 pm Monday to Friday, the area encompassing the Central Business District, Chinatown and Orchard Rd is a restricted zone where cars may only enter with an area licence sticker or if they carry at least four people. A licence costs S$3 per day or S$60 per month – not surprisingly this has dramatically reduced traffic problems in the rush hour! The licence requirement also applies to taxis, so if you want to take a taxi into the CBD during these hours you must pay for the taxi licence which costs S$3 – unless somebody else has already done so of course. The licence stickers are sold at booths just outside the district boundaries, or you can buy them at some post offices.

And if you should carelessly enter the CBD without a licence? There may well be inspectors standing by the roadside noting down the number plates of unlicensed cars as they enter the CBD. A fine will soon arrive at the car owner's address.

Parking in many places in Singapore is operated by a coupon system. You can buy a booklet of coupons at parking kiosks and post offices. You must display a coupon in your car window with holes punched out to indicate the time, day and date your car was parked.

Bicycle

Singapore's heavy traffic and good public transport system does not make bicycling such an attractive proposition. Bicycles can be hired at a number of places on the East Coast Parkway, but they are intended mostly for weekend jaunts along the foreshore. Mountain bikes, racers and tandems are available for around S$3 to S$5 per hour. See the East Coast section in Things to See & Do for details. Bikes can also be rented at Sentosa.

Walking

Getting around the old areas of Singapore on foot has one small problem – apart from the heat and humidity that is. The problem is the 'five-foot ways' instead of sidewalks or pavements. A five-foot way, which takes its name from the fact that it is roughly five feet wide, is a walkway at the front of the traditional Chinese shophouses, but enclosed, verandah-like, in the front of the building.

The difficulty with them is that every shop's walkway is individual. It may well be higher or lower than the shop next door or closer to or further from the street. Walking thus becomes a constant up and down and side to side, further complicated by the fact that half the shops seem to overflow right across the walkway, forcing you to venture into the street, and bikes or motorcycles are parked across them.

Even newer areas like Orchard Rd suffer from the five-foot-ways syndrome in places with shopping centres on different levels. The hazards are complicated by the flash, but very slippery, tiles out the front that are an essential part of shopping-centre architecture. After a rainstorm on Orchard Rd, count the tourists falling.

Boats & Ferries

You can charter a bumboat (motorised sampan) to take a tour up the Singapore River or to go to the islands around Singapore. Speedboats can be hired from Punggol Boatel to go across to the northern islands or for water skiing. There are regular ferry services from the World Trade Centre to Sentosa and the other southern islands, and from Changi Village to Pulau Ubin. Or you can take more luxurious junk tours around the harbour either by daylight or as an evening dinner cruise or disco.

TOURS

A wide variety of tours are available in Singapore. They can be booked at the desks of the big hotels or through the operators. The *Singapore Official Guide* lists tours and the operators. Any of Singapore's travel agents can also book tours for you, or you could contact the tourist office.

Tours include morning or afternoon trips around the city or to Jurong Bird Park, the east coast or the various parks and gardens in Singapore. Most tours go for around 3½ hours, though full-day tours are offered. Tours vary in price, depending on how long they last and the cost of admission to the attractions covered, but most cost between S$20 and S$40.

There are city tours, which vary but generally take in the colonial district and the CBD, Chinatown, Orchard Rd, Mount Faber, Little India or the Botanical Gardens and possibly a handicraft shop (take the 'very good discounts' with a grain of salt).

Historical tours cover some of the same areas as city tours but focus on the founding of Singapore. War tours are popular and cover the battlefields, Changi prison, war memorials, armed services bases etc. There are tours of Chinatown, Little India and Arab St, some involving touring by bicycle rickshaw.

Jurong Bird Park is covered by many operators and extended tours of Jurong also include Crocodile Paradise, Chinese Garden, Ming Village or a visit to the Tiger Brewery.

Other tours include the zoo, Tang Dynasty City, a nightclub tour, Sentosa, east coast, a horse-racing tour, Singapore Science Centre, the five-day Singapore Culinary Heritage Tour and a golf tour. In fact tours cover just about all of Singapore, so it is just a matter of finding one that covers your particular interests.

The Singapore Trolley (see buses above) allows you to put together your own tour of Central Singapore. It plies a set route and you can get on and off where you like. Helicopter tours are also available for a view of the city that even the Westin Stamford can't match. They cost S$150 for adults and S$75 for children, but photography is not allowed. Ring Safe Travel & Enterprises (☎ 220 8833) for details.

Don't forget the free city tour for transit passengers from Changi airport who have four hours to spare. Two-hour tours go at 2.30 and 4.30 pm and you can tour the city in sealed no-man's land, at least in theory. You don't clear customs and the interior of the bus could be classed as international territory.

Cruises

River Cruises One of the best ways to get a feel for central Singapore and its history is to take a river cruise. Singapore River Cruise & Leisure (☎ 336 6119) operates a half-hour river tour for S$6 per adult and S$3 per child. It leaves from in front of the Hill St Centre on North Boat Quay, not far from Clarke Quay. You can buy tickets at the booth there, and tours leave on the hour from 9 am to 7 pm. The tour goes upriver to the old godowns at Clarke Quay and then back down to the harbour and Clifford Pier. A taped commentary, complete with weak jokes, gives a good rundown on the history of the buildings along the river.

Harbour Cruises A whole host of operators have harbour cruises departing from Clifford Pier. There is no shortage of touts trying to sell you tickets, or you can buy them at the Clifford Pier booking offices. Two companies offer 'tongkang' (Chinese junk) cruises and three main companies offer regular cruises as well as a number of lunch and dinner cruises. Most of them do the rounds of the harbour, which involves a lot of time passing oil refineries, then a look at Sentosa, and a visit to the southern islands of St John's, Lazarus and Kusu. The short stop at Kusu is worthwhile and you will get some good views of the city and harbour.

Eastwind Organisation (☎ 533 3432) has 2½ hour tours at 10.30 am and 3 and 4 pm that cost S$20 for adults and S$10 for children. Watertours (☎ 533 9811) operates tours at the same times for the same price, and a dinner tour. Their gaudy Chinese junk looks like a refugee from Haw Par Villa, but despite its grotesqueness it is a comfortable option.

J&N Cruise (☎ 223 8217) plies the same route in a catamaran. The 1½-hour luncheon cruise at 12.30 pm costs S$35 for adults and S$20 for children, or the two-hour cruise at 3 pm costs S$30 for adults and S$17 for children. Phoenix Offshore (☎ 534 1868) has cruises at 9.10 am and 3.10 pm costing S$28 for adults and S$15 for children; their lunch cruise costs S$50 adults and S$35 children.

All four companies also operate dinner and/or evening cruises as does Resort Cruises (☎ 278 4677). Dinner cruises range from around S$40 to S$80.

It is also possible to charter boats – the Singapore Tourist Promotion Board (☎ 339 6622) can put you in touch with charter-boat operators.

Things to See & Do

Singapore's greatest attraction is its ability to offer a taste of Asian culture in a small, easy-to-get-around package. Minutes from the modern business centre and its towering air-conditioned office blocks are the narrow streets of Chinatown where the bicycle rickshaw is still the best way to get around. Meanwhile, across the river there is Little India (Serangoon Rd) and the Muslim centre of Arab St.

Further out of the city, the Jurong area has a number of gardens, theme parks and other attractions. The East Coast is most popular as a weekend beach destination for Singaporeans, but also has some points of cultural interest. The central hills to the north of the city are Singapore's green belt, containing some fine parks and the zoo. Sentosa is Singapore's most famous fun-park island, though quieter islands are scattered around Singapore.

COLONIAL SINGAPORE – map 3

The mark of Sir Stamford Raffles is indelibly stamped on central Singapore. His early city plans moved the business district south of the river and made the area north of the river the administrative area. This early framework remained the plan for central Singapore through generations of colonial rule and the republican years of independence. While Singapore is now a modern city, many reminders of old Singapore remain.

North of the river is colonial Singapore where you'll still find the imposing monuments of British rule – the stone grey edifices of the town hall, parliament and museum, the churches and Victorian architecture. Many of these buildings still serve their original purpose. The Central Business District is the commercial heart of Singapore, though its monuments are now the skyscrapers of modern finance. Dividing these two areas is the Singapore River, which has always been the centre of Singapore. It was the site of the first British arrivals and for a long time the main artery of Singapore's trade.

The colonial district is easily reached by MRT; get off at either City Hall or Raffles Place stations. From the Raffles Place MRT station it is a short walk to Cavenagh

Bridge and the Singapore River, a good starting point for a tour of the area.

River

Singapore River, once the thriving heart of Singapore, is a quiet pedestrian precinct – an escape for lunchtime office workers, the spot to cast a line for fish, a weekend haunt for wedding photography sessions, or the place to dine in one of the renovated terraces or godowns next to the river. The bustling activity of sampans, bumboats, cranes and yelling, sweating labourers have gone and the new riverfront is a recreational stretch of photo opportunities and colonial restoration.

At the mouth of the river stands Singapore's symbol of tourism, the **Merlion**, a much photographed water-spouting, half-lion/half-fish statue. Upstream, **Anderson Bridge** is the first of the old bridges that spans the river. Next is **Cavenagh Bridge**, built in 1869, now for pedestrians only. It offers good access to **Empress Place**, (named in honour of Queen Victoria), Singapore's oldest pedestrian area and surrounded by many reminders of British rule. Empress Place Building houses a museum, and nearby at Raffles Landing Site is **Raffles' Statue**, standing imperiously by the water. It's roughly in the place where Raffles first set foot on Singapore island. Naturally, there are plenty of places to eat along the river. Two busy foodstalls popular with lunchtime crowds are opposite each other near Cavenagh Bridge. On the south bank, **Boat Quay** is a picturesque area of restored old shops with soaring office buildings right behind them. The stretch of renovated terraces along to South Bridge Rd and Elgin Bridge is currently one of Singapore's most popular restaurant strips.

Crossing over, North Boat Quay leads upriver to **Clarke Quay**. The old godowns here have been completely rebuilt in the name of restoration and the new development is no doubt set to supplant Boat Quay as the next 'in' dining spot. This impressive complex houses has a variety of shops, restaurants, bars, food stalls, a children's play area and a river boat fun ride through 'old Singapore' that is housed in one of the godowns. Nearby, in front of the Hill St Centre, you can explore the real Singapore River on a river boat tour. See River Cruises in the Getting Around chapter for details.

Empress Place Museum

This museum has major rotating exhibitions focusing primarily on Chinese culture and various Chinese

dynasties. The museum is upstairs in the Empress Place
Building and open daily from 9.30 am to 7.30 pm; entry
is S$6 for adults and S$3 for children. If the exhibition
doesn't grab you, you can explore the building itself for
free. Built in 1865, it is an imposing Georgian structure
that was once a court house and later housed a number
of government offices. The ground floor has a small art
gallery and antiques, ranging from true collectables to
souvenirs. House of the Four Seasons is a chic restaurant
with a snack bar section.

The Padang

There is no more quizzical a symbol of British colonial-
ism than the open field of the Padang. It is here that
flannelled fools played cricket in the tropical heat,
cheered on by the members in the Singapore Cricket
Club pavilion at one end of the Padang. At the other end
of the field is the Singapore Recreation Club, set aside
for the Eurasian community. Cricket is still played on the
weekends; but segregation is, officially, no longer practised.

The Padang was a centre for colonial life and a place
to promenade in the evenings. Things haven't changed
all that drastically, and the Esplanade Park opposite the
Padang on the foreshore is still the place for an evening
stroll. The Padang also witnessed the beginning of the
end of colonial rule, for it was here that the invading
Japanese herded the European community together,
before marching them off to Changi Prison.

The Padang is ringed by imposing colonial buildings.
The **Victoria Concert Hall & Theatre**, built in 1862, was
once the town hall. It is now used for many cultural
events and is the home of the Singapore Symphony
Orchestra. Check performance times; tickets are often
very reasonably priced.

Parliament House is Singapore's oldest government
building. Originally a private mansion, it became a court
house, then the Assembly House of the colonial government and finally the Parliament House for independent
Singapore. High St, which runs next to Parliament
House, was hacked from the jungle to become Singapore's first street, and was an Indian area in its early
days.

The **Supreme Court** and **City Hall** are two other stoic
colonial buildings on St Andrew's Rd. Built in 1939, the
Supreme Court is a relatively new addition, and is
notable for what it replaced – the Grand Hotel de
L'Europe, which once outshone Raffles as Singapore's
premier hotel.

Top: Singapore River (PT)
Bottom: National Museum & Art Gallery (TW)

Top: Raffles Hotel (MF)
Middle: Raffles Hotel Arcade (RH)
Bottom: Main Courtyard, Raffles Hotel (RN)

Raffles Hotel

The Raffles Hotel on Beach Rd is far more than just an expensive place to stay or the best known hotel in Singapore. It's a Singapore institution, an architectural landmark which has been classified by the government as a part of Singapore's 'cultural heritage'.

The Raffles was opened in 1887 by the Sarkies brothers, three Armenians who built a string of hotels which were to become famous throughout the East. They included the Strand in Rangoon and the E&O in Penang as well as the Raffles. Raffles started life as a 10-room bungalow, but its heyday began with the opening of the main building in 1899.

The Raffles soon became a byword for oriental luxury and featured in novels by Joseph Conrad and Somerset Maugham. Rudyard Kipling recommended it as the place to 'feed at' when in Singapore (but stay elsewhere he added!), and in its Long Bar, Ngiam Tong Boon created the Singapore Sling in 1915.

More recently, the Raffles underwent extensive renovations and extensions; it had fallen from grace and could no longer compete with Singapore's modern hotels. It reopened in 1991, once again a top hotel, though for some it wasn't the same old Raffles. While it is true that the Raffles is now a slick exercise in tourism marketing, for many it still oozes the old-fashioned atmosphere of the East as Somerset Maugham would have known it.

The **lobby** of the restored main building is open to the public and high tea is served in the Tiffin Room, though the Writers' Bar next door is little more than an alcove. In the other wings, the **Long Bar** or the **Bar & Billiard Room** are the places to sip a Singapore Sling.

The Raffles Hotel Arcade is a collection of expensive shops, and hidden away on the 3rd floor is the **Raffles Hotel Museum**. It is well worth a look, especially the old postcards. Admission is free and it is open from 10 am to 9 pm. Raffles memorabilia are on sale at the museum shop, including the hotel crockery if you can't afford to stay at the Raffles and nick your own. Next to the museum, **Jubilee Hall** theatre puts on *Raffles Revisited*, a multi-media presentation on the history of the Raffles Hotel. Viewing times are at 10, 11 am, 1 and 2 pm, and cost S$5 for adults, S$3 for children.

Churches

The most imposing examples of colonial architecture between Bras Basah Rd and Coleman St are the churches.

Many are run down and their congregations depleted or nonexistent, but the Urban Redevelopment Authority has most of them earmarked for restoration.

St Andrew's Cathedral is Singapore's Anglican cathedral, built in Gothic style between 1856 and 1863. It's in the block surrounded by North Bridge Rd, Coleman St, Stamford Rd and St Andrew's Rd. The Catholic **Cathedral of the Good Shepherd** on Queen St is a stolid neoclassical edifice built between 1843 and 1846 and is a Singapore historic monument. The best religious buildings are the **Convent of the Holy Infant Jesus**, on the corner of Bras Basah Rd and Victoria St, and **St Joseph's Institution**, a former Catholic boys school near the corner of Bras Basah Rd and Queen St, which is to be restored and turned into a fine arts museum.

The oldest church in Singapore is the Armenian **Church of St Gregory the Illuminator** on Hill St which is no longer used for services.

Fort Canning

If you continue north-west up Coleman St from the Padang, you pass the Armenian Church and come to Fort Canning Hill, a good viewpoint over Singapore. Once known as Forbidden Hill, it contains the shrine of Sultan Iskander Shah, the last ruler of the ancient kingdom of Singapura. Archaeological digs in the park have uncovered Javanese artefacts from the 14th century Majapahit Empire.

When Sir Stamford Raffles arrived, the only reminder of any greatness that the island may once have claimed was an earthen wall that stretched from the sea to the top of Fort Canning Hill. Raffles built his house on the top of the hill, and it became Government House until the military built Fort Canning in 1860. There is little left of the historic buildings that were once on the hill, but it is a pleasant park and you can wander around the old Christian cemetery and see the many gravestones with their poignant tales of hopeful settlers who died young. On the top of the hill is the Fort Canning Centre, a former barracks which now houses the Singapore Dance Theatre.

National Museum & Art Gallery

The National Museum on Stamford Rd traces its ancestry back to Raffles himself who first brought up the idea of a museum for Singapore in 1823. The original museum opened in 1849, then moved to another location in 1862 before being rehoused at the present building in 1887.

The museum is not extensive but the exhibits are well worth seeing and focus on regional cultures, history, crafts etc. Exhibits include archaeological finds from the Asia region, articles relating to Chinese trade and settlement in the region, Malaysian and Indonesian arts and crafts, Peranakan artefacts and a wide collection of items relating to Sir Stamford Raffles. The museum also has a superb jade collection donated by the Aw brothers, of Tiger Balm fame. The family amassed not only this priceless collection of jade pieces but also a variety of other valuable pieces of art. Many of the exhibits are rotating, so it is pot luck as to what you see, but the exhibits are always well presented.

The art gallery has a permanent collection of contemporary paintings from Singaporean and other South-East Asian artists, and there are regular temporary exhibitions. The museum is open from 9 am to 5.30 pm, except Wednesdays from 10.30 am to 7.30 pm and Mondays when it is closed. Admission is S$2. There is a museum bookshop, and tours of the museum leave from the information counter at 11 am from Tuesdays to Fridays.

Bugis Street

For years Bugis St was famous as Singapore's raucous transvestite playground. In a country that banned juke boxes and long hair, Bugis St was proof that Singapore dared to be daring. Bugis St was never, officially, more than another food stall centre but, in practice, at the witching hour certain young men turned into something more exotic than pumpkins. It was the place to be until the early hours of the morning, to join the crowds and watch the goings on, that is until Bugis St was totally demolished during the building of the MRT. As is the case with so many of Singapore's attractions, the answer was to rebuild it, to make it newer and better than ever.

So now Singapore has a new Bugis St, just south-west of the MRT station, complete with new terrace lookalikes and new lock-up wooden stalls with new canvas walkway overhangs. Transvestites are not allowed, and of course Bugis St is a pale shadow of its former self. Nonetheless it is a pleasant, even if much quieter, place to hang out in the evenings. Some of the open air restaurants and a couple of karaoke bars stay open until 3 am or until the last customers go home. There are fruit and food stalls, and you can pick up a copy watch or a T-shirt. The Bugis MRT station is right across the way.

Kuan Yin Temple

This temple on Waterloo St is one of the most popular Chinese temples – after all, Kuan Yin is one of the most popular goddesses. This temple was rebuilt in 1982, but the flower sellers and fortune tellers out front make it one of the liveliest temples in Singapore. A few doors away is the Sri Krishnan Temple, which also attracts worshippers from the Kuan Yin Temple, who show a great deal of religious pragmatism by also burning joss sticks and offering prayers at this Hindu temple.

Central Business District – map 2

Once the vibrant heart of Singapore, **Raffles Place** is now a rather barren patch of grass above the MRT station surrounded by the giant high-rise buildings of the Central Business District. There are a few shopping possibilities nearby including Aerial Plaza, a collection of small shops and aggressive Indian tailors, from where you can cross Collyer Quay to **Clifford Pier**, the place to hire a boat or catch a harbour tour (see Tours in the Getting Around chapter). Singapore's harbour is one of the busiest in the world; there are always boats anchored offshore, with one arriving or departing at least every 15 minutes.

Further south along the waterfront, you'll find large office blocks, airline offices, more shops and the **Lau Pa Sat** festival market housed in the Telok Ayer Centre, a fine piece of cast-iron Victoriana that was once a market.

Central Business District (MF)

It was pulled down during the construction of the MRT but has been restored and now stands on its original site. It has a wide selection of eating places and craft stalls, and cultural performances are occasionally held here. It is lively in the evenings, when adjoining Boon Tat St is closed off and hawkers' carts are set up. Singapore's disappearing Chinatown is inland from this modern city centre.

CHINATOWN – map 2

One of the most fascinating areas of Singapore, and its cultural heart, is Chinatown. In today's Singapore, Chinatown provides a glimpse of the old ways – the ways of the Chinese immigrants that shaped and built modern Singapore.

Unfortunately, much of Chinatown has been torn down and redeveloped over the last 30 years. Nowadays Chinatown is undergoing a different kind of redevelopment. The old colonial shop fronts, which are synonymous with the Chinese on the Malay Peninsula, are being restored under the direction of the Urban Redevelopment Authority.

The redevelopments are faithful to the original, and it is wonderful to see the old buildings winning out over the concrete high-rises, but sadly these restorations pose a new threat to Chinatown. The restored buildings are now desirable properties commanding high rents for businesses, shops and restaurants. The traditional businesses are moving out and a new gentrified Chinatown is taking its place. Much of the old Chinatown is now fashionable restaurants and expensive shops.

Meanwhile, any time of day is a good time to explore Chinatown, but you'll probably find the early morning hours not only the most interesting but also the coolest. Chinatown is roughly bounded by the Singapore River to the north, New Bridge Rd to the west, Maxwell and Kreta Ayer Rds to the south and Cecil St to the east.

Walking Tour

You can start a Chinatown walking tour from Raffles Place MRT station in the Central Business District. From the station, wander west along Chulia St and south down Philip St to the **Wak Hai Cheng Bio Temple (A)**. This Teochew Taoist temple is quite run down but has some interesting scenes depicted under, and on top of, the roof of the main temple.

Continue down Philip St and over Church St to Telok Ayer St, where the real clamour of Chinatown begins.

Telok Ayer St was on the seashore in Singapore's early days and was something of a brawling area frequented by sailors, but despite this it has a profusion of temples and mosques representing Singapore's major faiths.

The **Fuk Tak Ch'i Temple (B)** is hidden away at 76 Telok Ayer St, and at first glance it looks like a shop. It is a Hakka temple, noted for statues of the God of Wealth and his horse, which attract worshipping gamblers. Just before the temple is a shop devoted almost entirely to selling incense to temple worshippers.

At the junction with Boon Tat St, you'll find the **Nagore Durgha Shrine (C)**, an old mosque built by Muslims from south India during 1829 and 1830. It's not that interesting, but just a little south-west down the street is the Chinese **Thian Hock Keng Temple (D)**, or Temple of Heavenly Happiness, one of the most interesting temples in Singapore (see below).

Continue walking along Telok Ayer St and you'll soon come to the **Al-Abrar Mosque (E)** which was originally

---

The Old Trades of Chinatown

When wandering around Chinatown, you may come across some disappearing trades that have been part of Chinatown since its inception.

The letter writer will set up a streetside table and pen letters for the old residents of Chinatown who have never learned to read or write. Traditionally the letter writer would deftly pen the Chinese characters in letters destined to relatives back in China, though these days he is more often than not a sign writer, producing the lucky scrolls with message of prosperity and luck that will be hung outside houses during the Chinese New Year.

The chop is a Chinese stamp that serves as a signature for documents, and a chop maker will carve them for his customers. Traditionally it is carved on bamboo or ivory, though these days plastic is often used. It has a unique imprint, bearing both a unique design and the style of its maker, and cannot be replicated.

Rickshaw drivers have been a part of Chinatown ever since the jinriksha, or man-pulled rickshaw arrived from Shanghai. They were later replaced by the bicycle rickshaw, which still ply the streets of Chinatown. Drivers take passengers for the short trips from the shopping centres to the nearby housing estates, or the goods rickshaw has a platform at the front and is still a convenient way to transport freight around the backstreets. ■

built in 1827 and rebuilt in its present form from 1850 to 1855. A right turn and then another right turn will bring you into Amoy St, a Hokkien area that once catered to sailors and the sea trade. This street has almost been totally modernised, but the last vestiges of old sea trade can be seen on the sign at No 89: 'Kwong Thye Hin, Native Passenger Lodging House'.

Continue up Amoy St over Cross St, and then turn left (north-west) up Pekin St to China St. This area is a fascinating conglomeration of shops and shopfront activity, and the bicycle rickshaw is still used to transport goods. It is one of the few enclaves of Chinatown untouched by redevelopment, and you will still have to negotiate your way on the five-foot ways. Walking on these covered walkways is always a continuous obstacle course. It's also amazing how on many of these old Chinese houses, bushes and even large trees seem to sprout straight out of the walls – an indication of the amazing fertility which Singapore's steamy climate seems to engender. A little further over, Chin Chew St especially seems intent on being reclaimed by the jungle before the developers move in.

If you walk south-west on China St and cross back over Cross St, the name changes to Club St. On the corner with Gemmill Lane are a few interesting **antique shops (F)** and in the lot opposite, a **thieves' market** is held on Sunday afternoons from around 2 pm. The quiet area around Club St, Ann Siang Rd and Ann Siang Hill was a clove and nutmeg plantation until it became a prime residential area for Hokkien merchants. This area was noted for its highly decorated terraces, a number of which housed the old Chinese guilds, though only a few remain now. On the corner of Club St and Ann Siang Hill watch out for the **Lee Kun Store**, which specialises in the intricate **lion dance masks (G)** made from paper and bamboo.

South-west down South Bridge Rd is the **Tanjong Pagar (H)** conservation area, wedged between Neil and Tanjong Pagar Rds. This was the first major restoration project in Chinatown. The beautifully restored terraces accommodate a variety of restaurants and bars. The old Jinrikisha station, on the corner of Neil and Tanjong Pagar Rds, is an interesting triangular building that was once the depot for the hand-pulled rickshaws. The **Tanjong Pagar Heritage Exhibition** in the 51 Neil Rd complex is a small, interesting exhibition with old photographs that shows what Chinatown used to be like. It is open from 11 am to 9 pm. Admission is free.

Near Tanjong Pagar, the Bukit Pasoh area is a traditional part of Chinatown. Bukit Pasoh Rd, where you'll

Fans & other Souvenirs, Chinatown (RN)

find the Majestic Hotel, is known as the street of the clans because of the many clan association houses here. Keong Saik Rd is a curving street of old terraces with coffee shops, clan houses and clubs. On weekend evenings it's a lively street, and Chinese musicians sometimes work up a sweat.

Heading back to the centre of Chinatown, north-east up to South Bridge Rd, you enter the Kreta Ayer district, the real heart of Chinatown. The street hawkers and many of the traditional businesses have gone, but some of the old atmosphere of Chinatown remains. The Chinatown Complex, on the corner of Trengganu and Smith Sts, is a lively local shopping centre and a popular meeting place outside in the cool of the evening. Along with Smith St, Temple, Pagoda and Mosque Sts are traditionally the heart of old Chinatown. New developments have destroyed a lot of the atmosphere but Mosque St has a good row of coffee shops and Pagoda

St has plenty of souvenir and trinket shops selling masks, reproduction bronzes, bamboo ware, carvings and silk dressing gowns. Bargain hard.

Upstairs at 14B Trengganu St is the **Chinaman Scholars Gallery (I)**. This living museum is styled as a Cantonese house of the 1930s and includes furniture, clothing, artefacts, photographs and musical instruments from the period. It is open from 9 am to 4 pm; admission is S$4 for adults, S$2 for children.

Also in this area is the **Sri Mariamman Temple (J)**, Singapore's oldest Hindu temple (see below). The **Jamae (or Chulia) Mosque** on South Bridge Rd is only a short distance from the Sri Mariamman Temple. It was built by Muslim Indians from the Coromandel Coast of Tamil Nadu between 1830 and 1855.

Across New Bridge Rd from Pagoda St is the huge People's Park Complex – a modern shopping centre, but with much more local appeal than the general run of Orchard Rd centres.

Further north-east along Eu Tong Sen St is the **Tong Chai Medical Institute (K)** on Eu Tong Sen St. This architecturally interesting building is classified as a national monument.

Heading north-west back towards the river is an old area of colonial terraces awaiting renovation or demolition. In these streets you'll find the **Melaka Mosque**, claimed to be Singapore's oldest mosque but otherwise unimpressive, and the delightful **Tan Si Chong Su Temple** on Magazine Rd near Clemenceau Ave and the Singapore River. Unfortunately, this temple and ancestral hall built in 1876 for the Tan clan is often closed and the Central Expressway right opposite does not add to the atmosphere.

Thian Hock Keng

The Temple of Heavenly Happiness on Telok Ayer St in Chinatown is the oldest and one of the most colourful temples in Singapore. The temple was originally built in 1840 and dedicated to Ma-Cho-Po, the Queen of Heaven and protector of sailors.

At that time it was on the waterfront and since many Chinese settlers were arriving by sea it was inevitable that a joss house be built where they could offer thanks for a safe voyage. As you wander through the courtyards of the temple, look for the rooftop dragons, the intricately decorated beams, the burning joss sticks, the gold leafed panels and, best of all, the beautifully painted doors.

Sri Mariamman Temple

The Sri Mariamman Temple on South Bridge Rd, right in the heart of Chinatown, is the oldest Hindu temple in Singapore. It was built in 1827 but rebuilt in 1862. With its colourful *gopuram*, or tower, over the entrance gate, this is clearly a temple in the south Indian Dravidian style. A superb collection of colourfully painted Hindu figures gazes out from the gopuram.

Around October each year, the temple is the scene for the Thimithi festival during which devotees walk barefoot over burning coals – supposedly feeling no pain, although spectators report that quite a few hotfoot it over the final few steps!

LITTLE INDIA – map 4

Although Singapore is a predominantly Chinese city, it does have its minority groups and the Indians are probably the most visible, particularly in the colourful streets of Little India along Serangoon Rd. This is another area, like Chinatown, in which you simply wander around and take in the flavours. Indeed, around Serangoon Rd it can be very much a case of following your nose because the heady aroma of Indian spices and cooking seems to be everywhere.

If you want a new sari, a pair of Indian sandals, a recent issue of *India Today* or the *Illustrated Weekly of India*, a tape of Indian music or a framed portrait of your favourite Hindu god, then Little India is the place to go.

It's also, not surprisingly, a good place to eat, and you'll see streetside cooks frying chapattis at all times of the day. Since many of Singapore's Indians are Hindu Tamils from the south of India, Little India has many vegetarian restaurants, and there are some superb places to eat vegetarian food – number one being the well-known Komala Vilas restaurant.

Walking Tour

Little India is not very extensive, and you can sample its sights, scents and sounds in an hour or two. Little India is roughly the area bounded by Bukit Timah Rd to the south, Lavender St to the north, Race Course Rd to the west and Jalan Besar to the east. The real centre of Little India is at the southern end of Serangoon Rd and the small streets that run off it. Here, the shops are wall-to-wall Indian, but only a hundred metres or so away the Chinese influence reappears.

Temple Doors, Thian Hock Keng Temple (TW)

Unfortunately, much of the western side of Serangoon Rd has been flattened and consists of open fields, but there are interesting temples further north. Race Course Rd has a few shops and some good restaurants down its southern end, but the housing estates have made an unmistakable contribution to its atmosphere.

The **Zhujiao Centre (A)** on Serangoon Rd near Buffalo Rd is Little India's market. It was known as the KK market (Kandang Kerbau, meaning 'cattle pens', as this was once a cattle-holding area), before it was rehoused in this modern building. Downstairs is a 'wet market', the Singaporean term for a produce market, and it is one of the liveliest local markets in Singapore, selling all types of fruit and vegetables as well as meat and fish. The hawkers' centre here has plenty of Indian food stalls. Upstairs, stalls sell a variety of clothes and everyday goods and you can also buy brassware and Indian textiles.

Across Serangoon Rd are sari shops such as the Govindasamy store, and nearby are **spice shops (B)** that sell fresh spices ground daily in their mills. Wander around the backstreets with the names of imperial India such as Clive, Hastings and Campbell. This is the heart of Little India with a variety of shops selling spices, Indian music cassettes, saris, religious artefacts and everyday goods for the Indian household.

This is also a restaurant area and the best place to sample south Indian vegetarian food. At 76 Serangoon Rd is the famous Komala Vilas restaurant and around the corner in Upper Dickson Rd is the equally good New Woodlands restaurant.

Sri Mariamman Temple (AR)

Apart from the ubiquitous gold shops (gold is a girl's best friend in Asia), there are a few interesting **jewellers (C)** on Serangoon and Buffalo Rds that make jewellery crafted with traditional designs.

The southern end of Race Course Rd has the best collection of non-vegetarian restaurants in Singapore, from the tandoori food of north India to Singapore's famous fish-head curry (sounds and looks terrible, tastes delicious).

On the corner of Belilios and Serangoon Rds is the **Veerama Kali Amman Temple (D)**, a Shaivite temple dedicated to Kali. It is always popular with worshippers, especially at dusk.

Further north-east along Serangoon Rd is the Serangoon Plaza. Architecturally, historically and culturally it's a write-off, but the department stores here are good places for bargains. The range may not be extensive, but the prices for electrical goods and other household items are usually as good as you'll find anywhere in Singapore.

The **Sri Srinivasa Perumal Temple (E)** is an extensive temple dedicated to Vishnu. The temple dates from 1855 but the impressive gopuram is a relatively recent addition, built in 1966. Inside the temple, you will find a statue of Perumal, or Vishnu, and his consorts Lakshmi and Andal, as well as his bird-mount Garuda. This temple is the starting point for devotees who make the walk to the Chettiar Hindu Temple during the Thaipusam festival.

Not far from the Sri Srinivasa Temple is the Sakya Muni Buddha Gaya Temple, better known as the **Temple** of 1000 Lights (F) (see below). It's a glitzy, slightly tacky Thai-influenced temple, but one of Singapore's best known, and it welcomes visitors. A more beautiful temple is the Leong San See Temple over the road. This Buddhist and Taoist temple has some fine ceramic carvings inside.

From Little India, you can wander across to Jalan Besar. The Indian influence is not so noticeable here; the fine old pastel-coloured terraces with intricate stucco and tiles are Peranakan in style. Of particular note are the terraces on Petain Rd, and those on the corner of Plumer Rd and Jalan Besar. The area around Jalan Besar and Petain Rd is popular with bird-lovers, especially on Sunday mornings when the birds often sing in competition. At night, Petain Rd is noted for less wholesome activities.

A number of traditional businesses are on and around Jalan Besar, and the area around Kelantan Lane and Pasar Lane is a place to look for antiques. On Sundays a lively flea market operates, selling everything from old shoes and computer chips to motorcycle parts, and if you rummage around you can find old coins, porcelain and brassware.

Just off Jalan Besar on Dunlop St, down towards Rochor Canal Rd, is the Abdul Gaffoor Mosque. It's an intriguing fairy-tale blend of Arab and Victorian architecture.

Temple of 1000 Lights

Towards the north-eastern end of Race Course Rd at No 366, close to the corner of Serangoon and Beatty Rds, is the Sakaya Muni Buddha Gaya Temple, or the Temple of 1000 Lights. This Buddhist temple is dominated by a brightly painted 15-metre-high seated figure of the Buddha. The temple was inspired by a Thai monk named Vutthisasara. Although it is a Thai-style temple, it's actually very Chinese in its technicolour decoration.

Apart from the huge Buddha image, the temple includes oddities like a wax model of Gandhi and a figure of Ganesh, the elephant-headed Hindu god. A huge mother-of-pearl footprint, complete with the 108 auspicious marks which distinguish a Buddha foot from any other two-metre-long foot, is said to be a replica of the footprint on top of Adam's Peak in Sri Lanka.

Behind and inside the giant statue is a smaller image of the reclining Buddha in the act of entering nirvana. Around the base, models tell the story of the Buddha's life, and, of course, there are the 1000 lights which give the temple its name.

Any bus going north-east along Serangoon Rd will take you to the temple.

ARAB ST – map 5

While Chinatown provides Singapore with a Chinese flavour and Serangoon Rd is where you head to for the tastes and smells of India, Arab St is the Muslim centre. Along this street, and especially along North Bridge Rd and along side streets with Malay names like Pahang St, Aliwal St, Jalan Pisang and Jalan Sultan, you'll find batiks from Indonesia and sarongs, hookahs, rosaries, flower essences, hajj caps, songkok hats, basketware and rattan goods.

Walking Tour

The easiest way to begin a tour of the Arab Street area is to take the MRT to Bugis station and walk up Victoria St to Arab St.

Arab St is traditionally a textile district, and while the big merchants inhabit the textile centre on Jalan Sultan, Arab St is still alive with textile shops selling batiks, silks and more mundane cloth for a sarong or shirt. A number of craft shops sell leather bags and souvenirs, and up the end of Arab St near Beach Rd are the caneware shops. Negotiate the five foot ways and haggle for the wares.

Sultan Mosque (see below), the focus for Singapore's Muslim community, is on the corner of Arab St and North Bridge Rd. It is the largest mosque in Singapore and the most lively. You'll also find good Indian Muslim food at restaurants across the street on North Bridge Rd. One street back towards the city is **Haji Lane**, a narrow picturesque lane lined with two-storey shophouses that contain a number of textile and other local businesses. At the end of Haji Lane turn left into Beach Rd.

If you have time for a detour north-east along Beach Rd, the **Hajjah Fatimah Mosque** is interesting. A national monument, it was built by a Malaccan born Malay woman, Hajjah Fatimah, on the site of her home around 1845. The architecture shows colonial influences.

Otherwise, turn back up Arab St. Heading north-east up Baghdad St from Arab St, you find more batik and craft shops and then you cross **Bussorah St**. During the month of Ramadan, when Muslims fast from sunrise to sunset, the area is alive with foodstalls, especially in Bussorah St where the faithful come to buy food at dusk. Bussorah St is destined to become the new yuppie Arab St. The old terraces are being renovated and palm trees have been planted to give that Middle Eastern oasis look.

Caneware, Arab Street (PT)

At 24 Baghdad St you'll find **stone carvers** crafting the small headstones for Muslim graves, and further along between Sultan Gate and Aliwal St are other stone carvers that also produce carvings for Chinese temples and graves. This area is slated to become the new Malaysia bus station.

If you turn left into Sultan Gate you come to the historic gates that lead to the **Istana Kampong Glam**. The *istana* (palace) was the residence of Sultan Ali Iskander Shah and was built around 1840. The Kampong Glam area is the historic seat of the Malay royalty, resident here before the arrival of Sir Stamford Raffles. In the early days of Singapore, it was allocated not only to the original Malays but also to Javanese, Bugis and Arab merchants and residents.

Sultan Mosque (PT)

The palace isn't open to visitors, but if you walk through the gateway and around to the left a doorway in the palace wall leads you to Kandahar St, behind the Sultan Mosque. Muscat St winds behind the mosque back to Arab St, or you can continue up Kandahar St to North Bridge Rd. Cross over North Bridge Rd and you'll find a number of merchants selling perfumed oils. The Malay art gallery at 737 North Bridge Rd specialises in semi-precious stones that are used in huge knuckle-duster rings, and the shop also has rows of decanters containing perfumes such as 'Ramadan' and 'Aidal Fitri' for the faithful, or 'Sweet Heart' for the less spiritual.

On the corner of Jalan Sultan and Victoria St is **Malabar Muslim Jama-Ath Mosque**, a beautiful little mosque covered in blue tiles that is at its fairy-tale best when lit up in the evenings during Ramadan. Behind it is the old **Kampong Glam cemetery**, where it is said that the Malay royalty is buried among the frangipani trees and coconut palms. Many of the graves have fallen into ruin and are overgrown, but more recent graves are tended, as is evidenced by the cloths placed over the headstones.

Sultan Mosque

The Sultan Mosque on North Bridge Rd near Arab St is the biggest mosque in Singapore. It was originally built in 1825 with the aid of a grant from Sir Stamford Raffles and the East India Company as a result of Raffles' treaty with the Sultan of Johor. A hundred years later, the original mosque was replaced by a magnificent gold-domed building. The mosque is open to visitors from 5 am to 8.30 pm daily, and the best time to visit is during a religious ceremony.

ORCHARD RD – map 6

Singapore's international tourists and its wealthy residents also have whole areas of Singapore to themselves. Orchard Rd is where the high-class hotels predominate, and beyond it you enter the area of the Singapore elite. Prior to independence, the mansions of the colonial rulers were built there, and today the wealthy of Singapore, as well as many expatriates, live in these fine old houses.

Orchard Rd itself is mostly a place to shop, eat and stay. Its rows of modern shopping centres hold a variety of stores selling everything from the latest in Japanese gadgetry to the antiques of the East. Here you'll also find the majority of Singapore's international hotels, many of Singapore's nightspots and a whole host of restaurants, bars and lounges. This area is a showcase for modern Singapore and the delights of capitalism, but it also has a few points of cultural interest where you don't need your credit card.

Peranakan Place

Amongst the glass and chrome is Peranakan Place, a complex of old Nonya-Baba shop-houses on the corner of Orchard and Emerald Hill Rds.

Peranakan culture is that of the Straits-born Chinese who spoke a Malay dialect and developed their own customs that are a fascinating hybrid of Chinese and Malay. 'Nonya' is the word for an adult Peranakan woman, 'Baba' her male counterpart. There is a **Show**

House Museum that exhibits Peranakan culture. This house is decorated with Peranakan artefacts, furniture and clothing and if traditional Straits Chinese culture interests you, it shouldn't be missed. The museum is hard to find. It is in a terrace a few doors back from Orchard Rd – there is no sign. Buy tickets at the Emerald Mall open-air restaurant. Interesting tours of the museum go on demand and cost S$4 for adults and S$2 for children. The museum is open from 10.30 am to 3.30 pm, Monday to Friday.

From Peranakan Place, wander north up Emerald Hill Rd, where some fine terrace houses remain. This whole area was once a nutmeg plantation owned by William Cuppage, an early Singapore settler. At the turn of the century, much of it was subdivided and it became a fashionable residential area for Peranakan and Straits-born Chinese merchants.

Peranakan Place is just north of the Somerset MRT station.

Istana

The Istana (palace) is the home of Singapore's president and is also used by the prime minister for ceremonial occasions. Formerly Government House, the Istana is set about 750 metres back from the road in large grounds. The closest you are likely to get to it are the well guarded gates on Orchard Rd, but the Istana is open to the public on selected public holidays, such as New Year's Day. If you are lucky enough to be in Singapore on one of these days, take your passport and join the queues to get in.

House of Tan Yeok Nee

On the corner of Clemenceau Ave and Penang Rd, near Orchard Rd, the House of Tan Yeok Nee was built in 1885 as the townhouse of a prosperous merchant in a style then common in the south of China. This national monument was the Salvation Army headquarters for many years, but it has recently changed hands and is now closed to the public.

Chettiar Hindu Temple

On Tank Rd at the intersection of River Valley Rd, not far from Orchard Rd, this temple was completed in 1984 and replaces a much earlier temple built by Indian chettiars, or money lenders. It is a Shivaite temple dedicated to the six-headed Lord Subramaniam and is at its most active during the festival of Thaipusam, when the procession ends there. Worshippers make offerings of coconuts which are smashed on the ground to crack them open.

JURONG – map 7

Jurong Town, west of the city centre, is more than just a new housing area. A huge industrial complex has been built on land that was still a swamp at the end of WW II. Today, it is the powerhouse of Singapore's economic success story. The Jurong area also has a number of tourist attractions, in Jurong Town itself and on the way to Jurong from the city centre.

Haw Par Villa

About 10 km west from the city centre on Pasir Panjang Rd, this Chinese mythological theme park features theatre performances, boat rides, and the exotic collection of concrete and plaster figures that made the original Tiger Balm Gardens so famous. This hillside park was built with the fortune the Aw brothers made from their miracle cure-all Tiger Balm, and featured a gaudy grotesquerie of statues illustrating scenes from Chinese legends, and the pleasures and punishments of this life and the next.

Recent renovations and high-tech additions have changed the face of this long-popular monument to bad taste, but the surviving statuary remains its major attraction. Favourite displays include the Ten Courts of Hell, where sinners get their gory comeuppance in the afterlife, and the 'moral lessons' aisle, where sloth, indulgence, gambling and even wine, women and song lead to their inevitable unhappy endings.

New additions include the Tales of China Boat Ride, which is a guided boat tour of some of the statuary, and Spirits of the Orient and Legends & Heroes theatres where the inevitable 'multi-media' displays narrate Chinese myths and legends. The Four Seasons Theatre has live performances popular with children and there is also a heart-in-the-mouth roller-coaster boat ride. Haw Par Villa is popular with Singaporean families – it's fun for the kids, teaches them Chinese mythology and the moral tales scare the bejesus out of them if they misbehave – but at S$16 for adults and S$10 for children, you need to spend most of the day there and have a strong interest in Chinese mythology to get your money's worth.

The gardens are open from 9 am to 6 pm Monday to Friday and 9 am to 9 pm on weekends and public holidays. To get there, take bus No 143 from Orchard Rd or bus No 51 from North Bridge Rd in the colonial district. The nearest MRT station is Buona Vista, from where bus No 200 goes to Haw Par Villa.

Jurong Bird Park

This beautifully landscaped 20-hectare park has over 7000 birds from 600 species and includes a two-hectare walk-in aviary with an artificial waterfall at one end. Exhibits include everything from cassowaries, birds of paradise, eagles and cockatoos to parrots, macaws and even penguins in an air-conditioned underwater viewing gallery. The nocturnal house includes owls, kiwis and frogmouths. The Southeast Asian Birds Aviary is a major attraction and features a simulated rainforest thunderstorm every day at noon. A number of other shows are held throughout the day including, among others, pelican feeding (9.30 am and 1.30 pm), penguin feeding (10.30 am and 3.30 pm) and 'King of the Skies' (4 pm), featuring birds of prey. Breakfast with the Birds is the park's answer to bird singing contests, and the S$12 buffet breakfast from 9 to 11 am is a pleasant way to start the day.

You can walk around the park or take the Panorail service – an air-con monorail that does a tour of the park, stopping at the Waterfall Aviary. The Panorail costs S$2 for adults, S$1 for children.

Admission to the park is S$7 for adults and S$2.50 for children. The park is open from 9 am to 6 pm, Monday to Friday, and 8 am to 6 pm on weekends and public holidays. To get there, take the MRT to Boon Lay station and then bus No 251, 253 or 255. The bird park is on Jalan Ahmad Ibrahim. You can climb up Jurong Hill, beside the park, from where there is a good view over Jurong.

Jurong Crocodile Paradise

Singapore's crocodile farms have spawned quite an industry in crocodile skin products and crocodile parks like this one. Right next to the Jurong Bird Park, this is the largest of the parks with the best set-up for tourists. It has crocodiles of all ages, alligators, a shop selling crocodile products, crocodile wrestling performances and even a seafood restaurant that has crocodile on the menu. The crocodile wrestling performances at 10.45 and 3 pm are not for nature lovers, but they are good theatre. It is open from 9 am to 6 pm daily and costs S$4.50 for adults and S$2.50 for children. It is easily combined with a trip to Jurong Bird Park.

Chinese & Japanese Gardens

Off Yuan Ching Rd at Jurong Park, the adjoining Chinese and Japanese gardens each cover 13.5 hectares. The Chinese Garden, which occupies an island in the Jurong Lake, is colourful and has a number of Chinese-style pavilions. The main attraction is the extensive *penjing* (Chinese bonsai) display. Linked by a bridge, the Japanese Garden has large grassed areas and a few buildings. Garden lovers will find the Botanical Gardens of more interest, but the Chinese Garden is very pleasant and a must for bonsai enthusiasts.

The gardens are open from 9 am to 7 pm Monday to Saturday and from 8.30 am to 7 pm on Sundays and holidays. Admission to both gardens is S$4 for adults and S$2 for children. The Chinese Garden MRT station is right by Jurong Lake and a five-minute walk away from the Chinese Garden.

Singapore Science Centre

On Science Centre Rd, off Jurong Town Hall Rd, the Science Centre is great fun. It attempts to make science come alive by providing countless opportunities to try things out for yourself. There are handles to crank, buttons to push, levers to pull, microscopes to look through and films to watch. The centre is primarily designed to encourage an interest in science among Singapore's school children, but it is amazing how many adults compete with the kids to have a go on the hands-on exhibits. The centre is open from 10 am to 6 pm Tuesday to Sunday and admission is S$2 (children 50c). Changi airport has a mini science centre in Terminal 2.

One of the main attractions is the Omni Theatre, next to the main science centre building, with full-blown three- dimensional whizz-bang movies covering topics from space flights to journeys inside the atom. Movies are screened from noon until 8 pm, every day except Monday, and cost S$9 for adults, S$4 for children. There is also a planetarium at the centre. Show times are at 10 and 11 am and cost S$6 for adults and S$3 for children.

The easiest way to get there is to take the MRT to Jurong East station and then walk 0.5 km west or take bus No 336 from the station. Otherwise, take bus No 197 from North Bridge Rd in the colonial district.

Tang Dynasty City

This multi-million-dollar theme park is a recreation of old Chang'an (modern day Xi'an), the Tang Dynasty capital, which was the centre of China's golden age from the 6th to 8th centuries AD. Behind the massive 10-metre-high walls, Tang Dynasty City's main street features a courthouse, geisha house and shops, and there are temples, restaurants and theatres, all built in Chinese style and attempting to recreate the period. 'Silk Road' camel rides, craft demonstrations, performances and antique displays, such as a jade suit and the reproduction of a life-size terracotta army, are all part of the experience.

The size and style of the buildings are impressive, though like most theme parks it is just a little plastic. At the time of writing, the park was only half finished and the main thing to see was the shops, such as the tea, antique and wine shops. Perhaps when the park is finished, it may be worth the S$15 admission (S$10 for children). Tang Dynasty City is open every day from 9.30 am to 6.30 pm. Buffet lunch and dinner shows, featuring performing troupes from China, cost S$20 and S$38 (S$15 and S$20 for children).

Tang Dynasty City is on the corner of Yuan Ching Rd and Jalan Ahmad Ibrahim, near the Chinese and Japanese gardens. Take the MRT to Lakeside station and then bus No 154 or 240, or it is a two-km taxi ride from the station.

New Ming Village & Pewter Museum

This pottery workshop at 32 Pandan Rd produces reproduction porcelain from the Ming and Qing dynasties. You can see the craftspeople create their pottery and, of course, you can buy their works. It is open every day from 8.30 am to 5.30 pm. Admission is free. The complete production process is done on the premises and guided tours go on demand for groups. Ming Village was recently acquired by Royal Selangor as their Singapore showroom. Consequently the village also has a small pewter museum with some interesting pieces, and the showroom sells an extensive selection of pewter as well as pottery. The pewter is made elsewhere, but the polishing and hand-beaten designs are demonstrated at the village.

To get there, take the MRT to Jurong East and then bus No 78 to Pandan Rd.

Singapore Mint Coin Gallery

This gallery, at Singapore's mint on Jalan Boon Lay just east of Boon Lay MRT station, exhibits coins and medals from Singapore and a few coins from around the world.

Top: Tiger Balm Gardens (TW)
Middle: Hornbills, Jurong Bird Park (BP)
Bottom: Crocodiles, Jurong Crocodile Paradise (STPB)

This place is essentially an outlet for the gold medallions that the mint sells, but a few mint sets of Singapore coins are also for sale. Only dedicated coin enthusiasts would want to make the trip out here. It is open Monday to Friday from 9.30 am to 4.30 pm.

CN West Leisure Park

This swimming pool centre in Jurong, near the entrance to the Japanese Garden, has a wave pool, water slide, water boat rides and a food centre. The best swimming facilities are in the members' section, while the public area and the wave pool are a little run down and often deserted. The East Coast has better swimming facilities. Admission is $2 (S$1 for children) from Tuesday to Friday and S$3 (S$1.50 for children) on weekends.

EAST COAST & CHANGI – maps 1, 8

East Coast Park is a popular recreational haunt for Singaporeans. It is the place to swim, windsurf, lie on the sand, rent a bike or, of course, eat. The stretch of beach along the east coast south of the East Coast Parkway was born of reclaimed land and won't win any awards as a tropical paradise, but it is by far Singapore's most popular beach and has good recreational facilities.

Further inland are the interesting areas of Katong and Geylang, largely Malay districts, which are rarely frequented by foreign visitors. Geylang is as close to a 'Little Malaysia' as you'll find; and Katong, centred on East Coast Rd, has Peranakan influences and interesting dining possibilities.

Changi is known for its renowned airport and infamous prison, both attractions in their own right, while further out is Changi Village, a pleasant residential area with a definite village feel, and its nearby beach.

Geylang & Katong

If Singapore has Chinese, Indian and Muslim areas – where is Singapore's Malay area? If you want to experience Malaysia, the real thing is just across the Causeway. However, there are Malay areas in Singapore, though Malay culture is not so obvious nor easily marketed as a tourist attraction.

Geylang Serai is a Malay residential area, though you are not going to see traditional *atap* houses and sarong-clad cottage industry workers. The area has plenty of high-rise buildings, though there are some older build-

The Peranakans

The Peranakans are the descendants of early Chinese immigrants who settled in Malacca and married Malay women. With the formation of the Straits Settlements, many moved to Penang and Singapore. Peranakan (meaning half-caste in Malay) culture and language is a fascinating hybrid of Chinese and Malay traditions. The Peranakans took the name and religion of their Chinese fathers, but the customs, language and dress of their Malay mothers. Baba is the term for a male Peranakan and nonya for females, but Peranakans also used the terms Straits-born or Straits Chinese to distinguish themselves from later arrivals from China, who they looked down upon.

Peranakans were often wealthy traders, and could afford to indulge their passion for sumptuous furnishings, jewellery and brocades. Peranakan terrace houses were gaily painted with patterned tiles embedded in the walls for extra decoration, and heavily carved and inlaid furniture was favoured. Nonyas wore fabulously embroidered *kasot manek* (slippers) and *kebaya* (blouses worn over a sarong) tied with beautiful *kerasong* brooches, usually of fine filigree gold or silver. Babas assumed Western dress in the 19th century, reflecting their wealth and contacts with the British, and their finery was saved for important occasions such as the wedding ceremony, a highly stylised and intricate ritual exhibiting Malay *adat* (traditional

ings around, especially in the *lorong* (alleys) that run off Geylang Rd.

Geylang Serai is easily reached by taking the MRT to Paya Lebar station. From here it is a short walk down Tanjong Katong Rd to Geylang Rd, the main shopping street. A short walk east along Geylang Rd will bring you to the **Malay Cultural Village**. This new complex of traditional Malay-style houses was built as a showpiece of Malay culture, and it was hoped it would become a major tourist attraction. It is certainly worth stopping to see, but apart from a few craft and clothes shops, an interesting antique shop and a good restaurant, the village is very quiet for most of the year except in the evenings during Ramadan.

Just next door to the cultural centre is the **Geylang Serai Market**. It's hidden behind some older-style housing blocks on Geylang Rd, and entrance is through a small laneway that leads to a crowded, traditional Asian market that hasn't yet been rebuilt as a concrete custom). Nonya cooking is perhaps the best metaphor for describing Peranakan culture – Chinese dishes with Malay ingredients and flavours.

The Peranakan patois is a Malay dialect but contains many Hokkien words, making it largely unintelligible to a Malay speaker. Fewer than 5000 people now speak it in Singapore. Western culture is supplanting Peranakan traditions among the young, and the language policies of the government are also helping in its decline. The Peranakans are ethnically Chinese; they study Mandarin as their compulsory mother tongue in schools, and increasingly use it at home, along with English. Many Peranakans marry within the broader Chinese community, resulting in the further decline of Peranakan patois.

Peranakan societies such as the Peranakan Association and the Gunong Sayang Association report growing interest in Peranakan traditions as Singaporeans discover their roots, but when the older generation passes it is likely that Peranakan culture and language will be consigned to history books.

For the visitor to Singapore, the Peranakan Place Museum offers a look inside a Nonya and Baba house from the turn of the century, while the Katong district has a number of Peranakan restaurants and the Katong Antique House on East Coast Rd, which has Peranakan artefacts. *Mas Sepuloh* by William Gwee is a book on the Peranakan language. ■

box. It is a good place to browse and much more interesting than most of Singapore's new markets. It reaches its peak of activity during Ramadan, when the whole area is alive with market stalls that set up in the evenings for the faithful after a long day of fasting.

From the market you can head down Joo Chiat Rd to the East Coast Rd and explore the Katong district. **Joo Chiat Rd** has a host of local businesses operating during the day, and at night it is a lively row of restaurants and music lounges. The streetscape has escaped both the developer and the restorer; some fine Peranakan-style terraces and some of the atmosphere of old Singapore remain.

The same can be said of **East Coast Rd**, a delightful strip of old (and some new) buildings that is the centre of Katong. Before land reclamation moved the beach, Katong was a quiet village by the sea. Now East Coast Rd bustles with city traffic and Singapore's modern developments have engulfed the East Coast, but Katong still retains its village atmosphere. East Coast Rd is noted for its Peranakan influence, mostly because of the opportunity to sample Peranakan food and the fascinating collection of Peranakan antiques in the Katong Antique House. The intricately hand-embroidered nonya slippers are hard to resist. Also on the itinerary for a tour of Katong is a visit to Katong Bakery & Confectionary, 75 East Coast Rd. Nonya cakes and pastries are served in this relic from pre-war Singapore.

It is also worth wandering the back streets of Katong around Joo Chiat and East Coast Rds where you'll find more terraces, coffee shops and temples. Just off East Coast Rd in Ceylon Rd is the Hindu Senpaga Vinayagar Temple, and about a km away in Wilkinson St is a Sikh temple, Sri Guru Nanak Sat Sangh Sabha.

East Coast Rd changes its name to Mountbatten Rd as it heads into the city and crosses Tanjong Katong Rd, which leads back to Geylang and the Paya Lebar MRT station. This area contains a number of grand old villas, such as the Villa Dolce at 164 Tanjong Katong Rd, and Mountbatten Rd also has some fine old houses.

From East Coast Rd, bus Nos 12 and 32 head into the city along North Bridge Rd in the colonial district, while bus No 14 goes down Stamford Rd and then Orchard Rd. Coming from the city, bus No 16 can be boarded in Orchard and Bras Basah Rds, and goes along Joo Chiat Rd, crossing East Coast Rd. From East Coast Rd it is also a short walk to the East Coast Park and the seaside.

East Coast Park

Stretching along Singapore's east coast on reclaimed land, East Coast Park comes alive on weekends with Singaporeans relaxing by the beach, eating at the seafood outlets or indulging in more strenuous sporting activities. The foreshore parkland has a track running right along the coast for bicycling, jogging or roller blading, and you can hire bicycles, canoes and sailboards. The beach is reasonable, with a continuous sandy stretch and calm waters, though like all of Singapore's beaches the water is hardly crystal clear.

The **Singapore Crocodilarium** is at 730 East Coast Parkway and has a large number of crocodiles crammed into concrete tanks. A shop also sells croc products. It's open daily from 9 am to 5.30 pm and admission is S$2 for adults and $1 for children.

Big Splash (☎ 345 1211), 902 East Coast Parkway, is a good water fun park with swimming pools and a huge water slide. It is open Monday to Friday from noon to 6 pm, and weekends and public holidays from 9 am to 6

pm. Admission is S$3 for adults and S$2 for children.
Next door mountain bikes can be hired for S$3.50 per
hour, 10-speed racers for S$2.50 an hour, or canoes for
S$5 and S$6 per hour. Operating hours are from 10 am
to 7.30 pm, though these tend to be shortened during the
week.

The **East Coast Recreation Centre** is the big place on
the East Coast Park with bowling, squash, crazy golf, fun
rides, a selection of restaurants and food stalls, and
bicycle and canoe hire. As well as racers (S$3 per hour)
and mountain bikes (S$4 per hour), tandems can be
hired at Cycland, which is open most days from 9 am to
7 pm, and until 11.30 pm on Saturdays.

One km further away from the city is the **East Coast
Lagoon**, noted for its seafood. The UDMC Seafood
Centre has a number of restaurants and the hawkers'
centre nearby on the other side of the lagoon has some
cheaper seafood stalls. Also here is the **East Coast
Sailing Centre** (☎ 449 5118), a private club which rents
sailboards to the public for S$20 for the first two hours
and S$10 for each subsequent hour. Bicycles and canoes
can also be hired at the kiosk near the food centre.

Bus No 401 operates from Bedok MRT station along
the service road in the park on Sundays and public
holidays. All other buses whizz by on the East Coast
Parkway expressway. Otherwise take bus No 16 from
Orchard Rd or Bras Basah Rd in the colonial district –
this service runs along Joo Chiat Rd to Marine Parade
Rd – and then walk. For the Singapore Crocodilarium,
bus No 16 can also be boarded on Orchard and Bras
Basah Rds and runs along Mountbatten Rd to East Coast
Rd. Get off at the Katong Swimming Complex and walk
from there.

Changi Prison Museum – map 1

Changi is still used as a prison but next to the main gate
is a museum with a bookshop and a poignant replica of
the simple thatched prison chapel built and used by
Allied prisoners of war during their horrendous internment at the hands of the Japanese during WW II. Pinned
to the chapel are notes from people who lost loved ones
in Changi. The small museum features drawings made
by the prisoners depicting life in Changi, as well as
photographs and other exhibits providing an overview
of the war in Asia. The museum is open Monday to
Saturday from 9.30 am to 12.30 pm and from 2 to 4.30
pm, though you can visit the chapel outside these hours.
A service is held at the chapel from 5.30 to 6.30 pm.

Changi Prison is on Upper Changi Rd near the airport and can be reached by bus No 2 from Victoria St in the colonial district.

Changi Village – map 1

Changi, on the east coast of Singapore, is a pleasant escape from the hubbub of downtown Singapore. Don't expect to find traditional *kampong* (village) houses – the buildings are modern – but Changi does have a village atmosphere. Changi's beach is not exactly a tropical paradise but it has a good stretch of sand and offers safe swimming. It's popular on weekends but almost deserted during the week. The food in Changi is an attraction, and there are some good seafood restaurants and foodstalls near the beach. A visit to Changi Village can be included with a trip to Changi Prison.

From Changi, you can catch ferries to Pulau Ubin (see the Other Islands section later in this chapter). Ferries also go to Pengerang across the strait in Malaysia (see the Getting There & Away chapter).

You can reach Changi on bus No 2 from Victoria St in the colonial district. If you have a few hours to kill at the airport, you can reach Changi Village in about half an hour; take bus No 24 to Upper Changi Rd, after you turn off the expressway, and then take bus No 2.

SENTOSA ISLAND – map 9

Sentosa Island, just off the south coast of Singapore, is the granddaddy of all Singapore's fun parks. It is Singapore's most visited attraction, especially popular with locals who flock there on weekends. A host of activities are spread around this landscaped island, and while, with its beaches of imported sand, it is a manufactured attraction, Sentosa is a good place for families and there is enough to keep adults occupied. Sentosa has museums, aquariums, beaches, sporting facilities, walks, rides and food centres. It is easy to spend a day at Sentosa but if that isn't enough there's a campground, a hostel and two luxury hotels.

Sentosa is open daily from 7.30 am until around 11 pm, or midnight from Friday to Sunday and on public holidays. Many of the attractions close at 7 pm but cultural shows, plays and discos are sometimes held in the evenings – check with the tourist office or ring the Sentosa Information Office (☎ 270 7888).

You can get around Sentosa by bicycle – rent a bike from the hire kiosk by the ferry terminal. The free bus service runs around the island roads with departures every 10 minutes. The free monorail loop service is the most scenic but slowest way to get around the island.

Basic admission to Sentosa is S$4 for adults and S$2.50 for children aged three to 12. This covers entry and all transport on the monorail and buses around Sentosa and the one-way bus ride from Sentosa to the mainland. Most of the attractions cost extra, and can really add up if you want to see them all. A Sentosa Saver's ticket, which includes entry to the Pioneers of Singapore/Surrender Chamber, Fort Siloso and Coralarium/Nature Ramble, costs S$9.50 for adults and S$5 for children.

There are a number of options for reaching Sentosa. Special Sentosa buses leave from the World Trade Centre (service A to Underwater World) and from the Tiong Bahru MRT station (service C to the ferry terminal on Sentosa, or service B to Central Beach on weekends and holidays). Hop on the bus and pay S$5 for adults, S$3 for children (exact cash or fare cards), which includes the return fare to Sentosa and the entry ticket. The other Sentosa bus operates from Orchard Rd (service E), and can be boarded on Orchard and Bras Basah Rds in the colonial district. The cost is S$6 for adults, S$4 for children, including return fare and entry to Sentosa. One-way bus fare only between Orchard Rd and the World Trade Centre is S$2. All of these buses run every 15 minutes during Sentosa's opening hours, though the Orchard Rd service has more limited operating hours, from 10 am to 7.30 pm.

The ferry from the World Trade Centre used to be the access to the island before the bridge was built. It is still one of the most pleasant ways to reach Sentosa and costs 80c one way. Ferries operate from 7.30 am to 10.45 pm.

The other alternative is to take the cable car. It leaves from the top of Mt Faber from 8.30 am to 9 pm, or you can board it at the World Trade Centre. The fare is S$5 for adults and S$2.50 for children, and you can buy tickets for separate stages. The cable-car ride, with its spectacular views, is one of the best parts of a visit to Sentosa. Take the ferry across and then the cable car back to Mt Faber – it is easier walking down Mt Faber than up.

Underwater World

This spectacular new aquarium is Sentosa's most popular attraction. Displays include the turtle pool, moray eel enclosure, reef enclosures with live coral, a theatre showing continuous films and a touch pool where visitors are invited to dip their digits into the pool and fondle the sealife. These excellent exhibits are just

Monorail & Cablecar, Sentosa Island (STPB)

entrees to Underwater World's main passageway, an acrylic tunnel with a 'travellator' that takes spectators through the main tanks as all manner of fish swim around you in all their natural technicolour glory. There is nothing like the sight of a huge manta ray, 60 kg grouper, or shark swimming up to you and then passing overhead.

Underwater World is open daily from 9 am to 9 pm and costs S$10 for adults and S$5 for children. It is always busy, but gets especially crowded on weekends and school holidays.

Pioneers of Singapore & Surrender Chamber

The Pioneers of Singapore wax-work museum relives history and recreates life in old Singapore. It gives an excellent account of Singapore's past and focuses on the traditional cultures of Singapore's main communities. The adjoining Surrender Chamber exhibit traces the history of Singapore's occupation during WW II up to the formal surrender by the Japanese forces in 1945. These days it is surprisingly popular with Japanese tour groups. The museum is very well done, in an old-fashioned sort of way – perhaps this means it will be renovated with multi-media displays, robotic figures and high-tech lighting effects. In the meantime, admission is a reasonable S$3 for adults and S$1 for children. It is open from 9 am to 9 pm.

Fort Siloso

Once used as a military base, the gun emplacements and underground tunnels of Fort Siloso, which date from the late 19th century, can be explored. The guns were all pointing in the wrong direction when the Japanese invaded in WW II and the island was then used by the victorious Japanese as a prisoner-of-war camp. A mini sound-and-light show relives the period immediately before the Japanese invasion, and a 'Behind Bars' exhibit focuses on prison life for the POWs under the Japanese.

From 1989 until 1993, Fort Siloso housed Sentosa's most unusual attraction, political prisoner Chia Thye Poh. Chia, arrested in 1966 under the Internal Security Act for allegedly being a communist, served 23 years in jail before being banished to complete his bizarre sentence amongst the holiday delights of Sentosa Island.

Fort Siloso is open from 9 am to 7 pm and costs S$1 for adults and 50c for children.

Butterfly Park & Insect Kingdom Museum

At the Butterfly Park, you can walk among live butterflies of over 50 species. In the museum there are thousands of mounted butterfly specimens, rhino beetles, *Dynastes Hercules* (the world's largest beetles), and scorpions, among other insects. The walk through the butterfly house is undoubtedly the highlight.

It is open from 9.30 am to 5.30 pm Monday to Friday, and 9.30 am to 6.30 pm Saturday, Sunday and public holidays. Entry costs S$4 for adults and S$2 for children.

Asian Village

Sentosa's newest attraction, Asian Village is a collection of craft shops and some food outlets reflecting Asia's various cultures: Japan, China, India, Thailand, Philippines and Malaysia/Indonesia. The theme park buildings are vaguely styled after traditional houses, and cultural performances are sometimes held, though the entertainment park rides are most popular. It is all a bit synthetic. Entry costs S$4 for adults and S$2.50 for children, which is a lot to pay to go shopping. It is open from 10 am to 9 pm, and the rides cost extra.

Other Attractions

The **Maritime Museum** (open 10 am to 7 pm; adults S$1, children 50c) has exhibits recording the history of Singapore's port and shipping, primitive craft, fishing and boat-building exhibits. The **Rare Stone Museum** (open 9 am to 7 pm; adults S$2, children S$1) is an odd concept for a museum and comprises stones resembling landscapes, historical personages and Chinese deities – that is if you squint a lot or you are stoned yourself. The **Coralarium** (open 9 am to 7 pm; adults S$1.50, children 50c) has a large display of sea shells, giant crabs, freshwater Asian fish and recreated natural habitats, but it has lost its popularity with the opening of Underwater World. The **Nature Ramble** is part of the Coralarium. **Orchid Fantasy** (open 9.30 am to 6.30 pm; adults S$3, children 50c) is an orchid garden with a Japanese theme.

Of the free attractions, the **Nature Walk** is in a more natural environment, except for the Dragon Trail section that has dragons and fossils to liven things up. Longtailed macaques are common, but hide your food from these aggressive monkeys. You can also wander around the impressive ferry terminal, Fountain Gardens, Flower Terrace and Waterfront Promenade with its 'ruined city'.

At night, the **Musical Fountain** spurts water to music and flashing, coloured lights, while the **Pasar Malam** (Night Market) stalls sell souvenirs. Nearby is the **Rasa Sentosa Food Centre** – naturally Sentosa has a hawkers' centre – and the ferry terminal also has some dining possibilities.

Other new attractions due to open soon are a water theme park, a gourmet centre, and even an adventure golf theme park. Then there is the high-tech 'multisensory' centre, which will explain the creation of earth and the evolution of life. Due to open in late 1994 and unfold the mysteries of the universe, it will of course also have rides, food and retail outlets!

Beaches & Recreational Facilities

Sentosa's southern coastline is devoted to beaches: Siloso Beach at the western end, Central Beach and Tanjong Beach at the eastern end. As a tropical paradise, Sentosa has a long way to go to match the islands of Malaysia or Indonesia, but in a case of 'if Mohammed won't come to the mountain' Singapore has imported its beach from Indonesia and planted coconut palms to give it a tropical ambience. The imported sand does make for a good beach, probably Singapore's best, and it won't be long before the palms mature.

The beaches have shelters and four rest stations with kiosks, changing facilities, deck chairs and umbrellas. Pedal cats, aquabikes, fun bugs, canoes and surf boards are all available for hire.

Sentosa has a 5.7-km-long bicycle track that loops the island and takes in most of the attractions. Bicycles can be hired at bicycle stations on the track, such as the kiosk at Siloso Beach or at the ferry terminal, and cost from S$2 to S$5 per hour.

Sentosa also has a roller-skating rink, which costs S$2 entry. There are two 18-hole golf courses: Serapong, for members only, and Tanjong which is open to the public and costs S$80 for a round on weekdays or S$120 on weekends.

OTHER ISLANDS

Singapore's other islands include Kusu and St John's, Pulau Sakeng, the Sisters' Islands (all south of Singapore), and islands such as Pulau Bukum, which are used as refineries and for other commercial purposes. South of Singapore's southern islands are many more islands – the scattered Indonesian islands of the Riau Archipelago. There are other islands to the north-east between Singapore and Malaysia.

You don't have to leave the island of Singapore to find beaches and indulge in water sports. Although the construction of Changi International Airport destroyed one of Singapore's favourite stretches of beach, there is still the huge East Coast Lagoon on the East Coast Parkway, not to mention the CN West Leisure Park at Jurong. Scuba diving enthusiasts will find coral reefs at Sisters' Islands and Pulau Semakan, while if you want to water ski, head to Punggol Point on the north coast.

St John's & Kusu Islands

Although Sentosa is Singapore's best known island, there are two others which are also popular with locals as a city escape. On weekends, they can become rather crowded but during the week you'll find St John's and Kusu fairly quiet and good places for a peaceful swim. Both islands have changing rooms, toilet facilities, grassy picnic areas and swimming areas.

St John's Island is much bigger than Kusu and has better beaches for swimming, though Kusu is the more interesting. Kusu has a Chinese temple, the Tua Pek Kong temple near the ferry jetty, and a Malay shrine (kramat) up a steep flight of steps to the top of a hill at the end of the island. Kramat Kusu is dedicated to Sahed Abdul Rahman, his mother Nanek Ghalib and his sister Puteri Fatimah. Though kramat worship is frowned upon by the Islamic clergy, this is Singapore's most popular shrine, especially for childless couples who pray for children, as evidenced by the pieces of cloth tied around trees on the way up to the shrine. Kusu is the site of an important annual pilgrimage, honoured by Taoists.

Most of the harbour tours pass St John's Island and stop at Kusu for 20 minutes or so (see Tours in the Getting Around chapter). You can walk around Kusu in 20 minutes.

To get to these islands, take a ferry from the World Trade Centre (WTC). It costs S$6 for the round trip and takes 30 minutes to reach Kusu and then the boats continue on to St John's.

Mondays to Saturdays

WTC	Kusu	St John's
10.00 am	10.45 am	11.15 am
1.30 pm	2.15 pm	2.45 pm

Sundays & Public Holidays

WTC	Kusu	St John's
9.10 am	9.45 am	10.00 am
10.40 am	11.15 am	11.30 am
12.10 pm	12.45 pm	1.00 pm
1.40 pm	2.15 pm	2.30 pm
3.10 pm	3.45 pm	4.00 pm
4.40 pm	5.15 pm	5.30 pm
6.10 pm	6.45 pm	7.00 pm
7.40 pm	8.15 pm	8.30 pm

Other Southern Islands

Many of the islands on Singapore's southern shore accommodate the refineries that provide much of Singapore's export income. Others, such as Salu, Senang, Rawai and Sudong are live firing ranges. However, there are a few off-the-beaten-track islands where you can find a quiet beach.

Pulau Sakeng is one of the few places where you can still see a traditional Malay village. The kampong here remains intact, and the stilt houses are built over the sea. Many of the villagers work at nearby Pulau Bukum where the Shell refinery is located.

Pulau Hantu is one of Singapore's most popular diving spots with coral reefs nearby. The Sisters' Islands, good for swimming, are also popular with divers. Other islands that can be visited include Lazarus Island (Pulau Sakijang Pelepah), Buran Darat, Terumbu Retan Laut and Pulau Renggit.

To reach these islands, you must rent a motorised 'bumboat' (sampan) from Clifford Pier or Jardine Steps

Kelongs

To the north-east of Singapore Island in the Johor Strait, particularly around Ponggul and Changi, are the *kelongs*, long arrow shaped fences erected to trap fish. The *kelongs* consist of *lawa* or fishing stakes that intercept the fish as they come inshore at night on the tidal currents and direct them down a shaft into a netted chamber, the *bunoh mati* or death chamber. The *lawa* are made from a palm that gives off a fluorescent glow, which helps direct the fish down into the nets. Powerful lights are used earlier in the evening to attract small fish and plankton into the chamber, which then attract larger fish. Once the large fish are in the *bunoh mati*, the kelong operators then drag them out with nets.

Kelongs are a Malay invention, but the majority of kelong operators are Teochow Chinese, who built larger kelongs with living quarters to make them commercially viable. These fascinating fishing traps are another disappearing sight since the Singapore government doesn't want any of these untidy things in the water and favours fish farms. Permits for kelongs are not being renewed once they expire, and the remaining kelongs number around 30. ■

at the World Trade Centre. Expect to pay at least S$30 per hour for a minimum of four hours, or S$200 per day. The boats will take six to 12 people. You can ask individual boat owners or contact the Singapore Motor Launch Owners' Association on the 2nd floor at Clifford Pier, just east of the Raffles Place MRT station.

Northern Islands

To get to the northern islands like Pulau Seletar, go to Punggol Boatel at Punggol Point or to Sembawang. The easiest northern island to visit is Pulau Ubin, which can be visited from Changi Village. Pulau Tekong, Singapore's largest island, tends to be forgotten because it is often cut off the eastern edge of Singapore maps (including the one in this book). It is now off-limits since the military took it over in the early '90s.

Pulau Ubin From Changi Village, you can wander down to the ferry jetty and wait for a bumboat to take you across to Pulau Ubin. You can tell that this is a different side of Singapore as you wait for the ferry to fill up – they go when a quota of 12 people is reached and there is no fixed schedule. Pulau Ubin has quiet beaches, a kampong atmosphere and some popular seafood restaurants. This rural island is as unlike 'Singapore' as you will find in Singapore. It is also a natural haven for many species of birds that inhabit the mangroves and forest areas.

The ferry to Pulau Ubin costs S$1, or S$12 to charter a whole boat if there are no other passengers to share a boat. Getting around the island is by taxi or bicycles can be hired.

NORTHERN & CENTRAL SINGAPORE – map 1

Singapore has been dubbed the Garden City and with good reason – it's green and lush, and parks and gardens are scattered everywhere. In part, this fertility is a factor of the climate; you only have to stick a twig in the ground for it to become a tree in weeks! The government has backed up this natural advantage with a concentrated programme that has even turned the dividing strip on highways into flourishing gardens – you notice it as you drive into Singapore from the Causeway.

Despite the never-ending construction, land reclamation and burgeoning HDB (Housing & Development Board) estates, Singapore has large areas of parkland and even natural forest. These areas are mostly found to the north of the city in the centre of Singapore Island.

Botanic Gardens

Singapore's 127-year-old Botanic Gardens are on the corner of Cluny and Holland Rds, not far from Orchard Rd. They are a popular and peaceful retreat for Singaporeans.

The Botanic Gardens contain an enormous number of species of plants, in both a manicured garden setting and in four hectares of primary jungle. The gardens also house the herbarium, where much work has been done on breeding the orchids for which Singapore is famous. The orchid enclosure contains over 12,000 orchids representing 2000 species and hybrids in all. In an earlier era, Henry Ridley, director of the gardens, successfully propagated rubber tree seeds sent from Kew Gardens in 1877, after they were smuggled out of Brazil. The Singapore Botanic Gardens pioneered the Malayan rubber boom.

The 54-hectare gardens are open from 5 am to 11 pm on weekdays and until midnight on weekends and public holidays; admission is free. Early in the morning, you'll see hundreds of Singaporeans jogging there.

The gardens can be reached on bus Nos 7, 14 or 174, which run along Stamford and Orchard Rds. Bus No 106 runs along Bencoolen St and Orchard Rd to the gardens.

Sunday Morning Bird Singing

One of the nicest things to do on a Sunday morning in Singapore is to go and hear the birds sing. The Chinese love caged birds as their beautifully ornate bird cages indicate. The birds – thrushes, *merboks*, *sharmas* and *mata putehs* – are treasured for their singing ability. To ensure the quality of their song, the doting owner will feed the bird a carefully prepared diet and once a week crowds of bird fanciers get together for a bird song session.

The bird cages are hung up on wires strung between trees or under verandahs. They're not mixed indiscriminately – sharmas sing with sharmas, merboks with merboks – and each type of bird has its own design of cage. Tall pointy ones for tall pointy birds, short and squat ones for short squat birds.

Having assembled the birds, the proud owners then congregate around tables, sip coffee and listen to their birds go through their paces. It's a delightful scene both musically and visually.

The main bird-concert venue is on Sunday mornings from around 8 to 11 am at the junction of Tiong Bahru and Seng Poh Rds (map 12), only a few hundred metres from the Havelock Rd hotel enclave. The coffee shop here is always well patronised on Sunday mornings.

To get there take the MRT to Tiong Bahru station, then walk east 0.5 km. By bus, take No 123 from Orchard Rd, No 103 from Bencoolen St or Nos 33, 62 or 103 from Raffles City to Tiong Bahru Rd, then walk.

Zoological Gardens

Located at 80 Mandai Lake Rd in the north of the island, Singapore's world-class zoo has over 2000 animals representing 240 species on display in natural conditions. Wherever possible, moats replace bars and the zoo is spread out over 90 hectares of lush greenery. Exhibits of particular interest are the Primate Kingdom, Wild Africa, the pygmy hippos and Children's World. As well as providing a play area, Children's World includes a domesticated animals section where children can touch the animals, see Friesian cow milking demonstrations and sheep dogs in action at the sheep roundup show.

There is a breakfast programme at 9 am and high tea at 4 pm, where you are joined by one of the orang-utans! There are also elephant rides and work performances. At most times of the day, you have a good chance of seeing one of the animal performances or one of the practice sessions in the zoo's outdoor theatre.

The Komodo dragons are another popular attraction and you can see their feeding frenzy on Sunday afternoons, though in fact they are not all that ferocious and need plenty more good feeds to reach full size.

The zoo's big new programme is the Night Safari. Set on a new 40-hectare site next to the zoo in secondary forest, trams negotiate the park and special lighting picks out the animals. Walking trails also criss-cross the park and allow a unique opportunity to view nocturnal animals. The park is divided into a number of habitats, focussing mostly on Asian wildlife. The Night Safari park is open from 6.30 pm until midnight.

The zoo is open daily from 8.30 am to 6 pm Monday to Saturday and 8 am to 6.30 pm on Sundays and public holidays. Admission is S$7 for adults and S$3 for kids. There is a zoo tram which runs from the main gate and costs S$2 for adults and S$1 for children.

To get to the zoo, take bus No 171 which runs along Stamford and Orchard Rds. This bus also stops at the Yishun MRT station. The Zoo Express shuttle bus is a much more expensive option that goes from many of the major hotels and includes a stop at the Mandai Orchid Gardens for S$29 (adults) and S$17 (children) including entry – call ☎ 235 3111 for information.

Mandai Orchid Gardens

Singapore has a major business in cultivating orchids and the Mandai Orchid Gardens, beside the zoo on Mandai Lake Rd, is the best place to see them – four solid hectares of orchids! The gardens are open daily from 9 am to 5.30 pm and admission is S$2 for adults, 80c for children.

Singapore Crocodile Farm

The croc farm on Upper Serangoon Rd takes the more commercial approach to crocodiles and turns them into handbags and other accessories. Check your government's customs regulations before you buy as some countries ban the import of crocodile skin products. The farm is open daily from 9 am to 6 pm and admission is free. Take bus Nos 81, 83, 97 or 111 from

Orchids, Mandai Orchid Gardens (STPB)

Selegie or Serangoon Rds. Bus No 111 also runs along Orchard Rd.

Bukit Timah Nature Reserve

Singapore is not normally associated with nature walks and jungle treks, but they can be enjoyed at this 71-hectare nature reserve. It is the only large area of primary forest left in Singapore, and is a haven for Singapore's wildlife. On Upper Bukit Timah Rd, 12 km from the city, the reserve also boasts the highest point in Singapore, 162-metre Bukit Timah.

The reserve is run by the National Parks Board and at the entrance to the reserve is an exhibition hall with interesting displays on Singapore's natural history. Adjoining the hall are changing rooms and showers. Oddly enough, the other national parks run by the board are the much more urban Fort Canning Park and Singapore Botanic Gardens.

Of the walks in the park, the most popular is the summit walk along a paved road to the top of Bukit Timah. Even during the week it attracts a number of walkers, though few venture off the pavement to explore the side trails. The road cuts a swathe through dense forest and near the top there are panoramic views across Peirce Reservoir.

The best trails to explore the forest and see the wildlife run off the summit road. Try the North View, South View or Fern Valley paths, where it is hard to believe that you are in Singapore. These paths involve some scrambling over rocks in parts, but are easily negotiated.

The park has over 800 species of native plants, including giant trees, ferns and native flowers. Wildlife is difficult to see, though long-tailed macaques and squirrels are in abundance. Flying lemurs, reticulated pythons, and birds such as the racquet-tailed drongo and white-bellied sea eagle inhabit the reserve. Try to pick up a copy of *A Guide to the Bukit Timah Nature Reserve* explaining the reserve's flora and fauna. There are in fact two good guides. One is produced by Mobil and the Nature Society, costs S$1 and is available from Mobil service stations and some bookshops. The other glossier and more extensive booklet, produced by BP and the Singapore Science Centre, costs S$5 and is available in bookshops.

The exhibition hall is open from 8.30 am to 6 pm and the reserve closes at 7 pm. Entry is free. It is a good idea to bring a water bottle if you intend going on some extended walks. A towel and even a change of clothes are also worth bringing as the walks are strenuous in parts and the conditions are hot and very humid.

To get to Bukit Timah, take bus No 171 or 182, which both run along Orchard and Stamford Rds in the colonial district. Other buses from the colonial district include No 181 from Beach Rd and the Johor Bahru bus No 170 from Queen St. Get off just past the 12-km mark at the large, yellow Courts Mammoth Super Store on Upper Bukit Timah Rd. The entrance to the park is on the other side, about one km along Hindhede Drive.

Other Parks

Despite Singapore's dense population, there are many small parks and gardens, and every traffic island or highway divide is turned into a green plantation.

MacRitchie Reservoir has a 12-hectare park area with a jogging track, exercise area, playground and tea kiosk. It is a pleasant retreat from the city, and popular with joggers. A band often plays on Sundays (check the newspapers). To the north of MacRitchie Reservoir is **Seletar Reservoir** where paddle boating is possible, and further east is **Sungei Seletar Reservoir** where you can go fishing.

Off Kampong Bahru Rd, the 116-metre-high **Mt Faber** is a pleasant park with fine views over the harbour and the city. To get there, take the cable car up from the World Trade Centre. Mount Faber can conveniently be visited in conjunction with a trip to Sentosa Island.

Pasir Ris Park on the north-east coast is for the most part a manicured park with a narrow stretch of beach. The park also has a wooden walkway that goes through a mangrove swamp area that is good for bird-watching. The park is often empty during the week, but comes alive on weekends and holidays, when the nearby trade-union-run NTUC Pasir Ris Resort fills up. To get there take the MRT to Pasir Ris station and then bus No 350 goes to the resort, only a short walk from the beach.

Bukit Batok, also known as Little Guilin, is a former quarry, now a park, that is compared to the spectacular limestone formations and lakes of Guilin in southern China, hence the name. This pleasant park is built around a hilly outcrop and lake, but it is a poor imitation of Guilin. It is near the Bukit Gombok MRT station, 14 km to the north-west of the city.

Bukit Turf Club

The horse racing calendar is part of the Malaysian circuit and races are held in Singapore once a month at the Bukit Turf Club on Bukit Timah Rd. At other times, races are broadcast on the huge video screen. The races are usually held on weekends and admission is S$5, or S$10 under the fans in the stand. If you are going to blow your dough at the races then you might as well spend S$20 for a seat in the air-conditioned members' stand – it gets very hot in the ordinary section on a crowded race day. Show your passport and buy a ticket to the members at the tourist information booth outside. The Bukit Turf Club produces a racing calendar available at the STPB tourist offices or ring ☎ 469 3611 for information. All betting is government-controlled, and the minimum win or place bet is S$5. A lot of money passes through the windows on race day. There are also off-course betting shops, such as the one in the Peace Centre on Selegie Rd.

Be sure to dress properly – no shorts, sandals or T shirts are allowed. The turf club also has a good hawkers' centre.

Holland Village

If you're wondering what the life of an expatriate is like, head for Holland Village. It's on Holland Rd, a westerly continuation of Orchard Rd, and services the garden belt suburbs of the well-to-do.

Holland Village is, in fact, just a suburban shopping centre where foreigners can shop, sip coffee and feel at home, but it has a definite village community atmosphere. It is best known for its host of trendy restaurants and watering holes, concentrated on Lorong Mambong, just back from the main road. The Holland Shopping Centre is a modern complex and one of the best places to buy antiques, furnishings and crafts such as porcelain ware, batik, wood carvings etc.

The nearest MRT station is Buona Vista, about a 15-minute walk along Buona Vista Rd from Holland Village. Or take bus Nos 7, 105 or 106 from Orchard Rd.

Temples

The central city areas of Singapore provide plenty of opportunities to experience Singapore's colourful temples, but a couple of temples of note are found in the outer areas.

Siong Lim Temple This is one of the largest temples in Singapore and includes a Chinese rock garden. It was built in 1908 but includes more recent additions. It features Thai Buddha statues and 2000-kg incense burners. There is a monastery next to the main temple, and next to the monastery is another temple featuring a gigantic Buddha statue. It's at 184E Jalan Toa Payoh, north of the city centre and out towards Paya Lebar Airport, about one km east from the Toa Payoh MRT station.

Kong Meng San Phor Kark See Temple This is the largest temple in Singapore and covers 12 hectares. It's on Bright Hill Drive A modern temple, it is impressive in its size and design, though its main function is as a crematorium; funerals, complete with paper effigies, are frequent. The attached old people's home is reminiscent of the old 'death houses' that used to exist in Chinatown's Sago St. Old folk were once packed off to death houses towards the end of their lives, thus avoiding the possible bad luck of a death in the home. The temple is about 1.5 km west of the Bishan MRT station.

Kranji War Memorial

Near the Causeway off Woodlands Rd, the Kranji War Memorial includes the graves of thousands of Allied troops who died in the region during WW II. The walls are inscribed with the names of those who died and a register is available for inspection.

Kong Meng San Phor Kark See Temple (PT)

Housing Estates

Still another side of Singapore is found in the modern HDB (Housing & Development Board) satellite cities like Toa Payoh, Pasir Ris, Tampines and Bukit Panjang. Nearly 90% of Singaporeans live in these government housing blocks and once again it's a programme that Singapore manages to make work.

While high-rise housing has become a dirty word in many countries, in Singapore it's almost universally popular. Many of the residents own their own flats, with subsidised interest rates provided by the HDB.

The MRT makes it simple to visit HDB areas. Just jump on a train and pop up somewhere like Toa Payoh. True, you won't see stunning architecture and breathtaking landscapes, you won't be spellbound by exotic ritual, but you will get a glimpse of what life is like for the overwhelming majority of Singaporeans. The estates are often good places to shop – straightforward, cheap and without the inflated prices and haggling that often go with the more popular tourist areas – and of course they have plenty of places to eat. You may find the best *ah balling* or the cheapest chicken rice in Singapore (try Yishun).

Kampongs

Recently the Singapore press announced that the last kampong in Singapore was due to be torn down, spark-

ing a debate about whether or not it should be preserved
and turned into a tourist attraction. There are in fact still
a few kampongs in Singapore, though they may have
iron roofs, electricity and a car parked next to the house.
The government has met strong resistance in the past
from the Malay community when villages have been
torn down to make way for HDB estates.

In the north-east of the island, for example near the
coast between Sembawang and Punggol, you can still
come across rural scenes, and you can still find kampongs. Some of the islands such as Pulau Ubin and Pulau
Sakeng are also rural and very Malay in character, and
they have kampongs that have so far escaped the
ravages of development.

Guinness World of Records

At the World Trade Centre you'll find this exhibition of
the biggest and best in the world. Computers, wax
dummies and audiovisual displays all help to convey
the pinnacles of human endeavour. There are displays
of sporting records, human feats and freaks, entertainment and a special Singapore and Asian section
focussing on number ones from the Lion City.

The exhibit can be visited on the way to Sentosa
Island. It is open from 9.30 am to 8.30 pm daily. Admission costs S$5 for adults and S$3 for children, which is
cheaper than the book but not as much fun.

Sun Yatsen Villa

This old villa was Sun Yatsen's residence in Singapore
before the overthrow of the Qing (or Manchu) Dynasty
that saw an end to imperial China and Dr Sat Yatsen
declared president of the new republic in 1912. His time
in Singapore was largely spent organising secret societies and fund-raising for the overthrow of the Qing
Dynasty. The house is a fine example of an old villa and
inside are personal items and photographs of the
Chinese revolutionary, while upstairs is a Chinese
library.

The villa is on Ah Hood Rd, about 0.5 km south of the
Toa Payoh MRT station. Bus no 145 goes from Balestier
Rd – get off at Ah Hood Rd.

SPORTS

Singapore's private clubs and country clubs have excellent sporting facilities but there are also fine public

facilities, such as those at Farrer Park near Little India, and a host of commercial ventures.

Archery

Contact the Archery Club of Singapore (☎ 258 1140) at 5 Bintang Walk.

Badminton

Badminton is popular in South-East Asia and the region has produced world champions in this sport. Courts at the Singapore Badminton Hall (☎ 344 1773) on Guillemard Rd are open from 8 am to 11 pm; bookings are essential.

Bowling

Tenpin bowling is very popular in Singapore. The cost per game is around S$3 to S$3.50; shoe hire is around 50c. Some alleys include:

Jackie's Bowl
    542B East Coast Rd (☎ 241 6519)
Orchard Bowl
    8 Grange Rd (☎ 737 4744)
Superbowl
    15 Marina Grove, Marina South (☎ 221 1010)
Victor's Superbowl
    7 Marina Grove, Marina South (☎ 221 0707)

Cricket

The Singapore Cricket Club holds matches every weekend on the Padang from March to October. The club is for members only but spectators are welcome.

Golf

Singapore has plenty of golf courses, though some are for members only, or do not allow visitors to play on weekends. A game of golf costs around S$90 on week-days, and from S$100 to S$200 on weekends. Club hire is expensive. The following courses have 18 holes, except for Changi, Seletar and Warren, which are nine-hole courses.

Changi Golf Club
    Netheravon Rd (☎ 545 1298)
Jurong County Club
    9 Science Centre Rd (☎ 560 5655)

Keppel Club
    Bukit Chermin (☎ 273 5522)
Raffles Country Club
    450 Jalan Ahmad Ibrahim (☎ 861 7655)
Seletar Country Club
    Seletar Airbase (☎ 481 4745)
Sembawang Country Club
    Sembawang Rd (☎ 257 0642)
Sentosa Golf Course
    Sentosa Island (☎ 275 0022)
Singapore Island Country Club
    Upper Thomson Rd (☎ 459 2222)
Warren Golf Course
    Folkstone Rd (☎ 777 6533)

Singapore has driving ranges at the Parkland Golf
Driving Range (☎ 440 6726), 920 East Coast Parkway; the
Marina Bay Golf & Country Club (☎ 221 2811), Marina
South, which also has putting greens; and Green Fair-
ways (☎ 468 8409), Bukit Turf Club, Fairways Drive.

Horse Riding

The Singapore Polo Club (☎ 256 4530), 80 Mount Pleasant Rd, has horse riding courses – ring for details. You
can also watch polo matches on Tuesdays, Thursdays
and weekends after 5.30 pm.

Squash

Most of the country clubs have squash courts. Some of
the public courts include:

East Coast Recreation Centre
    East Coast Parkway (☎ 449 0541)
Farrer Park
    Rutland Rd (☎ 299 4166)
National Stadium
    Kallang (☎ 348 1258)

Swimming

Singapore has a number of beaches for swimming – try
East Coast Park, Changi Village, Sentosa or the other
islands. On East Coast Parkway is the Big Splash
complex which has a number of pools including a wave
pool and a gigantic water slide. There is a similar
complex at the CN West Leisure Park, 9 Japanese Garden
Rd, Jurong.
    Singapore has plenty of public swimming pools;
admission is 60c. The Farrer Park Swimming Complex

in Dorset Rd is the closest to the Bencoolen St and Orchard Rd areas.

Tennis

Tennis courts cost from S$3 to S$6 per hour. Courts available for hire include:

Farrer Park Tennis Courts
  Rutland Rd (☎ 299 4166)
Singapore Tennis Centre
  1020 East Coast Parkway (☎ 442 5966)

Water Sports

The East Coast Sailing Centre (☎ 449 5118), 1210 East Coast Parkway, is the place to go for windsurfing and sailing. Sailboards cost S$10 per hour with a minimum of two hours hire; lessons are available. They also rent Laser-class boats for $20 per hour. Sailboards and aquabikes are also available for hire on Sentosa Island.

For water-skiing, William Water Sports (☎ 282 6879), at Ponggol Point in the north of the island, rents boats, a driver and gear for S$60 per hour.

Places to Stay

Singapore has a wide variety of accommodation in all price categories – you can get a dormitory bed in a guest house for S$6, a room in a cheap Chinese hotel for around S$25, pay over S$250 for a room in an 'international standard' hotel, or S$6000 for the best suite at the Raffles.

Hotels can be categorised into three groups. 'Top end' hotels are priced from around S$120 for a double. The main centre for these large hotels is along Orchard Rd. At the other end of the scale, most 'bottom end' hotels cost under S$50, and you can still find a room for under S$30. These cheaper places are found mainly in the colonial district, particularly along Beach Rd and Bencoolen St. 'Mid-range' hotels cover the ever-shrinking middle ground – some of them are better cheap Chinese hotels but most of them are smaller, relatively new air-con hotels. These hotels tend to be scattered throughout Singapore.

Singapore's hotel prices have fluctuated dramatically over the past few years. Hotel prices depend very much on what the market will bear, and when visitor numbers and hotel occupancy rates are high you will pay dearly at the top-end hotels. At other times, the big hotels offer large discounts. The same is true for mid-range and the cheaper top-end hotels, but price variations are less dramatic. On the other hand, prices for bottom end accommodation are very stable.

In the major hotels, a 4% government tax and 10% service charge is added to your bill. This is the dreaded 'plus-plus' which follows the quoted price (eg S$140++), while 'nett' means that price includes tax and service charge. The hotels stipulate that you should not tip when a service charge applies. The 4% government tax also applies to the cheaper hotels but this is usually added to the quoted price.

PLACES TO STAY – BOTTOM END

The budget accommodation is to be found in the cheap Chinese hotels and the guest houses or 'crash pads' as they have been known as for years by Asian travellers.

Singapore's guest houses are all mildly illegal since they're just residential flats or office space broken up into dormitories and cubicle-like rooms. But then this is Singapore and free enterprise is what counts! The trouble with them is that overcrowding tends to stretch the limited facilities, and the rooms really are small. In addition, everybody else there will be a traveller, just like yourself. On the other hand, they're good sources of information, good places to meet people and you won't find any cheaper accommodation in Singapore.

New guest houses are constantly opening up, and the services they provide are improving. Dormitory beds cost from S$6 or S$7 and rooms from S$15, though most rooms go for around S$20 and range up to S$50 for mid-range, hotel-standard rooms with air-con, attached bath and TV. Cheap rooms are often small spartan boxes with a fan. Free tea and coffee are standard offerings and a basic breakfast is usually thrown in. Singapore does not have an official youth hostel.

Guest houses do move around, usually in search of cheaper rents or under eviction notices initiated by other tenants in the building. The guest houses listed here are the more accessible and well-established ones. Others tend to come and go, so keep your eyes open, or just wander around Bencoolen St or Beach Rd with a backpack and you're sure to get plenty of offers. Touts at the airport and railway station will also offer accommodation. Some places don't advertise and are merely residential flats that rent out rooms on an ad-hoc basis. They can offer some of the best accommodation and are good options for long-term stayers.

The other main budget accommodation option is the cheap Chinese hotels. Most of the cheap hotels have seen better days, but they do have more character than the guest houses. They appear to be resigned to redevelopment and are, sadly, deteriorating each year. They are also declining in number, and you can be certain that there are no new hotels planned without air-con, bars, restaurants, high-speed lifts, swimming pools and all the other necessities of modern tourism. Rooms range from around S$25 to S$60. This will get you a fairly spartan room with a bare floor, a few pieces of furniture, a sink and a fan. Toilets are usually shared but you may even get hot water in the showers. Couples should always ask for a single room – a single usually means just one double bed, whereas a double has two.

Singapore has three YMCAs and a YWCA. All of the YMCAs in Singapore take men, women and couples. They are very good value and very popular, so advance bookings in writing with one night deposit are essential for the rooms. Book at least six weeks in advance for the YMCA International and around three weeks in advance for the others. Non-YMCA members must pay a small charge for temporary membership. Singapore also has two campgrounds.

The main area for budget accommodation is in the colonial district bounded by Bras Basah, Rochor, Beach and Selegie Rds. Bencoolen St has traditionally been the backpackers' centre in Singapore, and while it still has a number of guest houses, most of the old buildings and Chinese hotels have fallen to the wrecker's ball. Many backpackers' places have relocated to the Beach Rd area. Other cheap possibilities are found further north in Little India and nearby Jalan Besar, and in Chinatown.

Bencoolen St Area (map 3)

Bencoolen St has traditionally been the budget accommodation centre, and at almost any time of the night or day you can see travellers with backpacks seeking out a cheap hotel or guest house. Bencoolen St itself is has very little character left but it's within walking distance of the city centre, Orchard Rd and Little India.

From Changi International Airport, public bus No 390 will drop you on Stamford Rd. Get off near the National Museum, cross Stamford Rd and walk north through the small park to Bras Basah Rd and Bencoolen St. From the railway station, bus Nos 97 also stops on Stamford Rd and bus No 125 goes along Victoria St then Middle Rd where it crosses Bencoolen St. From the Lavender St bus station, bus Nos 64, 65, 81, 92, 97, 103, 106, 111, 122, 139 and 147 all run along Jalan Besar and go down Bencoolen St. The nearest MRT station is Dhoby Ghaut, about 10 minutes' walk from Bencoolen St.

Guest Houses You'll find one of the main backpackers' centres at 46-52 Bencoolen St, on top of a furniture store . There's no sign at all; go around the back and take the lift. The entire building is devoted to guest houses, the biggest of which is the *Lee Traveller's Club* (☎ 338 3149). Reception is at room 52 on the 7th floor but they have rooms on most of the floors. Like many of the guest houses, it's more a business than a homestay and you can stay for S$7 in a dorm with fan or S$8 in an air-con dorm. They have some good, hotel-style rooms with air- con and bath for S$40 or S$45, or air-con rooms without bath are S$35 to S$40. *Peony Mansions* (☎ 338 5638), one of the original crash pads, is on the 4th floor. Dormitory beds cost S$7 and rooms go for S$30 to S$45. The dorms aren't great but the rooms are reasonable.

There are other guest houses in the block, like *Latin House* (☎ 339 6308) on the 3rd floor at No 46,which is an anonymous place with run-down rooms.

On the other side of Bencoolen St, between the Strand and Bencoolen hotels, is *Bencoolen House* (☎ 338 1206) at No 27. The reception area is on the 7th floor. Dorm beds cost S$6 and most rooms cost from S$25, ranging up to S$45 for a very good air-con room. It is well managed and is one of the best guest houses.

The *Why Not Homestay* (☎ 338 0162, 338 6095), 127 Bencoolen St, is a popular place because of its good restaurant/travellers' meeting place downstairs. It's a rabbit warren with plenty of rooms upstairs and in the adjoining buildings. Most of the rooms are small, windowless boxes from S$26 with fan or from S$30 with air-con. The dormitories are better and a bed costs S$10 in a four-bed, air-con dorm.

At 171 Bencoolen St is another centre for guest houses. *Goh's Homestay* (☎ 339 6561), up a long flight of stairs to the 3rd floor at 171-A, is new and has a good eating/meeting area where you can get breakfast, snacks and drinks. The rooms are very clean but small and without windows. Rooms cost S$28 or a dorm bed costs an expensive S$12. *Hawaii Hostel* (☎ 338 4187) on the 2nd floor at 171-B has reasonable air-con singles/doubles for S$25/35.

Hotels Redevelopment in the area has seen the demise of most of the old hotels. The *San Wah* (☎ 336 2428) at 36 Bencoolen St is a little better than the cheapest Chinese hotels and many of the rooms are air-conditioned. It has a pleasant courtyard area. Singles or doubles cost S$40 or S$45 with air-con.

At 260-262 Middle Rd, near the corner of Selegie Rd, is the good, spotlessly clean *Sun Sun Hotel* (☎ 338 4911). It's a cut above the other traditional Chinese hotels and there's a bar and restaurant downstairs. Singles/doubles cost S$36/42, or air-con doubles cost S$48.

The *Victoria Hotel* (☎ 338 2381), next to the Allson Hotel at 87 Victoria Street, is a more modern hotel with clean, comfortable rooms. Air-con doubles with bath cost S$60, and there are a few rooms without bath for S$50.

The *South-East Asia Hotel* (☎ 338 2394) at 190 Waterloo St (which runs parallel to Bencoolen St) is a bit more costly, but all rooms have air-con with attached bathroom and it is quiet and fairly new. Singles/doubles are S$55/67.20. This is the hotel for the lazy sightseer – within 200 metres of the hotel you'll find a Buddhist temple, Hindu temple, market, food stalls and shopping centre. The street is also alive with flower sellers and fortune tellers during the day.

Beach Rd Area (map 3)

Beach Rd, a few blocks from Bencoolen St towards the (ever-receding) waterfront, is another centre for cheap hotels. If you aspire to the Raffles but can't afford it, at least you can stay nearby. Somehow, the several blocks north-east along Beach Rd from the Raffles have managed to remain a little enclave of old Singapore, unaffected by the demolition around them. From the airport, bus No 390 can drop you near the towering Raffles City complex, opposite the Padang, from where it's a short walk to Beach Rd. From the railway station and the World Trade Centre take bus No 100. Bus Nos 82 and 107 run down Beach Rd from the Lavender St Malaysia bus station, and pass the Thailand bus station on Beach Rd only a 10-minute walk from the cheap hotels. The Beach Rd area is about halfway between the City Hall and Bugis MRT stations.

Guest Houses *Lee Traveller's Club* (☎ 339 5490) is on the 6th floor of the Fu Yeun Building at 75 Beach Rd and they have more rooms on the 4th floor. It is a large place and popular, though it can get crowded. It costs $6 for a dorm bed, $8 in an air-con dorm, S\$15/25 for singles/doubles with fan or S\$35/40 for singles/doubles with air-con. *Willy's* (☎ 337 0916) is a smaller, friendlier place in the same building on the 4th floor. They have a few rooms and dorm beds in the common room – a common fault with guest houses. Dorm beds cost S\$6 and rooms cost around S\$25.

Willy's have two other branches in the same area, charging the same prices. Further along Beach Rd on the 3rd floor at 101 Beach Rd (☎ 338 8826) the other *Willy's* is one of the better guest houses; it is also a small place. *Raffles Home Stay* (☎ 334 1608) on the 3rd floor, 490 North Bridge Rd, is also part of the Willy's chain. It is on the top floor of an old Chinese shop. Enter through the shop, or from the lane at the rear after hours.

The *New Backpackers Lodge* (☎ 334 8042, 18A Liang Seah St, is spotlessly clean and has a little more character than the other backpackers' places. A dorm bed costs S\$7 and most rooms go for S\$25. The rooms are like freshly painted Chinese hotel rooms, chopped in half and without any furniture, but they are a cut above most other guest house rooms.

The *Das Travellers' Inn* (☎ 294 9740) on the 2nd floor at 87 Beach Rd is a long-running place that has been running a little too long. A bed in the large common dorm costs S$6, or S$8 in an air-con eight-bed dorm. Private rooms cost S$15 to S$30, and S$40 with air-con and shower.

Hotels The hotels here are all of a similar basic standard: traditional Chinese hotels with wire-topped walls, shuttered windows, a few pieces of furniture and a basin with running water. They are run-down but good for the price.

The *Shang Onn* (☎ 338 4153), at 37 Beach Rd on the corner of Purvis St, is a little more expensive than the other places. Single/double/triple rooms will cost you S$30/34/45. The rooms are reasonable and have character but not much else. At 54 Middle Rd is the *Lido* (☎ 337 1872) with singles/doubles at S$22/24. The rooms are large and good value.

At the corner of Liang Seah St and North Bridge Rd is the *Ah Chew Hotel* (☎ 336 3563), a very traditional old Chinese hotel. 'It's nothing to sneeze at', reported a guest. Rooms cost S$25 for a single or double.

Chinatown (map 2)

Chinatown, one of the most interesting areas to stay, has a few cheap hotels, most of which are within walking distance of the railway station and the Outram Park and Tanjong Pagar MRT stations.

Guest Houses The *Chinatown Guest House* (☎ 220 0671), 5th floor, 325D New Bridge Rd, opposite Pearl's Centre, has dorm beds for S$8 and a few rooms for S$30. There are better guest houses in Singapore, but this is the only cheap option if you want to stay in Chinatown.

Hotels The *Great Southern Hotel* (☎ 533 3223) at the corner of Fu Tong Sen and Upper Cross Sts is opposite the People's Park shopping centre. It is right in the heart of Chinatown and the rooms are reasonable, but it gets a lot of traffic noise. Rooms with fan start at S$35 and air-con singles/doubles with attached bath are S$50/60.

One of the best cheap hotels in Singapore is the well-kept *Majestic Hotel* (☎ 222 3377) at 31 Bukit Pasoh Rd on the south-western edge of Chinatown. Bukit Pasoh Rd runs between New Bridge and Neil Rds. It's a quiet street in an interesting, traditional area, right near the Outram Park MRT station. Air-con singles/doubles are S$45/59 without bath, S$57/69 with bath. The rooms without attached bathroom are the most pleasant, as they face the street and have balconies.

Not far away on Peck Seah St are a couple of carpeted, air-con hotels with more pretensions than the Majestic but not as good for the price. The *New Asia* (☎ 221 1861) is on Maxwell Rd at the corner of Peck Seah St. Most rooms are pokey and cost S$55, single or double. A couple of doors down at 10 Peck Seah St, the *Air View Hotel* (☎ 225 7788) is a bit better than the New Asia and costs $45/65 for singles/doubles, or S$50/70 with TV. All rooms have a shower cubicle.

Little India & Jalan Besar

Little India and Jalan Besar, near the Lavender St Malaysia bus station, also have a number of cheap hotels. It is not as convenient as the other areas, but it is close to the Lavender St bus station if you arrive by long-distance bus from Malaysia, and it is handy for exploring Little India and Arab St.

See the Little India map for the location of places to stay in this area.

Guest Houses The *Friendly Rest House* (☎ 294 0847) is at 357A Serangoon Rd, just past Kitchener Rd, but the door is actually around the corner on Perumal Rd. It's not very popular with travellers but it is close to Little India. The rooms are better than average and good value at S$15 and S$20.

The well-run *Little India Guest House* (☎ 294 2866) is just off Serangoon Rd in the heart of Little India at 3 Veerasamy Rd. It is more like a hotel than a guest house. Small rooms cost S$38/50/62 for singles/doubles/triples. It is a new place so the rooms and well-appointed shared bathrooms are spotless.

Hotels Little India has a couple of cheap Chinese hotels. Close to Serangoon Rd, the *Tai Hoe Hotel* (☎ 298 4911) is at 30 Verdun Rd on the corner of Kitchener Rd. Unattractive singles with fan cost S$24, though the air-con rooms are slightly better and cost $35 to S$45. The *Nan Yong Hotel*, 3 Roberts Lane, has dismal rooms for S$22 but the best room in the house is passable at S$30 with air-con.

Jalan Besar has a number of places to stay. The friendly *Boon Wah Boarding House* (☎ 299 1466), at 43A Jalan Besar on the corner of Upper Dickson Rd, has renovated rooms with air-con that really works, TV and attached bathrooms. It is as good as many of the mid-range places and costs S$60/70 for singles/doubles.

At 290A Jalan Besar, there's the *International Hotel* (☎ 293 9238) on the corner of Allenby Rd, with singles/doubles for $35/40. Doubles with bath cost S$45. The rooms are large, well kept and most have balconies. It's architecturally interesting and has a large restaurant downstairs. Further north down Jalan Besar at 383, right opposite Bugis Square Food Centre, is the *Kam Leng* (☎ 298 2289). It's a classic old hotel with wire-topped walls and old furniture. It has good, clean rooms at S$26 for a fan room and S$32 with air-con.

At the northern end of Jalan Besar at 407A-B, near Lavender St, is the spotlessly clean *Palace Hotel* (☎ 298 3108) with large, balconied double rooms for S$22. It is exceptionally good for the price and only a short walk from the Malaysia bus station on Lavender St.

Other Areas

Guest Houses *Airpower Services* (☎ 334 3496), 124-B Mackenzie Rd, is a quiet, relaxed place with a good atmosphere and popular with travellers. It is near Little India but is otherwise a little inconvenient. Dormitories cost S$7 or S$8 for air-con. There are a few rooms for S$20 to S$35.

Orchard Rd has a number of guest houses and private apartments that occasionally take in travellers. It is worth keeping an eye out for these places as they can be well located and offer a better class of guest house. *Skyvilla* is an apartment block on Cavenagh Rd where guest houses regularly crop up and then close down again for a while.

Hotels The *Mayfair City Hotel* (☎ 337 4542) is at 40-44 Armenian St near Orchard Rd, behind the National Museum in the colonial district. It's in one of Singapore's oldest streets and within walking distance of many attractions. Good rooms with air-con, shower and TV cost from S$52 to S$74.

The *Mitre Hotel* (☎ 737 3811), 145 Killiney Rd, is the cheapest hotel anywhere near Orchard Rd (half a km to the north). It would have to be the most dilapidated flea pit in Singapore, but that said it does have a good deal of character. It is in an old villa set back off the street in large grounds. The dinghy bar on the ground floor is popular with the oil-rig workers who stay here. Rooms range from S$23 for a rough single with fan to S$36 for a passable double with air-con and attached bath.

Just around the corner from the Mitre is the *Mario-Ville Boarding House* (☎ 734 5342), 64 Lloyd Rd. It is also set in a crumbling old villa but this hotel is in much better condition than the Mitre. Most of the rooms are newly partitioned and very clean. Singles cost S$45 but they don't have windows. Doubles with windows cost S$50 and are better for the price. Doubles with bath cost S$60.

At the railway station, the *Station Hotel* (☎ 222 1551), Railway Station, Keppel Rd, has seen better days and is a little inconveniently located. It may be ideal, however, if you've just finished a long train trip and can't face heading straight into the city. Singles cost S$44, and huge doubles cost S$55. All rooms have air-con and attached bathrooms and are good value by Singaporean standards.

0011654-

The Ys The *YMCA International House* (☎ 336 6000, fax 337 3140) is at 1 Orchard Rd (map 6). It is more like a top mid-range hotel and has rooms for S$60 single, S$70 double, S$80 family and S$90 superior room, plus 10% service charge. All rooms have air-con, TV, telephone and attached bathroom. A bed in the large dorm costs S$20. The facilities at this YMCA are exceptionally good with a fitness centre, roof-top swimming pool, squash and badminton courts, and a billiards room. There's also a restaurant which offers a cheap daily set meal and a McDonald's which actually offers room service! You can phone down to have a Big Mac delivered to your room.

The *Metropolitan YMCA* (☎ 737 7755, fax 235 5528, map 12), 60 Stevens Rd, also has well-appointed rooms, a pool and cafe. It is a good 15-minute walk north of Orchard and Tanglin Rds, and less conveniently located than the Orchard Rd YMCA. Singles/doubles/triples with bathroom, TV and air-con range from S$55/65/75 to S$80/90/100 for a 'pool view' room. A 5% service charge applies.

The *Metropolitan YMCA International Centre* (☎ 222 4666, fax 222 6467, map 12) is at 70 Palmer Rd, near the railway station and the Tanjong Pagar MRT station. If you want to be near Chinatown or the waterfront, this is your place. A dormitory bed is S$15 and singles with common shower are S$24, but these are for men only. Singles/doubles with shower are S$37/40, and triples are S$55. All rooms have air-conditioning, and a 5% service charge is applied. The facilities are good and there is a restaurant.

The *YWCA Hostel* (☎ 336 1212) at 6-8 Fort Canning Rd is behind the Supreme House, quite close to the Orchard Rd YMCA. A double room with air-con and shower costs S$45. Nice dorm rooms are available for S$15; they only take women or couples. It has been recommended by solo women travellers as safe and secure.

Camping The best place for camping is at Sentosa Island where pre-erected four-person tents with camp beds cost S$15 per night. They cater primarily for groups, but individuals can stay by booking in advance through the Sentosa Information Centre (☎ 270 7888). The nearby youth hostel is only open to organised groups and is also booked through the Sentosa Information Centre.

There's also the good *East Coast Campsite* on East Coast Parkway, at the five-km marker. It is run by the People's Association (☎ 340 5113), which has an office on Stadium Link, opposite the national stadium. Officially, you must first obtain a permit from the office (in person, three months in advance!) before you front up at the campground. If you can negotiate your way around the bureaucracy, a three-person tent costs S$15 per day (tents are provided) during the week and S$18 on weekends.

PLACES TO STAY – MIDDLE

The problem with Singapore is the lack of good middle-range accommodation. As with the bottom-end accommodation, there are no new middle-range places being built to fill the demand, and some have also fallen prey to redevelopment.

The hotels listed here are mostly second-string, relatively modern places which offer air-con, phone and TV, but could do with a face-lift. Others come close to matching the top-end hotels, but they lack the restaurants, bars and the Filipino band playing in the lobby. It is also worth looking at the cheaper top-end hotels, which may only be a few dollars extra after discount.

Some of the bottom-end hotels listed, like the excellent Orchard Rd YMCA, are really good quality middle-range hotels. Others like the Majestic in China-town or the South-East Asia Hotel in Waterloo St are comparable to the cheaper places listed here.

Colonial District (map 3)

The *New 7th Storey Hotel* (☎ 337 0251) at 229 Rochor Rd, at the northern end of the colonial district, is an upmarket cheapie. Good budget rooms with air-con, TV, telephone and carpeting go for S$59 nett or S$75 nett with attached bathroom.

Smaller modern hotels with air-con and bathrooms include the *Hotel Bencoolen* (☎ 336 0822), 47 Bencoolen St, situated amongst the rock-bottom guest houses. The rooms are cheaply put together and it costs S$76/80 nett. A notch up in quality with better facilities is the *Strand Hotel* (☎ 338 1866), 25 Bencoolen St, practically next door to the Hotel Bencoolen. It costs S$95 for a single or double.

The *Metropole Hotel* (☎ 336 3611), on Seah St behind the Raffles, is a fairly new hotel that was once a three-star place but it has its shine. It costs S$85/100 plus 10% service charge and tax for singles/doubles.

Little India (map 4)

The *Broadway Hotel* (☎ 292 4661), 195 Serangoon Rd, is one of the few hotels in Little India. The rooms have air-con, TV and attached bathrooms, but are musty and need maintenance. There's a good, cheap Indian restaurant downstairs. Singles/doubles cost S$80/90 and S$90/100 for superior rooms, plus 4% tax.

Orchard Road Area (map 6)

You can find a few reasonably priced hotels around Orchard Rd. At Kramat Rd, one block north of Orchard Rd, the *Supreme Hotel* (☎ 737 8333) is central and a good buy for the position. It is a good mid-range hotel and costs S$85 nett a single or double.

Lloyd's Inn (☎ 737 7309), 2 Lloyd Rd, is a small but modern hotel less than a 10-minute walk from Orchard Rd. It is in a quiet street among the old villas of Singapore and the rooms are spread out, motel style, around the reception building. The well-appointed rooms cost S$80 a double or S$90 a double with fridge, plus 14%, making them a good alternative to the major top-end hotels. Bookings are advisable.

In the quiet residential area to the north of Orchard and Tanglin Rds are some good hotels, but they are a little out of the way. The *Sloane Court Hotel* (☎ 2353311), 17 Balmoral Rd, is a pleasant Tudor-style hotel in a garden setting with an English pub. The rooms are comfortable but nothing special and cost S$80/90 for singles/doubles. A few hundred metres away is the *Hotel VIP* (☎ 235 4277), 5 Balmoral Crescent, which has a swimming pool. The rooms are a grade above those at the Sloane Court and cost S$115 single or double.

Next to the Shangri-La Hotel, the *RELC International House* (☎ 737 9044), 30 Orange Grove Rd, has large well-appointed doubles with balcony and fridge for a very reasonable S$102 to S$110. RELC stands for Regional English Language Centre, and the bottom floors are devoted to conference rooms and teaching facilities while the top floors are a good standard hotel.

Other Areas

Dragon Cityview Hotel (☎ 223 9228, map 2), 18 Mosque St in Chinatown, is one of those rarities – a new Chinese hotel without a pool, bars, restaurants and high-speed lifts. It is in a row of renovated shopfronts and the rooms are well appointed with air- con, attached bathroom, TV and mini fridge. The rooms are quite small and most cost from S$100 to S$120, though 'small, small' singles are available for S$70. Their published rates are higher – too high – so ask for a discount.

Other mid-range places can be found in less convenient locations. Towards the east coast in the Geylang and Katong areas you'll find a few moderately priced hotels that are comparable to the cheaper top-end places. It is an interesting area to stay but a long way from most of Singapore's attractions. In the Geylang district, the *Lion City Hotel* (☎ 744 8111), 15 Tanjong Katong Rd, is one of the best in this area. The hotel has been recently renovated and offers very good rooms, but the big bonus is that it is only a short walk from the Paya Lebar MRT station. Singles or doubles cost S$120. The *Sea View Hotel* (☎ 345 2222), Amber Close in Katong, is a good hotel with singles for S$140 and doubles for S$160. The *Duke Hotel* (☎ 345 3311), 42-46 Meyer Rd, also in Katong, costs S$106 plus service charge and tax.

The *Great Eastern Hotel* (☎ 284 8244), 401 MacPherson Rd, is seven km to the north-east of the city on MacPherson Rd. Singles or doubles cost S$143. The *Mount Emily Hotel* (☎ 338 9151), 10a Upper Wilkie Rd, is between Little India and Orchard Rd and costs S$99/109 for singles/doubles.

PLACES TO STAY – TOP END

The rates for Singapore's international standard hotels constantly change as they ride the roller coaster of supply and demand. In the mid-'80s hotel rates bottomed out, rose steadily and peaked in the early '90s, while recently most top-end hotels offered large discounts on their advertised rates, making them good value for the facilities on offer. Discounts are not usually available if you walk in off the street, but it is always worth asking. If you arrive by air, the Singapore Hotels Association (☎ 542 6955) operate a stall at Changi International Airport and keep an up-to-the-minute list of available rooms. You don't pay extra for the service, and you will be quoted the current discount rates, which are usually a much better deal than the walk-in rates. STA Travel (☎ 734 5681) in the Orchard Parade Hotel can also make bookings at discounted rates for a selection of cheaper luxury hotels. Of course, if you visit Singapore on a package or on a stopover, travel agents overseas should be able to offer good deals on accommodation. If you book in advance yourself, fax or phone the sales offices of the hotels and ask for the corporate or discount rates to avoid paying walk-in rates.

As a rough demarcation line, 'top end' refers to hotels where a standard double room costs over S$120 a night. Singapore's best hotels generally cost over S$200 a night, and many were designed to cater for expense-account travellers. Naturally, all these hotels will be air-conditioned, all rooms will have bathrooms, TV and mini-bar and in almost all cases there will be a swimming pool and a variety of restaurants, coffee shops and bars. They are all of international standard and often there is little to distinguish one from the other – the choice boils down to price and where you want to stay.

The hotels at the bottom end of this range are of a good standard but are either getting a little old or lack the extensive facilities of the larger hotels. Singapore has a number of 'super luxury' hotels that in price and standards rise a cut above the mere international-standard hotels. Singapore also has a couple of hotels with definite old Eastern flavour and style, notably the Goodward Park in the Orchard Rd area and, of course, the Raffles in the colonial district. A few new boutique hotels have sprung up in the renovated terraces of Chinatown and while they don't have pools or a host of restaurants and bars, they have character, which so many of the concrete-and-glass high-rise hotels lack.

Orchard Rd

Orchard Rd is where everyone wants to stay, and consequently hotels tend to be a little more expensive than those in other areas. This is very much the tourist centre of Singapore with hotels, airline offices and shopping centres in profusion. Orchard Rd is easily reached by bus from Changi International Airport – bus No 390 runs along Penang Rd and Orchard Blvd, parallel to Orchard Rd, and then loops back along Tanglin Rd and Orchard Rd itself. Orchard Rd is also well serviced by the MRT, with Somerset and Orchard stations on Orchard Rd, and Newton station at the top (north-eastern) end of Scotts Rd. Orchard Rd has its fair share of expensive hotels, however, you can find the full range of top-end accommodation, including some moderately priced hotels of a high standard.

The *Cockpit Hotel* is just off Orchard Rd at the city end. It is looking a little weary and the facilities are limited but it is well located and moderately priced. The *Hotel Grand Central* is indeed central to Orchard Rd and has good facilities, though is not particularly grand. On Claymore Drive, which runs parallel with Orchard Rd, the *Hotel Negara* was one of the first international hotels in Singapore, but is now a relatively small hotel compared to the huge new hotels. It is currently undergoing revovations.

Other cheaper hotels can be found to the north and west of the western end of Orchard Rd, near Scotts and Tanglin Rds. Most are smaller hotels just beyond an easy walk to the action. On Nassim Hill, the *Hotel Premier* is used as a training centre for hotel and catering staff. The standards of service are therefore usually better than the small size might indicate, and the two good restaurants are a bonus. The rooms are good but will need upgrading soon. The rates are always reasonable. Nearby on Lady Hill Rd, the *Ladyhill Hotel* is a slightly more expensive low-rise hotel in an attractive garden setting. The best rooms with private balconies overlooking the pool are in the chalet block and cost an extra S\$20 to S\$40. The *Garden Hotel*, further away from Orchard Rd on Balmoral Rd, is another smaller hotel with a pleasant covered courtyard/atrium area and a courtyard pool. The well-appointed rooms are very good value. The *Hotel Asia* is more expensive but more conveniently located on Scotts Rd. Smaller and older than its flash neighbours, it lacks the facilities of most other big hotels.

The centrally located hotels in Orchard Rd are more popular and generally more expensive. On the corner of Tanglin and Orchard Rds, the *Orchard Parade Hotel* is moderately priced for its location and facilities. More expensive hotels nearby are the recently renovated *Boulevard* and the *Orchard*. Heading back (south-east) down Orchard Rd is the more luxurious *Crown Prince Hotel* at the corner of Bideford Rd. A few minutes' walk from Orchard Rd is the *Cairnhill Hotel* on Cairnhill Circle, a notch below most of the other hotels but reasonably priced. The relatively small *Holiday Inn Park View* is well positioned and has good discounted rates but the central expressway has spoiled its park view. Further down Orchard Rd, the French-run *Le Meridien* has a shopping centre where all prices are quoted in yen. It is a good hotel but only worth it if you can get a large discount. Across from the Meridien on Penang Rd, *Hotel Phoenix* is at the lower end of the range for Orchard Rd and lacks

Orchard Road (PT)

a lot of facilities. The big plus is that it sits over the
Somerset MRT station. The *Imperial Hotel* on Jalan
Rumbia enjoys a hilltop location near River Valley Rd
and is within walking distance of the city end of Orchard
Rd. It is also cheaper.

Most of the top hotels are at the top end of Orchard
Rd around Scotts and Tanglin Rds. Just off Tanglin Rd
are the renovated *Omni Marco Polo*, which is moderately
priced for its superior facilities, and the impressive
Regent, which is edging into the super luxury category.
Just off Tanglin Rd on Nassim Hill, the *ANA* is another
of the more expensive hotels and has gone for the old-
world look in decor. The *Shangri-La* is set in five hectares
of garden on Orange Grove Rd, just a few minutes' walk
from the north-western end of Orchard Rd. The rooms
in the Garden Wing each have their own balcony overflowing with plants. This super luxury hotel recently
polled as one of the best business hotels in the world.

On the corner of Scotts and Orchard Rds, the *Dynasty
Hotel* is a gaudy Chinese-style hotel in a strange sky-
scraper-topped-by-a-pagoda. This well-appointed hotel
offers 'Asian opulence' and is priced accordingly.
Similar in oriental style, but more restrained, is the *Mandarin*, one of Singapore's top hotels halfway along
Orchard Rd.

The international hotel chains are well represented.
The slightly worn *Hilton*, on Orchard Rd, and the *Royal
Holiday Inn Crowne Plaza*, on Scotts Rd, are both mid-
range luxury hotels. The *Hyatt Regency* on Scotts Rd is

one of the most expensive hotels in Singapore and definitely in the super luxury class. It caters for expense-account business travellers and has good business facilities. Further along Scotts Rd, the *Sheraton Towers* is one of Singapore's most opulent hotels and another favourite for business trips.

Next to the Sheraton Towers and near the Newton MRT station is *Melia at Scotts* (map 12). It is popular with tour groups, and travel agents can usually get good discounts at this well- appointed hotel. Other hotels around Scotts Rd include the renovated *York Hotel* on Mt Elizabeth Rd, and in the same street the brand new *Elizabeth Hotel*.

The beautiful, old-fashioned *Goodwood Park Hotel* on Scotts Rd was designed by the same architect that designed Raffles. Its architecture is more ornate and, if anything, even more delightful than the Raffles. It began life as the Teutonia Club for the German community in Singapore, but was used by the Australian army after WW II when they investigated Japanese war crimes. It is set on six hectares, and is one of Singapore's most expensive hotels.

Colonial District (map 3)

The colonial district also has a good selection of luxury hotels. The real estate may not be as prestigious as Orchard Rd, but if anything these hotels are more conveniently located for most of Singapore's attractions.

The *Bayview Inn* is a good three-star hotel in Bencoolen St amongst the backpackers' guest houses. It doesn't have a huge lobby and a profusion of restaurants, but it has a roof-top swimming pool and good rooms. The low tariffs make it a best buy.

On Coleman St, over towards the business centre of Singapore, the *Peninsula Hotel* and its sister hotel the *Excelsior* are moderately priced hotels. The *New Otani* is an immoderately priced Japanese-run hotel on River Valley Rd, opposite Fort Canning Park.

The *Carlton* is a relatively new hotel on Bras Basah Rd with excellent facilities. It regularly offers large discounts on its high advertised rates. The *Allson Hotel* on Victoria St is another very good hotel with reasonable rates for the standards on offer. Both are close to the City Hall MRT station.

On top of the Raffles City shopping centre and the City Hall MRT station is the tallest hotel in the world and Singapore's largest, the 73-storey *Westin Stamford Hotel*, and its sister hotel the *Westin Plaza Hotel*, with countless restaurants and lounges, and two roof-top swimming pools. These hotels are among the best in Singapore.

Nearby on the edge of the colonial district, the massive Marina Square complex is a testament to rampant capitalism that has risen from the wasteland of reclamation. Here you'll find the *Marina Mandarin, Oriental* and *Pan Pacific*, with competing lobbies that owe their inspiration to Hollywood special effects movies. The Marina Mandarin's towering lobby (complete with 21-storey Hanging Gardens of Babylon atrium) gets the mega-starship award. They are expensive, super luxury hotels, with the Oriental being the most popular for business executives. The swimming pools even have underwater sound systems!

At the junction of Bras Basah and Beach Rds, the venerable *Raffles* is as much a superb tourist attraction as it is a fine old hotel. The hotel has been through massive renovations to restore its grandeur and it is now ringed by new extensions. To the purist it ain't the old Raffles, but the restorations are faithful to the original and the extensions are in keeping with the style. The bars and restaurants can still conjure up some of the mysteries of the orient and what other hotel can claim that a tiger was once shot in the billiards room? The limited number of beautiful antique-decorated rooms are only for those with money to burn. The fabulously rich can stay in the magnificent suites, available for a mere S$6000 per night. Don't expect discounts at the Raffles. The accommodation area is only accessible to guests with security keys, so they won't be bothered by the riff-raff.

Chinatown (map 2)

If you want to experience the atmosphere of Chinatown, the futuristic *Furama Hotel* on Eu Tong Sen St is right in the centre of things. The *Amara Hotel* on Tanjong Pagar Rd is on the edge of Chinatown not far from the railway station, and nearby on Anson Rd is the *Harbour View Dai-Ichi*. Both are well-appointed business hotels, near the Tanjong Pagar MRT station.

Two new boutique hotels have taken up residency in the renovated terraces of Chinatown. The *Duxton Hotel* in the Tanjong Pagar area, is undoubtedly the pick of these. Rooms are furnished in opulent, antique style. The suites have a mezzanine bedroom, and while they are not overly large, are worth the extra dollars. The hotel has a good French restaurant and a bar.

Inn of the Sixth Happiness has standard rooms on the ground floor that run off a winding passageway with attractive open courtyard areas, but the rooms are small and windowless. The superior and deluxe rooms upstairs are much better. All rooms are well appointed though not quite international standard. The suites have spa baths and traditional Chinese beds with mahogany canopies, but are expensive.

Havelock Rd (map 12)

Over on Havelock Rd, south of Orchard Rd, is another hotel enclave. Chinatown is within walking distance, and the Singapore Explorer shuttle operates from the hotels to Orchard Rd, but basically these hotels are in the middle of nowhere. Consequently they tend to be cheaper and are generally good value. While not super luxury hotels they are all of a good standard, and include the *Apollo*, *King's*, *Miramar*, *River View* and *Concorde* hotels. The pick of these are the River View, right on the Singapore River, and the Concorde with its impressive lobby and superior facilities.

Other Areas

In Little India (map 4) and Arab Street (map 5) are a few good hotels that are reasonably priced. The *New Park Hotel*, on Kitchener Rd in Little India, was recently renovated and is popular with tour groups. The *Golden Landmark Hotel*, on the corner of Victoria and Arab Sts right next to the Bugis MRT station, has middle-eastern inspired architecture to match its location. The rates are very competitive. At the end of Arab St on Beach Rd, the *Plaza Hotel* is very well appointed and also handy to the MRT.

On Bukit Timah Rd, about two km north of Orchard Rd, are the *Hotel Equatorial*, and just across the road, the *Novotel Orchid*. The Novotel has the better facilities. These hotels have shuttle bus services to Orchard Rd, but because they are a long way from anywhere they often offer big discounts, especially the Novotel. They are certainly worth considering if you have a car and want to travel around the island as they are handy for Singapore's expressways. Also north of Orchard Rd is the *Royal* on Newton Rd, next to United Square and near the Newton MRT station. It is also moderately priced for the facilities on offer.

Sentosa Island (map 9) has two luxury hotels if you want to get away from it all. The *Beaufort* is the more luxurious and its low-rise buildings are built around courtyards and surrounded by two golf courses. The

Restored Shophouse (JC)

new *Rasa Sentosa Beach Resort* is a high-rise built at the end of the beach and is good for sporting activities.

On the other side of the city in the East Coast district is the *Paramount Hotel* on Marine Parade. It is one of the cheaper hotels in the top-end range. *Le Meriden Changi* is eight km from the airport in quiet Changi Village.

Top-End Details

The following list contains details of all top-end hotels. Unless otherwise stated, all prices are '++', ie add 10% service charge and 4% government tax. The rate quoted is the published rate for a standard single/double room, except for a few that offer a discount as a matter of course for walk-in customers, in which case that price is quoted. These hotels usually have more expensive 'deluxe' and 'superior' rooms, which are normally larger or have a better view, and many also have suites. These prices should be used as a guide only, as Singapore hotel rates are subject to large variations. At the time of writing most hotels had discount rates of 20% or more (sometimes much more) on the published rates and only the super luxury hotels charged over S$200 for a standard room.

Allson Hotel (☎ 336 0811, fax 339 7019), 101 Victoria St. Pool, restaurants, shops, entertainment, business centre, health club, handicapped facilities, conference facilities. S$190/210.

Amara Hotel (☎ 224 4488, fax 224 3910), 165 Tanjong Pagar Rd. Pool, restaurants, shops, entertainment, business centre, health club, squash, tennis, conference facilities. S$300/320.

ANA Hotel (☎ 732 1222, fax 235 1516), 16 Nassim Hill. Pool, restaurants, shops, entertainment, business centre, health club, conference facilities. S$270/300.

Apollo Hotel (☎ 733 2081, fax 733 1588), 405 Havelock Rd. Restaurants, shops, entertainment, business centre, health club, conference facilities. S$210 single or double.

Hotel Asia (☎ 737 8388, fax 733 3563), 37 Scotts Rd. Restaurants, entertainment, conference facilities. S$120/140.

Bayview Inn (☎ 337 2882, fax 338 2880), 30 Bencoolen St. Pool, restaurants, entertainment, conference facilities. S$115/125.

Beaufort Hotel (☎ 275 0331, fax 275 0228), Bukit Manis Rd, Sentosa. Pool, restaurants, entertainment, business centre, health club, squash, tennis, conference facilities. S$305/330.

Boulevard Hotel (☎ 737 2911, fax 737 8849), Cuscaden Rd. Pool, restaurants, shops, entertainment, business centre, health club, conference facilities. S$240/270.

Cairnhill Hotel (☎ 734 6622, fax 235 5598), 19 Cairnhill Circle. Pool, restaurants, shops, entertainment, health club, conference facilities. S$136/152.

Carlton Hotel (☎ 338 8333, fax 339 6866), 76 Bras Basah Rd. Pool, restaurants, shops, entertainment, business centre, health club, conference facilities. S$175/185.

Cockpit Hotel (☎ 737 9111, fax 737 3105), 6/7 Oxley Rise. Restaurants, entertainment, conference facilities. S$138 single or double.

Concorde Hotel (☎ 733 0188, fax 733 0989), 317 Outram Rd. Pool, restaurants, shops, entertainment, business centre, tennis, conference facilities. S$170 single or double.

Crown Prince Hotel (☎ 732 1111, fax 732 7018), 270 Orchard Rd. Pool, restaurants, entertainment, business centre, conference facilities. S$180/210.

Dynasty Hotel (☎ 734 9900, fax 733 5251), 320 Orchard Rd. Pool, restaurants, shops, entertainment, business centre, health club, conference facilities. S$270/300.

Duxton Hotel (☎ 227 7678, fax 227 1232), 83 Duxton Rd. Restaurants, entertainment, business centre. S$260/290.

Hotel Equatorial (☎ 732 0431, fax 737 9426), 429 Bukit Timah Rd. Pool, restaurants, shops, entertainment, business centre, conference facilities. S$160 single or double.

Excelsior (☎ 338 7733, fax 339 3847), 5 Coleman St. Pool, restaurants, shops, entertainment, business centre, health club, conference facilities. S$170/S$185.

Furama Hotel (☎ 533 3888, fax 534 1489), 60 Eu Tong Sen St. Pool, restaurants, shops, entertainment, business centre, health club, conference facilities. S$170/187.

Garden Hotel (☎ 235 3344, fax 235 9730), 14 Balmoral Rd. Pool, restaurants, entertainment, conference facilities. S$108/126.

Golden Landmark Hotel (☎ 297 2828, fax 298 2038), 390 Victoria St. Pool, restaurants, shops, entertainment, business centre, conference facilities. S$125/135.

Goodwood Park Hotel (☎ 737 7411, fax 732 8558), 22 Scotts Rd. Pool, restaurants, shops, entertainment, business centre, conference facilities. S$355 single or double.

Hotel Grand Central (☎ 737 9944, fax 733 3175), Kramat Lane & Cavanagh Rd. Pool, restaurants, shops, entertainment, business centre, health club, conference facilities. S$140 single or double.

Harbour View Dai-Ichi (☎ 224 1133, fax 222 0749), 81 Anson Rd. Pool, restaurants, shops, entertainment, business centre, health club, conference facilities. S$200/220.

Hilton International Hotel (☎ 737 2233, fax 732 2917), 581 Orchard Rd. Pool, restaurants, shops, entertainment, business centre, health club, conference facilities. S$280 single or double.

Holiday Inn Park View (☎ 733 8333, fax 734 4593), 11 Cavenagh Rd. Pool, restaurants, shops, entertainment, business centre, conference facilities. S$260/290.

Hyatt Regency Hotel (☎ 733 1188, fax 732 1696), 10-12 Scotts Rd. Pool, restaurants, shops, entertainment, business centre, health club, squash, tennis, conference facilities. S$360 single or double.

Imperial Hotel (☎ 737 1666, fax 737 4761), 1 Jalan Rumbia. Pool, restaurants, shops, entertainment, business centre, health club, conference facilities. S$180/200.

Inn of the Sixth Happiness (☎ 223 3266, fax 223 7951), 33 Erskine Rd. Restaurants. S$130 single or double.

King's Hotel (☎ 733 0011, fax 732 5764), Havelock Rd. Pool, restaurants, shops, entertainment, conference facilities. S$180/200.

Ladyhill Hotel (☎ 737 2111, fax 737 4606), 1 Lady Hill Rd. Pool, restaurants, entertainment, conference facilities. S$155/175.

Le Meridien Changi Hotel (☎ 542 7700, fax 542 5295), 1 Netheravon Rd. Pool, restaurants, shops, entertainment, business centre, health club, conference facilities. S$270/300.

Le Meridien Singapore Hotel (☎ 733 8855, fax 732 7886), 100 Orchard Rd. Pool, restaurants, shops, entertainment, business centre, health club, conference facilities. S$270/300.

Mandarin Hotel (☎ 737 4411, fax 732 2361), 333 Orchard Rd. Pool, restaurants, shops, entertainment, business centre, health club, squash, tennis, conference facilities. S$300/340.

Marina Mandarin Hotel (☎ 338 3388, fax 339 4977), 6 Raffles Blvd. Pool, restaurants, shops, entertainment, business centre, health club, squash, tennis, conference facilities. S$315/355.

Melia at Scotts (☎ 732 5885, fax 732 1332), 45 Scotts Rd. Pool, restaurants, shops, entertainment, business centre, health club, conference facilities. S$245/270.

Hotel Miramar (☎ 733 0222, fax 733 4027), 401 Havelock Rd. Pool, restaurants, entertainment, business centre, health club, conference facilities. S$140/S$170.

Hotel New Otani (☎ 338 3333, fax 339 2854), 117A River Valley Rd. Pool, restaurants, shops, entertainment, business centre, health club, conference facilities. S$260 single or double.

New Park Hotel (☎ 291 5533, fax 297 2827), 181 Kitchener Rd. Pool, restaurants, shops, entertainment, conference facilities. S$180/200.

Novotel Orchid Hotel (☎ 250 3322, fax 250 9292), 214 Dunearn Rd. Pool, restaurants, shops, entertainment, business centre, health club, conference facilities. S$180/200.

Omni Marco Polo Hotel (☎ 474 7141, fax 471 0521), 247 Tanglin Rd. Pool, restaurants, shops, entertainment, business centre, health club, conference facilities. S$200 single or double.

Orchard Hotel (☎ 734 7766, fax 733 5482), 442 Orchard Rd. Pool, restaurants, shops, entertainment, business centre, squash, tennis, conference facilities. S$190/230.

Orchard Parade Hotel (☎ 737 1133, fax 733 0242), 1 Tanglin Rd. Pool, restaurants, shops, entertainment, business centre, health club, conference facilities. S$220/240.

Oriental Hotel (☎ 338 0066, fax 339 9537), Marina Square, 5 Raffles Ave. Pool, restaurants, shops, entertainment, business centre, health club, squash, tennis, conference facilities. S$250/270.

Pan Pacific Hotel (☎ 336 8111, fax 339 1861), Marina Square, 7 Raffles Blvd. Pool, restaurants, shops, entertainment, business centre, health club, tennis, conference facilities. S$300/340.

Paramount Hotel (☎ 344 5577, fax 447 4131), 25 Marine Parade Rd. Pool, restaurants, shops, entertainment, business centre, health club, conference facilities. S$180 single or double.

Peninsula Hotel (☎ 337 8080, fax 339 6236), 5 Coleman St. Pool, restaurants, shops, entertainment, business centre, health club, conference facilities. S$160/175.

Hotel Phoenix (☎ 737 8666, fax 732 2024), 277 Orchard Rd/Somerset Rd. Restaurants, shops, conference facilities. S$142/165.

Plaza Hotel (☎ 298 0011, fax 296 3600), 7500A Beach Rd. Pool, restaurants, shops, entertainment, business centre, health club, squash, conference facilities. S$200/220.

Hotel Premier (☎ 733 9811, fax 733 5595), 22 Nasim Hill. Pool, restaurants, conference facilities. S$120 single or double (no government tax is charged).

Raffles Hotel (☎ 337 1886, fax 339 7650), 1 Beach Rd. Pool, restaurants, shops, entertainment, business centre, health club, conference facilities. S$600 single or double.

Rasa Sentosa Beach Resort (☎ 275 0100, fax 275 0355), 101 Siloso Rd, Sentosa. Pool, restaurants, shops, entertainment, business centre, health club, conference facilities. S$180/200.

Regent of Singapore (☎ 733 8888, fax 732 8838), 1 Cuscaden Rd. Pool, restaurants, shops, entertainment, business centre, health club, conference facilities. S$325 single or double.

River View Hotel (☎ 732 9922, fax 732 1034), 382 Havelock Rd. Pool, restaurants, entertainment, business centre, health club, conference facilities. S$170/190.

Hotel Royal (☎ 253 4411, fax 253 8668), 36 Newton Rd. Pool, restaurants, shops, entertainment, health club, conference facilities. S$130/150.

Royal Holiday Inn Crowne Plaza (☎ 737 7966, fax 737 6646), 25 Scotts Rd. Pool, restaurants, shops, entertainment, business centre, health club, conference facilities. S$270/310.

Shangri-La Hotel (☎ 737 3644, fax 733 7220), 22 Orange Grove Rd. Pool, restaurants, shops, entertainment, business centre, health club, squash, tennis, conference facilities. S$300/330.

Sheraton Towers (☎ 737 6888, fax 737 1072), 39 Scotts Rd. Pool, restaurants, entertainment, business centre, health club, conference facilities. S$380 single or double.

Westin Plaza Hotel (☎ 338 8585, fax 338 2862), 2 Stamford Rd. Pool, restaurants, shops, entertainment, business centre, health club, squash, tennis, conference facilities. S$290/330.

Westin Stamford Hotel (☎ 338 8585, fax 337 1554), 2 Stamford Rd. Pool, restaurants, shops, entertainment, business centre, health club, squash, tennis, conference facilities. S$250/290.

York Hotel (☎ 737 0511, fax 732 1217), 21 Mount Elizabeth. Pool, restaurants, shops, entertainment, business centre, conference facilities. S$220/245.

LONG TERM

For medium to long-term stays, Singapore has a number of serviced apartments, or it is possible to rent rooms in private apartments. Rents are very high in Singapore, and an apartment in the sought-after areas close to the city are S$1000 and up per week. Cheaper apartments and even small houses can be rented much further out for lower rents, but rates are still high.

For many foreign workers on term contracts, serviced apartments are a no-fuss form of accommodation and as cheap, if not cheaper, than renting an apartment. The cheapest option of all is to rent a room in an apartment with a local family, and the guest houses usually know of some options, though many travellers simply stay in the guest houses. Expect to pay around S$200 per week for a room in an apartment, though this varies depending on the standards and amenities on offer.

As well as private apartment blocks many of the hotels have serviced apartments. For your money you get the amenities of a hotel, laundry facilities and car parking, and the apartments will be suites with separate bedroom, small kitchens and a living/dining room. The cheaper places have essential furniture and cooking utensils, but are fairly bare. Many have one-month minimum stays, though some can be rented by the week, making them good alternatives to hotel rooms.

Of the hotels, the *Novotel Orchid* has one-bedroom apartments from S$3000 per month, the *Imperial* is slightly more expensive and the *Plaza* has apartments starting at S$3600. Two-bedroom apartments usually cost an extra 50%. The better hotels have more luxurious suites for around S$4500 to S$6000 per month. The *Orchard*, *Carlton*, *Oriental* and *Pan Pacific* hotels all have suites.

Other serviced apartment blocks usually have swimming pools, gyms and most of the amenities of hotels. The rates are similar to the hotels and some to try include: *Liang Court Regency* (☎ 337 0111), 177 River Valley Rd; *Palm Court* (☎ 235 0088), 15 Cairnhill Rd; *Karakouen Orange Court* (☎ 738 1511), 6C Orange Grove Rd.

Places to Eat

Singapore is far and away the food capital of Asia. When it comes to superb Chinese food, Hong Kong may be a step ahead but it's Singapore's sheer variety and low prices which make it so good. Equally important, Singapore's food is accessible – you haven't got to search out obscure places, you don't face communication problems and you don't need a lot of money.

Alternatively, if you want to make gastronomic discoveries, there are lots of out-of-the-way little places where you'll find marvellous food that few visitors know about. The Singaporean enthusiasm for food (and economical food at that) is amply illustrated by the competitions newspapers run every so often to find the best hawker's stall in the city. A recent food story to hit the press was the S$1 chicken-rice war. This hawkers' price war in the outlying areas attracted large queues and customers from all over Singapore.

To get to grips with food in Singapore, you firstly have to know what types of food are available, and then where to find them. The *Singapore Official Guide*, a free booklet, has a food section with numerous restaurant recommendations. *Foodstops* by Margaret Chan is the best guide to food in Singapore and well worth S$9.90 for those with more than a passing interest in Singaporean food. She writes with wit and great love for her topic, and includes extensive suggestions for good dining in all price ranges. *Singapore's 100 Best Restaurants* is a selection of fine restaurants, chosen by a survey of *Singapore Tattler* magazine subscribers, a decidedly well-to-do bunch. Some moderately priced restaurants are included.

Dining possibilities range from streetside hawkers' stalls to fancy five-star hotel restaurants with a whole gamut of possibilities in between. In a hawkers' centre you can eat well for under S$5. The food is excellent. Next up the scale are the coffee shops, or *kopi tiam* (kopi is Malay for coffee and tiam is Hokkien for shop). These spartan, open-fronted restaurants with marble-topped tables often have similar food to the hawkers' centres and within each coffee shop you may find two or three different stalls serving their own specialities. Other coffee shops are more restaurant-like and the menus are more extensive; the food may be as good as a top restaurant and cost a fraction of the price. The old coffee shops, typically housed in a terrace or under an old hotel, are a dying breed.

Restaurants run the full range from glorified coffee shops to luxury restaurants. The price increases with the quality of the decor and the efficiency of the service. Unlike most Asian cities where Western chain food is a luxury item, Singapore's Asian and Western chain restaurants are reasonably priced. All the luxury hotels have a selection of restaurants, and they house most of Singapore's fine dining establishments.

Mid-range and expensive restaurants will normally add a 10% service charge and 4% tax (add 14% to the prices quoted here, except for hawkers' food and the cheapest restaurants). Many restaurants offer good-value set lunches and more expensive set dinners. *Kiasu* diners should keep an eye out for buffets, which allow you to try a number of dishes as you stuff yourself to the eyeballs.

Hawkers' Food

Traditionally, hawkers had mobile food stalls (pushcarts), set up their tables and stools around them and sold their food right on the streets. Real, mobile, on-the-street hawkers have now been replaced by hawkers' centres where a large number of stationary hawkers can be found under the one roof. These centres are the baseline for Singapore food, where the prices are lowest and the eating is possibly the most interesting.

Scattered amongst the hawkers are tables and stools, and you can sit and eat in any area you choose – none of them belongs to a specific stall. A group of you can sit at one table and all eat and drink from different stalls.

One of the wonders of food-centre eating is how the various operators keep track of their plates and utensils – and how they manage to chase you up with the bill. The real joy of these food centres is the sheer variety; while you're having Chinese food, your companion can be eating a biryani and across the table somebody else can be trying the satay. As a rough guide, most one-dish meals cost from S$1.50 to S$3, but the price is higher for more elaborate dishes.

There are hundreds of hawkers' centres all over Singapore, and many new shopping complexes and housing blocks set aside areas for the hawkers. Even Changi International Airport has a pretty good food centre in the basement! Many new hawkers' centres are air-conditioned and more like cafeterias with slightly higher prices. All centres are government-licensed and subject to health department regulations.

City Centre (map 2) In the business centre, *Empress Place* beside the Singapore River and *Boat Quay* directly across from it on the other bank are pleasant places to sit beside the river and have a meal. They are both very busy at lunchtime; Boat Quay closes in the evening.

Near the waterfront towards Chinatown is *Lau Pa Sat*, on Raffles Quay near the Raffles City MRT station. It is housed in the renovated Telok Ayer market building, a wonderful example of intricate Victorian cast-iron architecture in the railway-station mould. It has some souvenir stalls and occasionally stages cultural exhibits, but the main emphasis is on the favourite Singaporean pastime – food. Hawkers inside serve nonya, Korean and Western food, as well as more usual fare, and the famous Zam Zam restaurant has opened a very popular Indian Muslim stall. Restaurants with bars are also found here. It is more sanitised and expensive than the usual hawkers' centres, but as part of the recreation of old Singapore, quasi-mobile hawkers set up in the evenings on Boon Tat St, where the dining is cheaper and cooler than inside. If you crave a more traditional hawkers' centre, the *Telok Ayer Transit Centre* is hidden behind a park just on the other side of Raffles Quay and houses the original hawkers of the Telok Ayer centre before it was dismantled.

Orchard Rd (map 6) *Newton Circus Hawker Centre* is at the top (north-eastern) end of Scotts Rd, right near the Newton MRT station. It is very popular with tourists and therefore tends to be a little more expensive, but it is lively and open until the early hours of the morning. For a minor extravagance, try the huge prawns.

South-east down Orchard Rd is another popular food centre upstairs in the *Cuppage Centre*. The downstairs section is a vegetable and produce market with a wonderful selection of fruit. It is mainly a daytime centre and closes around 8 pm.

The *Scotts Picnic Food Court* in the Scotts Shopping Centre on Scotts Rd, just off Orchard Rd by the Hyatt Hotel, is quite a different sort of food centre. It's glossier and more restaurant-like than the general run of food centres, and the stalls around the dining area are international – as well as a variety of Chinese possibilities (including Peking Duck-rice) there is also Indian, Western and vegetarian food available. Orchard Rd has a number of similar food centres. The *Orchard Emerald*

The Hawkers' Variety

Some typical hawkers' food you may find includes carrot cake, or *chye tow kway*, (S$1.50 to S$3) – also known as radish cake, it's a vegetable and egg dish, tasting something like potato omelette, and totally unlike the Western health-food idea of carrot cake.

Indian biryanis cost from S$2 to S$4 or you can have a murtabak for around S$2. Naturally, chicken rice and *char siew*, or roast pork, will always be available in food centres (S$2 to S$3). All the usual Cantonese dishes like fried rice (S$1.50 to S$3), fried vegetables (S$3), beef & vegetables (S$5), and sweet & sour pork (S$3 to S$5) are available, plus other dishes like fish heads with black beans & chilli from S$3 to S$5.

There will often be Malay or Indonesian stalls with satay from 30c to 35c a stick, *mee rebus* from S$1.50 to S$2, and *gado gado* or *mee soto* at similar prices. *Won ton mee*, a substantial soup dish with shredded chicken or braised beef, costs from S$2 to S$3. You could try a *chee chong fun*, a type of stuffed noodle dish, which costs from S$1.50 to S$3 or more, depending on whether you want the noodles with prawns, mushrooms, chicken or pork. *Hokkien fried prawn mee* costs from S$1.50 to S$3, *prawn mee soup* from S$1.50 to S$3, *popiah* (spring rolls) $1 and *laksa* (spicy coconut based soup) from S$2 to S$3. There's also a whole variety of other dishes and soups.

Or, you can even opt for Western food like sausage, egg & chips for S$3.50, burgers for S$3 or fish & chips for S$3. Drinks include a large bottle of beer for S$6.50, soft drinks from 70c, ais kacang for 80c or sugar-cane juice from 50c to S$1 depending on the size. Fruit juices such as melon, papaya, pineapple, apple, orange or starfruit range from 80c to S$1.50. To finish up you might try a fruit salad for S$2 or a *pisang goreng* (fried banana) for 50c. ■

Food Court in the basement of the Orchard Emerald shopping centre has a varied selection of Asian food. In the same vein are the food stalls downstairs in *Orchard Towers*, on the corner of Orchard and Claymore Rds, and the very small but good centre in the basement of *Wisma Atria*. The busy hawker centre on the 6th floor of *Lucky Plaza* has a good range of the local hawkers' favourites and is as cheap as you'll find anywhere.

Colonial District (map 3) The *Albert Centre* on Albert Rd between Waterloo and Queen Sts is an extremely good, busy and very popular centre which has all types of food at low prices. On the corner of Bencoolen St and Albert St, in the basement of the Sim Lim Square complex, is the *Tenco Food Centre*, a very clean establishment.

Victoria St Food Court, next to the Victoria Hotel, is a notch up from most food centres. It has an air-con section at the back and a bar with draught beer. The food is cheap and good, and you can get Western-style breakfasts here. *Food Paradiz*, in the basement of the Paradiz Centre on Selegie Rd is another good air-con hawkers' centre.

The *Tropical Makan Palace* in the basement of the Beach Centre, 15 Beach Rd, is close to Raffles and the budget accommodation area. It has food stalls in the air-conditioned section or you can eat outside.

Just north of the river on Hill St, the large *Hill St Food Centre* is popular, and across the road the *Funan Centre* has a more upmarket air-conditioned food-stall area on the 7th floor.

The famous *Satay Club*, not far from the waterfront at the foot of Stamford Rd near Raffles Hotel, is a colourful place to dine. The satay here is the best in Singapore; just make sure you specify how many sticks (30c a time) you want or they'll assume your appetite is much larger than you will. It's only open in the evenings.

Little India (map 4) On Serangoon Rd at the start of Little India, the large *Zhujiao Centre* is a market with a number of food stalls. As you would expect, Indian food dominates.

Over on Jalan Besar are two food centres, the *Berseh Food Centre* halfway down on the corner of Jalan Berseh and the lively *Bugis Square Centre* at the end of Jalan Besar near Lavender St.

Chinatown (map 2) The Chinatown area has a number of excellent food centres. The *People's Park Complex* has a good, large food centre, and the *Maxwell Food Centre* is an old-fashioned centre on the corner of South Bridge and Maxwell Rds.

Some of the best Chinese food stalls in town are on the 2nd floor at the *Chinatown Complex* on the corner of Sago and Trengganu Sts, where there is also a market. Try the *Fu Ji Crayfish*, stall No 02-221, where crayfish *hor fun* costs only S$3, or a superb crayfish (actually scampi) or prawn claypot with vegetables and rice costs around S$5.

The *Fountain Food Court* at 51 Craig Rd is a different type of food centre in keeping with the new Chinatown. You can dine in air-con comfort, and the nouveau decor includes sand-blasted and bag-painted walls. The food is good, but some dishes are at restaurant prices. They have satay and other Malay food, *popiah and kueh* (cakes), and good (and cheap) congee.

Other hawkers' centres can be found alongside the *Tanjong Market*, not far from the railway station, and at the *Amoy St Food Centre*, where Amoy St meets Telok Ayer St.

Other Areas (map 1) The *Rasa Singapura Food Court* is a collection of hawkers selected in a special competition to find the best stalls for each dish. It used to be on Tanglin Rd but most of the hawkers have moved to the Bukit Turf Club on Turf Club Rd and they have taken the name with them. During the week, it's open for lunch and dinner until 11 pm. On weekends, it's open all day until midnight but you have to pay entry to the races until 6 pm.

The *Taman Serasi Food Centre* has one of the best settings – it is next to the Botanic Gardens north-west of the city centre on Cluny Rd, just off Napier Rd. The stalls are predominantly Malay.

Chinese Food

Singapore has plenty of restaurants serving everything from a south Indian rice plate to an all-American hamburger, but naturally it's Chinese restaurants that predominate. Many Chinese restaurants cater for family and work groups and offer banquets for eight or more people. For groups they offer a wonderful opportunity to try a whole range of dishes at a reasonable price. Even at the à la carte restaurants, dishes are meant to be shared, and restaurants offer small, medium and large servings to cater for different size groups. The prices of dishes quoted here are for small servings.

Cantonese The famous *Fatty's Wing Seong Restaurant* (☎ 338 1087), at 01-33 Albert Complex on Albert St, near the corner of Bencoolen St (map 3), has been a popular with Westerners ever since Fatty became a favourite with British troops stationed in Singapore during the Emergency. The extensive menu unfortunately lacks prices but the food is consistently good and moderately priced. Most dishes cost around S$5 to S$8, and go up to S$20 or more for crab. The restaurant is always crowded, but the ever-busy staff turn the tables around quickly so you shouldn't have to wait long.

The *Hillman* (☎ 221 5073, map 2) at 159 Cantonment Rd, near the Outram Park MRT station at the edge of

Chinatown, is a straightforward open-fronted restaurant where you can have a good meal for under S$15 per person, though seafood and more exotic dishes such as shark's fin will cost more. The picture of Paul Bocuse, signed with a glowing recommendation from the master chef, is nowfaded but the food is fresh and still good.

The *Xiang Man Lou Seafood & Shark's Fin Restaurant* (☎ 338 7651), on the 1st floor of the Bras Basah Complex (map 3), near the Raffles Hotel in the colonial district, has good food in a glittering, gaudy setting. It is not as expensive at the decor would lead you to believe, and apart from the specialities, cheaper main dishes are available for S$4 to S$10. The *Esquire Kitchen* (☎ 336 1802), 02-01 Bras Basah Complex, is another moderately priced air-con place with Chinese decor and good food. Most small mains cost from S$6 to S$10. The menu is not extensive, except for the ice creams and spiders which are a speciality.

Grand City (☎ 338 3622), 07-04 Cathay Building, 11 Dhoby Ghaut (map 6), is a more expensive restaurant and has a varied menu with good seafood and chicken dishes. Set menus start at S$38 for two. Peking Duck costs S$40 for two. It is near the Dhoby Ghaut MRT station, right at the start of Orchard Rd.

Tsui Hang Village (☎ 338 6668), 02-142 Marina Square, 6 Raffles Boulevard (map 3), is a popular Hong-Kong-style restaurant. You can fill yourself on a good set lunch for around S$40 for two, or the set dinners costs from S$60; à la carte meals are available. They also have a branch at the Asia Hotel, 37 Scotts Rd, near Orchard Rd

For dim sum a good bet is the *Tiong Shan Eating House*, an old-fashioned coffee shop on the corner of New Bridge and Keong Saik Rds in Chinatown (map 2). A plate of dim sum is around S$1.50, and as good as you'll find anywhere. They have other dishes here as well. *Tai Tong Hoi Kee*, 2/3 Mosque St, is another coffee shop in Chinatown that has dim sum for breakfast. Later in the day until the early hours of the morning, the menu switches to standard Cantonese fare at cheap prices. More expensive dim sum can be had in more luxurious air-con surroundings at the *Regency Palace* (☎ 338 3281) in the Plaza by the Park, 51 Bras Basah Rd, in the colonial district. The prices are reasonable and most plates cost about S$2 to S$4. Many of the big restaurants offer dim sum, but remember that dim sum is a lunchtime or Sunday breakfast dish – in the evening these restaurants change to other menus.

Teochew Teochew food is a widely available cuisine. Among the many coffee shops in Chinatown's Mosque

St (map 2) you'll find a good selection of Teochew food.
These very traditional restaurants are good places to
sample simple Teochew food in the atmosphere of old
Chinatown. Menus are hard come by but a request for
suggestions and prices will be readily answered, and the
prices are low. The *Chui Wah Lin* (☎ 221 3305) at 49
Mosque St has very good porridge. Try the duck porridge for S$3. *Liang Heng Teochow Eating House* (☎ 223
1652) at 48 Mosque St is another good Teochew eatery.
The Ellenborough St market , near Boat Quay in Chinatown, is noted for its Teochew food stalls.

For moderately priced Teochew food in more luxurious surroundings, try the *Teochow City Seafood Restaurant*
(☎ 733 3338), 05-16 Centrepoint, 176 Orchard Rd (map
6).

Hainanese Chicken-rice is a common and popular
dish all over town. Originally from Hainan in China,
chicken-rice is a dish of elegant simplicity, and in Singapore they do it better than anywhere else. *Swee Kee* (☎ 337
0314, map 3) at 51 Middle Rd, close to the Raffles Hotel,
is a long-running specialist with a very good reputation.
Chicken-rice served with chilli, ginger and thick soya
sauce is S$3.30. They also do steamboats; a S$20 version
has a stock enriched by various Chinese herbs and Mao
Tai wine.

A stone's throw from Swee Kee you'll find *Yet Con*
(☎ 337 6819, map 3) at 25 Purvis St which some claim is
the best of all Singapore's chicken-rice places. This area
west of Beach Rd is something of a Hainanese stronghold.

Hokkien Hokkien food is not all that popular despite
the large number of Hokkiens in Singapore, but *Beng
Hiang* (☎ 221 6684, map 2) at Food Alley, 20 Murray St,
is renowned for its Hokkien food. In fact Food Alley is a
great place to try all of Singapore's various cuisines. It
features around 10 mid-range restaurants representing
most Chinese cuisines and Indian food.

Beng Thin Hoon Kee (☎ 553 7708) is on the 5th floor of
the OCBC Centre on Chulia St (map 2); it is a short walk
from Raffles Place MRT station and has moderately
priced dishes, including Hokkien seafood.

Szechuan Szechuan, or Sichuan, restaurants are
common though not cheap; this spicy food is popular
with Singaporeans. *Chinatown* (☎ 737 1666) in the Imperial Hotel, 1 Jalan Rumbia (map 6), has daily lunch and
dinner buffets for S$22 per person. The *Golden Phoenix*

(☎ 732 0431) in the Hotel Equatorial, 429 Bukit Timah Rd (map 12), is a long-running restaurant with consistently good food. You can dine à la carte for around S$30 per person. The *Min Jiang* (☎ 737 7411) in the Goodwood Park Hotel, 22 Scotts Rd (map 6), is one of the best Szechuan restaurants and not outrageously priced for the location.

Vegetarian On Bencoolen St, the Fortune Centre (map 3) is a good place for cheap vegetarian food. On the ground floor you'll find the *ABC Eating House* and *Yi Song* food stalls, which have cheap vegetarian food in air-con surroundings. Upstairs on the 4th floor is the *Eastern Vegetarian Food* coffee shop, offering rice or noodles with three selections from S$2. It is open on Sundays and public holidays.

At 143, 147 and 153 Kitchener Rd in Little India, the *Fut Sai Kai* (☎ 298 0336) (which translates as 'monk's world') is a spartan old coffee shop and an air-con restaurant next door. Most main dishes cost around S$8 to S$10. Similarly priced is the *Kwan Yim* (☎ 338 2394), another traditional, long-running vegetarian restaurant. It's at 190 Waterloo St in the South-East Asia Hotel (map 3) in the colonial district.

Chinatown (map 2) has some moderately priced vegetarian restaurants, including the *Happy Realm* (☎ 222 6141) on the 3rd floor of Pearl's Centre on Eu Tong St, one of the best around. Main dishes cost around $5 to S$6 and they have good claypot dishes. *Loke Woh Yeun* (☎ 221 2912), 20 Tanjong Pagar Rd, is another in Chinatown where you can have a meal for under S$15. While it is mostly vegetarian they also have chicken and prawn dishes.

Hong Kong Bodhi (☎ 337 0703), 03-140 Marina Square, 6 Raffles Blvd (map 3), is a branch of the popular Hong Kong chain. It is more upmarket but reasonably priced – set dinners are available from $24 for two, and most main meals cost S$8 to S$12, except for the shark's fin and bird's nest dishes, which stretch the definition of vegetarian.

Seafood Singapore has another variation on Chinese food. Seafood in Singapore is simply superb, whether it's prawns or abalone, fish-head curry or chilli crabs. Most of the specialists are some distance out from the city centre but the trip is worthwhile. Seafood isn't cheap, and a whole fish, crab or prawns start at just under S$20 per dish. Many places don't have set prices,

but base them on 'market price' and the size of the fish.
Make sure you check the price first.

Loo Tien Food Centre (☎ 336 7891, map 3), 2 Purvis St
near Raffles Hotel, is a Teochew coffee shop-style restaurant with open-air tables around the side. There is no
menu – choose your fish from the tanks for around S$20
and up, and you can get chilli crabs starting at S$18. Side
dishes of vegetables and fried rice are cheap. This is a
good place for a seafood banquet amongst a group of
people. The restaurant is open from 3 pm to 3.30 am.

The *UDMC Seafood Centre* (map 8), at the beach on East
Coast Parkway, has a number of seafood restaurants and
is very popular in the evenings. The food and the setting
are good, but they tend to hustle a bit at some of these
places, so definitely check the prices first. Cheaper is the
hawkers' centre nearby on the other side of East Coast
Lagoon, which has some good moderately priced
seafood stalls as well as the usual hawkers' selection.
Bugis St also has a couple of hustling seafood places, but
it is a pleasant place to dine under the stars and people
watch. Other, cheaper dishes at fixed prices are available
from the menus.

At 610 Bedok Rd, the *Long Beach Seafood Restaurant*
(☎ 344 7722), one of Singapore's best known seafood
restaurants, is famous for its black pepper crabs and 'live
drunken prawns' (soaked in brandy). It is casual and
you can dine outside or in the air-conditioned section.
Tanah Merah is the nearest MRT station.

Ng Tiong Choon Sembawang Fish Pond (☎ 754 1991) is a
different style of restaurant built on stilts over an old fish
pond. It is two km off the Mandai Rd out past the zoo in
a beautiful rural setting. The seafood is excellent. You
need a car, or ring for details of the minibus service.

Punggol Point (map 1) is a Singapore seafood institution. It is in a quiet setting on the north-east of the island
overlooking the Straits of Johor, far removed from the
bustle of downtown Singapore. The last few km into
Punggol along Punggol Rd go through a surprisingly
rural area of market gardens and chicken farms. Punggol
was set to be redeveloped but there was such a public
outcry that it won a temporary reprieve – one of the few
examples of people power winning the day, but then
food is an important issue in Singapore. *Punggol Restaurant* at 896 Punggol Rd and the consistently good *Choon
Seng* at 892 Punggol Rd are the places to eat, and the
seafood is as cheap as you'll find anywhere. To get to
Punggol take bus No 82 from Beach Rd.

Something Different Tanjong Pagar (map 2) has a
number of Chinese tea houses, where the emphasis is on

Chinese Food Seller (STPB)

the art and presentation of tea drinking. Take your shoes off at the door, and as you sit on cushions on the floor the waitress will bring you a tea set, complete with burner and kettle of boiling water, and demonstrate the art of tea preparation. *Tea Chapter* (☎ 226 1175), 9A-11A Neil Rd, boasts Queen Elizabeth and Prince Philip among the clientele. Dim sum snacks are served for around S$2 per plate, and the extensive range of Chinese teas cost from S$6 to S$15. It is open from 11 am till 11 pm. A few doors away, *Yixing Yuan* offers a small dim sum lunch for around S$7, or otherwise you can have dim sum for around S$2 to S$3 per plate, washed down with the tea of your choice. Both tea houses have shops that sell expensive tea and tea paraphernalia.

Snackworld (☎ 732 6921) 01-12/13 Cuppage Plaza, and the annexe outside on Cuppage Terrace off Orchard Rd (map 6), has crocodile on the menu, starting at S$25 a plate. If you can stomach the thought of eating the wildlife (actually it is farmed and, of course, it is supposed to taste like chicken) they have a wide range of dishes at some of the best prices in town.

The *Imperial Herbal Restaurant* (☎ 337 0491) in the Metropole Hotel, 41 Seah St near Raffles Hotel (map 3), is an unusual restaurant with an extensive range of dishes cooked with medicinal herbs. You can order dishes recommended by the resident herbalist, who will take your pulse and prescribe a suitable meal for your ills. Expect to pay about S$35 per person. You can get a lunch special menu for around S$50 for two.

Indian Food

There are three types of Indian food in Singapore: south Indian, Indian Muslim and north Indian.

South Indian food is mostly vegetarian and Little India is the main centre for it. You can get a thali, an all-you-can-eat rice plate with a mixture of vegetable curries, for less than S$5.

Indian Muslim food is something of a hybrid. It is the simpler south Indian version of what is basically north Indian food. Typical dishes are biryani, served with chicken or mutton curry, roti and murtabak. It can be found all over Singapore but the main centre is in North Bridge Rd opposite the Sultan Mosque. Indian Muslim food is also well represented in the hawkers' centres; you can have a superb chicken biryani from just S$2.50 to S$3.50.

For the rich north Indian curries and tandoori food, you have to go to more expensive restaurants. They can be found all around Singapore, but Little India has a concentrated selection of very good restaurants on Race Course Rd where you'll pay considerably less than Indian restaurants in the more fashionable areas.

To sample eat-with-your-fingers south Indian vegetarian food, the place to go is the Little India district off Serangoon Rd (map 4). The famous and very popular *Komala Vilas* (☎ 293 6980) at 76 Serangoon Rd was established soon after the war and has an open downstairs area where you can have masala dosa (S$1.50) and other snacks. The upstairs section is air-conditioned and you can have their all-you-can-eat rice meal for S$4.50. Remember to wash your hands before you start, use your right hand and ask for eating utensils only if you really have to! On your way out, try an Indian sweet from the showcase at the back of the downstairs section.

Two other rice-plate specialists are *Sri Krishna Vilas* at 229 Selegie Rd and *Ananda Bhavan* at 219-221 Selegie Rd. There are several other Indian eateries on and off Serangoon Rd and a main contender in the local competition for the best south Indian food is the *Madras New Woodlands Cafe* (☎ 297 1594) at 14 Upper Dickson Rd off Serangoon Rd, around the corner from Komala Vilas. A branch of the well-known Woodlands chain in India, New Woodlands serves freshly prepared vegetarian food in very clean air-conditioned rooms. The yoghurt is particularly good. Prices are about the same as at Komala Vilas.

Race Course Rd, a block north-west from Serangoon Rd, is the best area in Singapore for nonvegetarian curry. Try the *Banana Leaf Apolo Restaurant* (☎ 293 8682) at 56 Race Course Rd for superb nonvegetarian Indian food, including Singapore's classic fish-head curry. The very popular *Muthu's Curry Restaurant* (☎ 293 7029) at 78 Race Course Rd also specialises in fish-head curry and other seafood dishes. Rice plates vary from S$3.50 to S$6 depending on what you choose from the counter, or fish-head curry is S$15 to S$23 for a serve to be shared amongst a table of diners.

In the same block of Race Course Rd are good north Indian restaurants with typically dark decor. They serve the cheapest, and some of the best, Indian tandoori food in Singapore. *Delhi Restaurant* (☎ 296 4585) at 60 Race Course Rd has Mughlai and Kashmiri food, with curries from S$7 to S$10. Expect to pay S$15 to S$20 per person with bread and side dishes. The food is excellent and this restaurant is always popular. If it is full, the sister restaurant a few doors down at No 48, *D' Deli Pubb & Restaurant* (☎ 294 5276), has the same fare with a bar at the front. *Nur Jehan* (☎ 292 8033) at 66 Race Course Rd is slightly cheaper and also has good tandoori and other north Indian food. *Maharajahs's Tandoor* (☎ 293 0865, 70 Race Course Rd, has similar prices and food to the others.

Just around the corner is *Chakra* (☎ 299 1930) at 41 Kerbau Rd, with tasteful decor in a renovated Peranakan terrace. Most curries cost $5 to $6. Vegetarian and non-vegetarian set meals cost around S$6, but you won't get their best curries. The most popular part of the restaurant, however, is the foodstall area in a beer garden setting out the front.

Another cheap north Indian restaurant in Little India is the small *Bombay Restaurant*, in the Broadway Hotel at 195 Serangoon Rd. It has curries and kormas from S$4.50 to S$6 and breads such as naan for S$1.20.

For Indian Muslim food (chicken biryani for S$3.50, as well as murtabak and fish-head curry), there is a string of venerable establishments on North Bridge Rd, near the corner of Arab St, opposite the Sultan Mosque (map 5). Each of them has the year of founding proudly displayed on their signs out front, and they are great places for biryani and other Indian dishes at very low prices. The *Victory* (established 1910) is at 701 North Bridge Rd, the *Zam Zam* (established 1908) is at 699 and the *Singapore* (established 1911) is at 697 North Bridge Rd. Further along is the *Jubilee* at 771 North Bridge Rd and at 791-797 the *Islamic* is very similar.

There's a small, basic Indian Muslim place called *Sahib Restaurant* (map 3) at 129 Bencoolen St near Middle Rd, across from the Fortune Centre. They have very good food and specialise in fish dishes, including fish-head curry, but have chicken and vegetable items too. Meals are around S$4 and they are open 24 hours.

The *Moti Mahal Restaurant* (☎ 221 4338, map 2), another upmarket north Indian place, proudly proclaims it is 'one of the best Indian restaurants anywhere (*Far Eastern Economic Review*)' on the sign out front. It doesn't quite live up to the review but the food is good and costs around S$25 per person. It's in Food Alley at 18 Murray Terrace in Chinatown.

In the Orchard Rd area (map 6), *Maharani* (☎ 235 8840) is on the 5th floor of the Far East Plaza, 14 Scotts Rd. The north Indian food and the service are good in this casual restaurant. You can eat well for S$20 per person. The ritzy *Rang Mahal* (☎ 737 1666), Imperial Hotel, 1 Jalan Rumbia, is the place to go if are hungry. Don't bother with the expensive menu, go for the excellent North Indian buffet, which costs S$28 for daily lunch and S$35 for dinner on Saturdays and Sundays. The Orchard Rd area also has a vegetarian Woodlands restaurant, the *Bombay Woodlands Restaurant* (☎ 235 2712), B1-01 Tanglin Shopping Centre, 19 Tanglin Rd. The decor is Orchard Rd and the prices are about three times what you pay in Little India.

A couple of new and expensive North Indian restaurants are very 'in' at the moment. *Hazara* (☎ 467 4101), 24 Lorong Mambong, Holland Village (map 7), is a small 'north Indian frontier restaurant' with fashionable decor and efficient service. The food is very good though the serves are small. Expect to pay at least S$35 per person. *Royal Bengal* at 72 Boat Quay (map 2) is lavishly decorated in colonial style, as are the staff. It is one of Singapore's most expensive Indian restaurants.

Malay & Indonesian Food

Malay food is scattered throughout Singapore, though Malay restaurants are not abundant. The occasional stall or two at some of the food centres serve Malay food, and satay is easily found. Geylang in the East Coast area is a

Malay stronghold and therefore a good place to go. Indonesian food shares many similarities with Malay cuisine, though some dishes such as gado gado are uniquely Indonesian.

The Orchard Rd area (map 6) has a number of good restaurants. *Bintang Timur* (☎ 235 4539), 02-Far East Plaza, 14 Scotts Rd, has excellent Malay food at excellent prices. You can try a good range of dishes and eat your fill for under S$20. *Tambuah Mas* (☎ 733 3333), 04-10/13 Tanglin Shopping Centre, 19 Tanglin Rd, is a cheap Indonesian restaurant with a good selection of seafood dishes and Indonesian favourites such as rendang, gado gado and cendol. Another good Indonesian restaurant is *Sanur* (☎ 734 2192), 04-17/18 Centrepoint, 176 Orchard Rd. Most mains are S$7 to S$10 and range up to S$20 for whole fish. More expensive is *Azizas Restaurant* (☎ 235 1130), 36 Emerald Hill Rd, at Peranakan Place. It serves authentic Malay meals and is regarded as one of Singapore's top Malay restaurants.

Pancha Sari (☎ 338 1032), 03-239 Marina Square, is a reasonably priced Indonesian restaurant in the colonial district (map 3). Most mains cost S$6 to S$10 and you can eat well for under S$20. The small lunch set menu is S$6.50. *Nasi William* (☎ 227 7822, map 2), 118 Telok Ayer St in Chinatown, has good lunchtime fare. Most dishes are S$2 or S$3, but you'll need a few to fill up, and make sure that you don't get given the 'dinner' menu.

If you like the fiery food of north Sumatra, there are a few nasi padang specialists, the best known being *Rendezvouz*, 02-19 in the Raffles City Shopping Centre (map 3) on Bras Basah Rd. *House of Sundanese Food* (☎ 345 5020, map 8), 218 East Coast Rd, specialises in the cuisine from West Java. Try a number of dishes, nasi padang style, many of which cost around S$3. The chicken dishes are particularly good, or try charcoal-grilled whole fish for around S$15 to S$20.

The Geylang district in the East Coast area (map 8) has plenty of Malay eateries. For Malay food during the day, go to the *Geylang Serai Market* on Changi Rd. This is the predominantly Malay area in Singapore, and it's worth a visit just to see the market, which is more traditional than the new complexes. To get there, take the MRT to Paya Lebar station and walk east along Sims Ave to Geylang Serai. You can find a good stretch of cheap restaurants further along Changi Rd, one km east of the Malay Cultural Village. The decor is straightforward, the food cheap and excellent. *Makan House* (☎ 742 2677), 259 Changi Rd, is more in vogue than most, but the food is authentic and good. To get there, take the MRT to Eunos station. Walk east along Sims Ave, turn right at Jalan

Eunos, then left at Changi Rd. From the station to Makan House is only a five-minute walk and if you keep going east along Changi Rd, you'll find more good restaurants.

Nonya Food

Nonya & Baba Restaurant (☎ 734 1382) is one of the best restaurants to try nonya food at reasonable prices. Most mains cost around S$6 for small claypots up to S$15 for large serves. A variety of snacks and sweets are also available. It is at 262-264 River Valley Rd, near the corner of Tank Rd and directly behind the Imperial Hotel (map 6). The Dhoby Ghaut MRT station at the start of Orchard Rd is a 15-minute walk away.

There are Nonya buffets at the King's and Apollo hotels in Havelock Rd (map 12), and the Bayview Inn (map 3) in Bencoolen St has a good lunchtime buffet for S$13.80 on Wednesdays, Saturdays and Sundays. In Holland Village (map 7), the *Baba Cafe* (☎ 468 9859) at 25B Lorong Liput has good-value food in an attractive setting. In the basement of Plaza Singapura on Orchard Rd (map 6), the food plaza has a good selection of nonya cakes and savoury pastries for take away snacks.

One of the best places to go for Nonya food is east of the city in the Geylang and Katong districts (map 8). Along (and just off) Joo Chiat Rd, between East Coast and Geylang roads in particular, is a good hunting grounds for all kinds of Asian foods, and this area has one of the liveliest local night scenes in the city. *Guan Hoe Soon* (☎ 344 2761), 214 Joo Chiat Rd, is a long-running, moderately priced nonya coffee shop famous for its nonya dishes.

East Coast Rd in Katong is a great place to try nonya food. The *Peranakan Inn & Lounge* (☎ 440 6194), 210 East Coast Rd, is one of the cheapest places in Singapore to eat nonya food in an air-con setting. Most dishes cost S$4 to S$6, and more expensive seafood dishes such as prawn sambal or *ikan terabok* cost S$12 to S$18. On the corner of East Coast and Ceylon Rds, the *Hok Tong Hin Restaurant* (☎ 344 5101) is a coffee shop where you can get superb laksa. During the day, try the nonya kueh and curry puffs at the *Katong Bakery & Confectionary* (☎ 344 8948), 75 East Coast Rd. This wonderful old-fashioned cake shop is a throwback to the Singapore of yesterday. If you prefer sanitised surroundings, East Coast Rd also has plenty of new cake shops for takeaways. The best bus for East Coast Rd is No 14, which goes along Orchard and Bras Basah Rds in the colonial district. Bus Nos 10, 12 and 40 will also get you there from the colonial district.

Other Asian Food

The Golden Mile Complex at 5001 Beach Rd – the north-easter end – is a modern shopping centre catering to Singapore's Thai community where you'll find a number of small coffee shops serving Thai food and Singha beer. Prices are cheap – you can get a good meal for S$4 – but there are no menus in English and it can be difficult ordering what you want. Here you'll also find the *Pornping Thai Seafood Restaurant* (☎ 298 5016), which has a wide variety of good Thai food including Isaan dishes. Small main meals cost around S$6 to S$10 and more expensive seafood dishes around S$15. It is open from 9.30 am to 11 pm and there is a bar section next door at the back.

There are several Thai restaurants along Joo Chiat Rd in the Katong district – *Haadyai Beefball Restaurant* (☎ 344 3234) at 467 Joo Chiat Rd is a moderately priced air-con place with authentic Thai food.

Closer to town, *Parkway Thai* (☎ 737 8080) in Centrepoint, 176 Orchard Rd (map 6), has an extensive menu – small mains range from S$6 up to $15 for seafood. *Cuppage Thai Food Restaurant* (☎ 734 1116, map 6), 49 Cuppage Rd, is not the greatest Thai restaurant but the low prices and pleasant al fresco setting just off Orchard Rd are hard to beat. The set lunch for two is S$10 and the set dinner for two is S$28. There are plenty of other Thai restaurants in town, all serving the obligatory chicken feet salad, but it is difficult to find authentic Thai food and many serve a Chinese variant. *Siamese Fins* (☎ 227 9759, map 2), 45 Craig Rd in Chinatown, is one such restaurant specialising in Thai shark's fin dishes. The food is good but make sure you are dining on an expense account.

Singapore has experienced a Japanese restaurant boom, which reflects the Japanese tourist boom. While you can spend a small fortune at a Japanese restaurant, you can also find food at moderate prices. Small Japanese restaurants displaying their plastic-glazed meals in the window can be found all around Singapore. *Restaurant Hoshigaoka* is a chain of Japanese restaurants, with branches at 03-45 Centrepoint and 04-02 Wisma Atria on Orchard Rd (map 6), on the 2nd floor of the Apollo Hotel on Havelock Rd (map 12), and 03-237 Marina Square (map 3). Most set meals are under S$20, eg tempura costs S$15 and sushi meals cost from S$12 to S$22, though the servings are small. In Holland Village (map 7), *Mapuku Tei Japanese Restaurant* (☎ 462 3420) at 29 Lorong Mambong is popular and most set menus cost S$14 to S$20. *Momiji* across the road at 24 Lorong Mambong is slightly cheaper. For top-of-the-range Japanese food, try the *Nadaman* (☎ 737 3644), a branch of the Japanese chain in the Shangri-La Hotel (map 6) in Orange Grove Rd.

Seoul Garden is a Korean chain with branches at 05-01 Shaw Centre, 1 Scotts Rd (map 6); B1-07 Orchard Point, 160 Orchard Rd (map 6); and 03-119 Marina Square, 6 Raffles Blvd (map 3), among others. The Korean BBQ set lunches for around S$12 and the slightly more expensive set dinner are good value, while dining à la carte is only slightly more expensive. Tanjong Pagar Rd in Chinatown (map 2) also has a number of Korean restaurants.

Then there's Taiwanese food. Try the reasonably priced *Goldleaf* (map 2) at 24-24A Tanjong Pagar Rd in Chinatown. A speciality is chicken covered in whole fried chillies. You can eat very well for less than S$20.

If you are hankering after spicy Asian food but can't decide what type of cuisine, try *Spice Express* (☎ 734 8835), B1-20/21 Forum shopping centre, 583 Orchard Rd (map 6). Indian, Thai, Malay, Chinese, and Vietnamese dishes are all on offer and despite the diversity they are all good. The à la carte menu is moderately priced, but the best bet is the lunch buffet for S$18.50 or the buffet dinner on Fridays and Saturdays for S$22.50. Changi International Airport also has a branch of Spice Express in Terminal 2.

Western Food

Fast Food Yes, you can get Western food in Singapore too. There are nearly 40 *McDonald's*, found all over town. It's good to see that the corporate smile and 'have a nice day' haven't really caught on in Singapore, and you can be served with the same brusque efficiency as you would find in any Singaporean coffee shop.

There are also *A&W Restaurants, Kentucky Fried Chicken, Burger King, Dunkin' Donuts, Dennys, Pizza Hut, Baskin Robbins* and *Swensen's Ice Cream* outlets, so there's no shortage of Western fast food.

Italian If you want good Italian food in Singapore, steer clear of the chain stores run by youths suffering from corporate brainwashing and serving soggy pizza and pasta with insipid sauces.

Pete's Place (☎ 733 1188) in the Hyatt Regency (map 6) has good Italian food in a rustic setting with a good salad bar. Most pasta dishes cost around S$15 and a main course salad is S$10.50. *Pasta! Ristorante* (☎ 467 0917), 23 Lorong Mambong, Holland Village (map 7), has home-made pasta and is reasonably priced.

Al Forna Trattoria (☎ 722 5121, 01-07 Novena Ville, 275 Thomson Rd in Novena, is an excellent, authentic Italian restaurant with pasta dishes from around S$11 to S$15, small but good pizzas for around S$12, and the deserts are worth waiting for. To get there, take the MRT to Novena station, two stops past Orchard, and as you come out of the station on Thomson Rd, the restaurant is about 200 metres to the right in the block of shops on the other side of the street. *Ristorante Bologna* (☎ 338 3388) in the Pan Pacific Hotel, in the Marina complex (map 3) is the top Italian restaurant in town.

French A number of restaurants do a pretty good job of convincing you that you're in France, even though you're almost on the equator. *Le Restaurant de France* (☎ 733 8855) in the Le Meridien Hotel (map 6), 100 Orchard Rd, is one of the best French restaurants in Singapore and has an eight-course set meal for S$100, or take your credit card to *Maxim's de Paris* in the Regent Hotel (map 6), 1 Cuscaden Rd.

L'Aigle d'Or (☎ 227 7678) in the Duxton Hotel (map 2), 83 Duxton Rd, is new and trying hard to be Singapore's No 1 French restaurant. It will cost about S$80 per person for an à la carte three-course meal, or the set lunch is exceptional value for S$28.

Other Western Food *Hard Rock Cafe* (☎ 235 5232, map 6), 50 Cuscaden Rd, near the corner of Orchard and Tanglin Rds, is one of the most popular places for American-style steaks, BBQ grills and ribs. Main meals cost around S$20, and snacks such as burgers cost around S$8. The restaurant finishes around 10.30 pm when the bands start, but there is a small snack bar that stays open.

Bob's Tavern (☎ 467 2419), 17A Lorong Liput, Holland Village (map 7), is an English-style pub popular with expats who for some reason miss English food. It does good steaks, fish & chips etc. Main meals cost around S$15 to S$20. You can drink at the bar, or dine outside on the veranda. The *Third Man* (☎ 334 1985), in the Capitol Building, 11 Stamford Rd near Raffles City, is a pub-style place that does set lunches and dinners for around $15.

Singapore steak houses are mostly run by chains such as the *Ponderosa* (☎ 336 0139) in the 02-13 Plaza Singapura, 68 Orchard Rd (map 6); 02-232 Marina Square (map 3); and 02-20 Raffles City shopping centre (map 3). A steak and a salad bar serving costs around S$20. The *Sizzler* chain is also moving into Singapore but the biggest chain is *Jack's Place* with restaurants all over town, including 03-18/19 Wisma Atria, 435 Orchard Rd (map 6), and 01-01 Bras Basah Complex in the colonial district (map 3). Grills cost S$14 to S$20, while pasta and chicken dishes cost around S$10.

In Bencoolen St, the *Golden Dragon Inn* is a Chinese coffee shop on the 2nd floor of the Fortune Centre (map 3) that does a reasonable job of Western grills. You can get steak or prawns with chips and eggs served on a sizzler for only S$6, or if you crave cholesterol for breakfast, ham and eggs costs S$3.

For upmarket Western food at bargain prices, the Singapore Hotel Association's Training & Educational Centre (☎ 235 9533) at 24 Nassim Hill (map 6) has two restaurants, *Bouganville* and *Rosette*. Open to the public, the place is really a training centre for hotel dining room food preparation and presentation. They offer set meals at S$12 for lunch and S$25 for dinner.

Many other cuisines are represented in Singapore. For German food, there is the *Brauhaus Restaurant & Pub* (☎ 250 3116), United Square, 101 Thomson Rd (map 12). The *Treffpunct Cafe*, B2 09, Tanglin Shopping Centre(map 6), is a small deli with German sausages. *Movenpick* (☎ 235 8700) B1-01 Scotts Shopping Centre, 6 Scotts Rd (map 6), is a Swiss restaurant with grills for around S$25, bratwurst for S$17.50, or the set lunch is around S$20. There is also a branch at 30 Robinson Rd (map 2).

El Felipes Cantina (☎ 733 3551), 02-09, International Building, 360 Orchard Rd and at 34 Lorong Mambong in Holland Village, is an old favourite that has large serves and moderate prices. *Cha Cha Cha* (☎ 462 1650), 32 Lorong Mambong in Holland Village, is the most popular Mexican restaurant in town, as much for the margaritas as the good food.

Saxophone Bar & Grill (☎ 235 8385, map 6), 23 Cuppage Terrace just off Orchard Rd, is a pleasant place to dine al fresco and listen to the music coming from inside. The food is continental. *Alkaff Mansions* (☎ 278 6979), west of the city at 10 Telok Blangah Green, has ambience plus-plus. This restored old mansion offers Dutch rijstaffel (buffet 'rice table') served with a touch of colonial theatre for S$32 – this dish is popular with tour groups, though not with Singapore's gourmets and pretty people, who favour the more expensive continental à la carte fare.

Breakfast, Snacks & Delis

The big international hotels have their large international breakfast buffets of course (around S$18 to S$20) but there are still a few old coffee shops which do cheap Chinese and Indian breakfasts – take your pick of dosa and curry or *yu-tiao* and hot soy milk. Roti chanai with a mild curry dip is a delicious and economical breakfast available at *Sahib Restaurant* (map 3), 129 Bencoolen St in the cheap hotel area. Most of the coffee shops will rustle you up toast and jam without too much difficulty.

There are many places which do a fixed-price breakfast – continental or American. Try the *Silver Spoon Coffee House* in Supreme House (map 6) on Penang Rd off Orchard Rd, or the *Chameleon* on the ground floor of Orchard Plaza (map 6) where an American breakfast costs S\$5.50. *McDonalds* and *A&W* do fast-food breakfasts, you can have a McDonald's 'big breakfast' for S\$3.90 or hotcakes and syrup for S\$1.50. *Arcadia Cafe*, 01-42 Lucky Plaza in Orchard Rd (map 6), is a Chinese/Western greasy spoon with breakfast for S\$3.50; at other times steaks cost S\$8 and fish & chips are S\$5. One of the nicest breakfasts is undoubtedly *Breakfast with the Birds* (☎ 265 0022) at Jurong Bird Park (map 7). The buffet breakfast costs S\$12 (admission is extra), the waffles are great and the birds will tell your fortune for free.

For Western-style pastries, head for the *Café d'Orient de Delifrance* at Peranakan Place on Orchard Rd (map 6) – the croissants and coffee are hard to beat for breakfast. This is the original store with the best setting, but you can find branches everywhere in Singapore.

A lot of the coffee shops in the big hotels do 'high tea', featuring local cakes and snacks and all the tea or coffee you can drink. The *Cafe Oriental* in the Amara Hotel near Chinatown (map 2), has a high tea buffet for S\$7. *Old Chang Kee* is a chain that specialises in that old favourite – curry puffs. There is one at Lau Pa Sat (map 2), on Raffles Quay, but the best is at the corner of MacKenzie and Niven Rds, near Selegie Rd in the colonial district. Try their range, washed down with coffee in an old-style kopi tiam. The small *L E Cafe* at 264 Middle Rd, under the Sun Sun Hotel (map 3) almost at Selegie Rd, is an old-fashioned place with European and oriental cakes and pastries for takeaways. *Sweet Secrets*, at the back of Centrepoint in Orchard Rd (map 6), is a Western-style coffee shop with a magnificent array of cakes.

Singapore has plenty of delis that cater for lunching office workers and snacking shoppers. Most are in the central business district and Orchard Rd. Try cakes, cookies, yoghurt and muesli in *Steeple's Deli*, 02-25 Tanglin Shopping Centre (map 6) on Tanglin Rd. This is one of Singapore's original delis and they do great sandwiches from S\$8 to S\$10. *Chef's Deli*, also in the Tanglin Shopping Centre, is another good place for sandwiches. *Sandwich Express*, 45 Boat Quay (map 2), is in the new row of trendy eateries by the river. Sandwiches cost around S\$3 to S\$6, a good breakfast of egg, toast and ham is S$3.40, and salads and set meals are available. *Mr Cucumbur*, 02-02 Clifford Centre (map 2), 24 Raffles Place, has good pastrami sandwiches amongst others (S$4 to S$8), and cheap breakfasts are also served. *Seah Street Deli* in the Raffles Hotel (map 3) is slightly mis-named. This is Singapore's answer to a New York deli – pastrami, bagles and rye at higher than average prices.

There are plenty of supermarkets in Singapore with everything from French wine and Australian beer to yoghurt, muesli, cheese and ice cream. You can get a beer (S$3 to S$3.50) at almost any coffee shop but there are also plenty of bars as well as the big hotels.

Entertainment

Singapore has plenty of night life, although it's certainly not of the Bangkok or Manila sex and sin variety. Almost every four-star hotel has a Filipino band playing in the lobby, every five-star hotel has a jazz band in the lobby, while even many three-star hotels can muster up a piano bar. For better bands, you have to go to the clubs and discos, where a cover charge normally applies. Dress is usually smart casual, drinks are expensive and the bands mostly play covers.

There is no shortage of bars, and more are springing up everywhere, especially in the newly renovated terraces along the riverfront and in Chinatown's Tanjong Pagar. Many of the bars are also karaoke lounges. Smoking is permitted in bars, though if food is also served smoking is restricted until after meal hours.

Highbrow entertainment in the form of classical music, ballet and theatre can be enjoyed in Singapore, as well as Chinese opera and tourist-oriented cultural shows.

Live Music

While there are local bands, many are imports – mostly Filipino bands and occasionally Western musicians – playing jazz, pop covers, old favourites or even something more risqué like the blues. In Singapore, punks are usually disobedient youngsters who won't do their homework. There are hardcore post-punk bands like Stompin' Ground, but they won't be playing in Orchard Rd. It is difficult to see original Singaporean performers singing about life in the HDB estates, or dissatisfaction with the oppressive nature of Singaporean society, but they do exist and Singaporean music is developing its own identity. *Substation* (map 3) in Armenian St in the colonial district occasionally puts on concerts of original local performers. Popular artists such as Dick Lee and Kopi Kat Klan perform songs with Asian themes sung with a Singaporean voice.

Some venues don't have a cover charge, but drinks are expensive and you can expect to pay around S$8 for a glass of beer. Those that do have a cover charge usually include the first drink free. For most venues, 10% service charge and 4% government tax are added to the drinks and the cover charge. Most have happy hours until around 8 pm when the beers are up to half price but the music doesn't start until later.

The free tourist magazines have gig guides, and so do the local newspapers. The *Straits Times* has a good gig guide on Thursdays. Many of Singapore's bars also have bands – see the bars section below.

The Orchard Rd area (map 6) is the main centre for live music, and one of the biggest places is *Fire*, 04-19 Orchard Plaza, 150 Orchard Rd. The resident band, Energy, live up to their name and are one of the best in town. If the pace gets too frenetic for you, the other lounges and disco music in the three-floor complex offer different styles. The cover charge is S$12 for women (S$21 on weekends), S$15 for men (S$24 on weekends).

Orchard Towers at 400 Orchard Rd has a concentration of venues. On the 1st floor, *Club 392* features a variety of music, including good jazz bands. It has an interesting, slightly seedy atmosphere and gets very crowded late in the evening. Happy hours are from 4 to 9 pm, and there is no cover charge. *Top Ten* on the 4th floor is a large barn of a place with Manhattan skyline decor and an affluent clientele. It is primarily a disco but a band alternates brackets with the disco music. Entry costs S$20 for the first drink on Fridays, S$25 on Saturdays and S$15 for the rest of the week. *Cinivy*, on the 2nd floor of Orchard Towers, has two types of music – country and western. This is the place for macho Singapore cowboys.

Anywhere on the 4th floor of the Tanglin Shopping Centre, 19 Tanglin Rd, is a long-running rock 'n roll place. The band, Tania, has been playing here for nearly 15 years and features a cross-dressing lead singer. The band has a regular following of mostly expats, and while it is sometimes hard to see why, the band can belt out a song when they try and this place does have a casual, convivial atmosphere. There is no cover charge.

Hard Rock Cafe, 50 Cuscaden Rd, has the usual rock memorabilia and good atmosphere. It has better bands than most venues, and occasionally imports some big names from overseas. The music and cover charge starts, and the ash trays come out, after 10.30 pm when the dining stops. Entry is S$15, except Sundays, or get there early. It stays open until around 2 or 3 pm.

Brannigans in the Hyatt Regency, 10-12 Scotts Rd, is a popular pick-up spot for expat and Singaporean professionals. This is more of an intimate pub than other venues and the music is jazz. The band plays until 1 pm, and happy hours are from 4 to 8 pm.

Nearby, the *Saxophone Bar & Grill*, 23 Cuppage Terrace near the corner of Orchard Rd, is a small place with blues and jazz music. It's so small that the band has to play on a platform behind the bar, but it's unpretentious and you can also dine outside and listen to the music. There is no cover charge.

One of Singapore's best jazz venues is *Somerset's* in the lobby bar at the Westin Stamford, Raffles City, 2 Stamford Rd (map 3). A minimum charge of S$12 applies on Fridays and Saturdays.

Discos

Singapore has no shortage of discos. They often have a cover charge of around S$15 to S$20 on weekdays and S$20 to S$30 on weekends, but this usually includes the first drink. Women often pay less. They tend to be big on decor and are yuppie hang-outs with strict dress codes.

The *New Warehouse*, 338 Havelock Rd, is next to the River View Hotel (map 12) and is housed in an old godown. The *Library* in the Mandarin Hotel on Orchard Rd (map 6) is a subterranean club where nonmembers can dance after 9 pm. *Scandals* in the Westin Plaza Hotel (map 3) is one of the most sophisticated discos and has impressive sound and light effects. It is open until 3 am and has a cover charge.

Chinoiserie in the Hyatt Regency (map 6) and *Xanadu* in the Shangri-La Hotel (map 6) are upmarket places that attract a wealthy clientele.

For a disco with a difference, the *Equator Dream* (☎ 533 2733) is a floating disco that tours the harbour before docking at Clifford Pier for the rest of the evening. The cost is S$20 on weekdays and S$30 on weekends; you have to book.

Bars

Singapore has plenty of bars, and most of the major hotels have bars with jazz and easy listening bands. The time to drink is during the happy hours, usually around 5 to 8 pm, when drinks are as cheap as half price, or keep a eye out for promotional all-you-can-drink extended happy hours for around S$20. Most of the bars also serve food and the serious drinking is done outside meals times, but you can grab a stool at the bar anytime.

A good place for a pub crawl is the Tanjong Pagar area (map 2). Tanjong Pagar Rd, Duxton Rd and Duxton Hill all have a number of bars, and the beers are a little cheaper than elsewhere. *Elvis' Place*, 1A Duxton Hill, is lined with Elvis memorabilia and plays the King's hits and '50s music nonstop. It's always crowded and popular with expats, and stays open until around 1 am.

A few doors away at 6 Duxton Hill, *Chicago Bar & Grill* is another popular place which often has a band.

The renovated Boat Quay (map 2) is another good area to look for bars. *Harry's,* 28 Boat Quay, is one of the best and very popular at the moment. It's a crowded but pleasant place to have a drink by the river, if you can get a table, or you can sit inside, and sometimes listen to jazz bands.

Wala Wala Bar & Grill, on Lorong Mambong in Holland Village (map 7), has one of those sin machines that were banned for many years in Singapore – a juke box. It is an American-style restaurant and bar, and they sometimes have extended happy hours. *Charlie's* is at the eastern end of Singapore Island at Block 2, Changi Village (map 1). This is Singapore's most casual bar with the best selection of beers from around the world. It is behind the hawkers' centre, and its long bar and stools have an ambience to match the location. Burgers, steaks, fish & chips and hot dogs are also served. It is closed on weekends and public holidays.

Of course you can have a drink at the *Raffles* (map 3), at the Long Bar or the Bar & Billiard Room where that infamous tiger was supposedly shot. One of the favourite pastimes in the elegant Long Bar is throwing peanut shells on the floor – swinging stuff. The billiard room is laid back, and you can recline in the wicker chairs, tickle the ivories or chug-a-lug outside on the patio. In the evenings both bars have light jazz (no boogie woogie, please) from 7.30 pm, and food is served. Sip your beers – there are no happy hours. The *Compass Rose* on the 70th floor of the Westin Stamford Hotel (map 3), 2 Stamford Rd, has stunning views and prices to match. After 8.30 pm a minimum charge of S$15 applies. This is not the place to don jeans.

Another place for throwing peanut shells is the *Front Page,* 9 Mohammed Sultan Rd. As the name suggests it attracts journalists. A few doors away is *Next Page,* another cosy, easy going place in an old terrace. Mohammed Sultan Rd runs off River Valley Rd, not far from the corner of Tank Rd, and is a 10-minute walk from the southern end of Orchard Rd.

The bar in the lobby at the *Marina Mandarin* (map 3) has jazz in the evenings in salubrious and impressive surroundings. You can be served by leggy hostesses in split Chinese gowns, and if that fails to interest you, you can lie back and contemplate the wonders of hotel lobby architecture.

For a quiet drink in English pub ambience, try *Bob's Tavern,* 17A Lorong Liput, Holland Village or the cosy *Third Man,* in the Capitol Building, 11 Stamford Rd near

Raffles City (map 3). Another is the *Flag & Whistle*, 10 Duxton Hill in Chinatown's Tanjong Pagar (map 2).

A less pretentious and much cheaper place to drink is at the new *Bugis St* (map 3). You can have a beer at the foodstalls under the stars late in the evening until 3 am, or whenever everyone goes home. If you want to pay more, there are a couple of places that have karaoke – *Boom Boom* and *Ding-Dong A-Go-Go* – which also have some bad Filipino bands playing.

Karaoke

Singaporeans are karaoke mad and every second bar has a karaoke set up, complete with big video screen and a list of songs for you to choose from. You can sing along to your old favourites and impress or amuse your friends, though it is unlikely you will be laughed at. Some of the lounges have their regulars who can really belt out a song, while others are free-for-alls where any drunk can grab the microphone. Karaoke bars can be great fun, and you can expect to be asked to sing, but the soppy ballads pall after a while.

It's not hard to find a Karaoke or 'KTV' lounge in Singapore. There are hundreds of them, probably too many, as some are often empty and karaokeless due to lack of interest. Tanjong Pagar in Chinatown (map 2) has a selection of karaoke lounges. such as *Sun City* and *Unchained Melody*, or *Kin Kawa Karaoke Lounge* in Cuppage Plaza is on Orchard Rd (map 6). Bugis St (map 3) also has karaoke lounges, of which *Ding-Dong A-Go-Go* is the best, and there's a disco and live band.

Java Jive, 17D Lorong Liput, Holland Village, is one of Singapore's best karaoke lounges. It is unlikely you will be asked to sing as the regulars dominate the microphone. The would-be professional singers, who like to hit crystal-shattering notes, are often accompanied by the DJ, herself a professional singer, who provides harmonies or rescues songs that stray from the tune.

Singstation in the Plaza Hotel (map 5), opposite Arab St on Beach Rd, is an upmarket karaoke lounge with a number of theme rooms for rent, or there is the main lounge where a cover charge applies.

Cinema

There are plenty of cinemas in Singapore, with the main fare being Hollywood hits, or you can catch a Chinese kung-fu film or see an all-singing, all-dancing Indian movie. Recently alternative cinema has found an outlet

Snake Charmers (STPB)

in Singapore; the Cathay Cinema's *Picture House*, 6 Handy Rd, Dhoby Ghaut, at the city end of Orchard Rd (map 6), regularly shows art house movies, as does *Jade Classics* in Shaw Towers, 100 Beach Rd (map 3). Multi-theatre cineplexes are at Shaw Towers on Beach Rd, and at the Shaw Centre on Scotts Rd, near the corner of Orchard Rd (map 6).

Singapore has an annual film festival and the various expatriate clubs also show movies. The Alliance Française often has movies open to the public, some with English subtitles.

Recently, as part of Goh Chok Tong's liberalisation moves, Singapore introduced an R rating, where movies showing nudity, which would have previously been banned, are allowed screening if the content is of artistic merit. These movies are for over-21-year- olds.

Theatre

Singapore's nascent theatre scene is starting to come of age as Singaporeans become more interested in expressing, and discovering, their identity. More local plays are being produced, and alternative theatre venues such as the *Substation* (☎ 337 7800, map 3), 45 Armenian St in the colonial district, are helping to foster an interest in theatre. Plays, workshops, poetry readings and visual arts exhibits are held here, and at the back the Garden has craft and art works for sale.

The main venues for theatre are the *Drama Centre* (☎ 336 0005, map 6) on Canning Rise, the *Victoria Theatre* (☎ 336 2151, map 3), Empress Place, and *Kallang Theatre* (☎ 345 8488), opposite the National Stadium on Stadium Rd. Performances range from local and overseas plays performed by a variety of local theatre companies, to the blockbusters such as *Phantom of the Opera* (which had a less than blockbuster run in Singapore). Some of the hotels, such as the Hilton and Raffles, also stage theatre shows from time to time.

The Singapore Festival of Arts, which features many drama performances, is held every second year around June. Music, art and dance are also represented at the festival, which includes a Fringe Festival featuring plenty of street performances.

Chinese Opera

In Chinatown or in the older streets of Serangoon Rd and Jalan Besar, you may chance upon a *wayang* – a brilliantly costumed Chinese street opera. In these noisy and colourful extravaganzas, overacting is very important; there's nothing subtle about it at all. The best time of year to see one is around September during the Festival of Hungry Ghosts. They are often listed in the 'What's On' section of the *Straits Times*.

Cultural Shows

At the Mandarin Hotel (map 6) on Orchard Rd there is ASEAN night every night at 8 pm. It features dancing and music from all over the region. The show costs S$19 for adults and S$14 for children; including dinner it is S$38 for adults and S$23 for children.

At the Singa Inn Seafood Restaurant (☎ 345 1111), 920 East Coast Parkway (map 8), a 45-minute *Instant Asia* show is held in the evenings at 8 pm for diners..

The Cockpit Hotel (map 6) puts on the *Lion City Revue*, which includes the acrobatic lion dance. The cost is S$38 for adults and S$26 for children, including dinner.

Other Entertainment

The big hotels have cocktail lounges and there are some Chinese nightclubs. The *Neptune Theatre Restaurant*, Collyer Quay (map 2), has a Chinese cabaret, Cantonese food and hostesses. It is glitzy but just this side of seedy and the shows are as risqué as Singapore will allow. The *Red Lantern Beer Garden* downstairs is definitely seedy and has a band in the evening, and cheap meals, good prices for beer and a band at lunchtime. *Lido Palace* in the Concorde Hotel (map 12) on Outram Rd also has a Chinese cabaret and dance hostesses. In the same vein is *Golden Million Nite-Club* in the Peninsula Hotel (map 3) on Coleman St.

Decidedly more high-brow entertainment can be found at the *Victoria Concert Hall* (☎ 338 1230, map 3), the home of the Singapore Symphony Orchestra. Tickets are very reasonably priced starting at S\$5, or more depending on the visiting musicians. Concerts of classical Chinese music are also performed by the Singapore Broadcasting Corporation's Chinese Orchestra (☎ 256 0401 ext 2732).

After Dark

If you're worried that Singapore is simply too squeaky clean for belief, you may be relieved to hear that there's a real locals-only, low-class, red-light district stretching along Desker Rd between Jalan Besar and Serangoon Rd. It's a depressing sight – rows of blockhouse rooms with women standing in doorways while a constant stream of men walk through inspecting the wares. Outside, hawkers sell condoms and potency pills, and makeshift tables are set up with card games to gamble on.

The predominantly Malay district of Geylang is full of houses and bars operated by organised Chinese gangs who employ women of all nationalities, including Indonesians, Indians and the occasional Caucasian. They are found in the *lorongs* off Sims Ave. Of course, Singapore caters to business needs, and there is no shortage of 'health centres' and escort services.

The Tropicana, Singapore's most famous strip club, has gone and all the action is now across the Causeway in Johor Bahru, though even here the clubs are periodically cleaned up by the Malaysian government. It is ironic that Singaporeans venture to Islamic Malaysia for risqué nightlife. *Mechinta* at 1 Jalan Skudai, Johor Bahru, is the best known of these clubs.

Shopping

One of Singapore's major attractions is, of course, shopping. There are plenty of bargains to be had on all sorts of goods, but there are also a number of guidelines to follow if you want to be certain to get your money's worth. First of all, don't buy anything unless you really want it and don't buy anything where the hassle of getting it back home will cost you more than the savings you make. Remember that 'duty free' and 'free port' are somewhat throwaway terms. Firstly, not everything is loaded down with import duty in your own country, and secondly, Singapore also has some local industries to protect.

Price

Before you leap on anything as a great bargain, find out what the price really is. If you're going to Singapore with the intention of buying a camera or a tape recorder for example, check what they would cost you back home first. Then, when you reach Singapore, first find out what the 'real' price is. It's no triumph to knock a starting price of S$200 down to S$150 if the real price was S$150 to start with.

To find out what something should cost, you can check prices out with the main agent or showroom in Singapore, or you can check a big fixed-price department store where the price is unlikely to be rock bottom, but is most likely to be in the ball park. Most importantly, ask around. Never buy in the first shop you come to; always check a few places to see what is being asked.

If you arrive by air, *Shopping & Eating* is a free guide to Changi International Airport that lists the prices of goods available at the duty-free shops. Use it to compare the prices of electronic goods, watches, clothing etc at the shops around town. Except for truly duty-free items like cigarettes and alcohol, you can expect prices in the shops around Singapore to be 10% to 20% less than at the airport. However, quite often you'll find that the prices at the airport compare very favourably, especially for cheaper items, and after hours of trudging around town trying to get the best price, you may only have saved yourself a few dollars off the airport price. You can buy duty-free goods at the airport on arrival before you go through customs.

Bargaining

In Singapore, bargaining is the rule. There is no rule as to the bargaining technique used: you may be quoted double the right price, 30% more or a good price first up with little or no reduction, no matter how hard you bargain.

If you have no idea of the right price, your only alternative is to shop around and offer well under the starting price. You can gradually keep raising your price; after a while you should know what is a good price. This can be a frustrating and time-consuming process, for you and the shopkeepers. Remember that it is possible to bargain too hard, and be wary of prices that are too low.

The secret of successful bargaining is to keep it good-humoured and try to make them move rather than you. Your first gambit can be 'is that your best price', for their opening offer almost certainly won't be. Then when you have to make an offer go lower than you are willing to spend but not so low that you seem totally uninterested.

You have to try and give the impression that if the price isn't right you can quite happily do without the goods, or that if the price isn't right the shop next door's price probably will be. Also remember that when you've made an offer, you've committed yourself. If you really don't want something don't offer anything or you might just end up buying it with a totally ludicrous offer.

Don't assume that because an item has a price tag that you cannot bargain. This is particularly true in the craft and souvenir stores that cater mainly to tourists. Even in the department stores, 'discounts' are sometimes available

The Singapore Tourism Promotion Board has introduced a new price tagging scheme where shops display tags marked as fixed price or recommended price. 'I'm tagged with a recommended price' means bargaining is allowed.

Guarantees

Guarantees are an important consideration if you're buying electronic gear, watches, cameras or the like. You must be sure that the guarantee is an international one – usually this is no problem but check it out before you start haggling. A national guarantee is next to useless – are you going to bring your calculator back to Singapore to be fixed? Finally, make sure that the guarantee is filled out correctly with the shop's name and the serial number of the item written down.

As important as the guarantee is the item's compatibility back home. You don't want a brand or model that has never found its way to your home country.

Buyer Beware

Singapore has consumer laws and the government wants to promote the island as a good place to shop; however, you should be wary when buying.

This is particularly true in the smaller stores and when you try to get too good a deal. A shopkeeper may match your low price but short-change you by not giving you an international guarantee or the usual accessories. For example, you may be offered a very low price for a camera, only to find that the guarantee is only good for Singapore, the batteries and case are extra and the price quoted is for a brand-name body with a no-name lens.

Make sure you get exactly what you want before you leave the store. Check your receipts and guarantees – make sure they are dated and include serial numbers and the shop's stamp.

Check for the right voltage and cycle when you buy electrical goods. Singapore, Australia, New Zealand, Hong Kong and the UK use 220 to 240 volts at 50 cycles while the US, Canada and Japan use 110 to 120 volts at 60 cycles. Check the plug – most shops will fit the correct plug for your country.

Singapore enforces international copyright laws so being palmed off with pirated goods is not really a problem. You should be wary but the only real instances of this are the copy watch sellers who will offer you a 'Rolex' for ridiculously low prices and make no pretence that they are genuine.

If you have any problems take your purchases back to the store or contact the Consumers' Association of Singapore (☎ 270 5433) or the Singapore Tourist Promotion Board (☎ 339 6622).

Service

You buy in Singapore on one basis only – price. The goods (high-technology goods that is) are just the same as you'd get back home, so quality doesn't enter into it. You're not going to come back for after-sales service, so service doesn't come into the picture either. You're not there to admire the display or get good advice from the assistants. In Singapore it's price, price, price.

Consequently, Singapore's shops can be quite unexciting places – 99 times out of 100 it's simply a case of pack the goods in. Nor are the staff always that helpful or friendly – they may be a long way behind Hong Kong shop assistants when it comes to out- and-out rudeness, but a few shopping trips in Singapore will soon indicate why the government runs courtesy campaigns so often!

WHERE TO SHOP

Singapore is almost wall-to-wall with shops, and while there are certain places worth heading to for certain items, shopping centres usually have a mixture of stores selling electronics, clothes, sporting goods etc. Shopping centres are found all over town, but of course Orchard Rd is famous for its profusion of shopping possibilities.

Orchard Rd (map 6)

The major shopping complexes on and around Orchard Rd have a mind-boggling array of department stores and shops selling whatever you want. The prices aren't necessarily the best, but the range of goods is superb, and this is certainly a good place for high-quality, brand-name items. The following is an overview and by no means exhaustive.

Starting at the city end, Park Mall on Penang Rd, which runs parallel to Orchard Rd, is the place for international designer clothes and brand-name style. The International Food Gallery in the basement is a good collection of mid-range restaurants.

Plaza Singapura on Orchard Rd is good for golfing gear and musical instruments. Orchard Point, Orchard Plaza and Cuppage Plaza are clustered together and have a variety of shops and food outlets. Next along is Centrepoint, one of the liveliest shopping centres, with good bookshops on the 4th floor, carpets on the 5th floor, and Marks & Spencer and Robinsons department stores. The Cuppage Centre behind has food outlets and an adjoining wet market. Past Peranakan Place, Orchard Emerald has watches and electronics and the basement has a large supermarket, food stalls and restaurants. Next door, OG is a straightforward department store.

Across Orchard Rd next to the Somerset MRT station the Specialist's Shopping Centre is older and quieter. It has the John Little department store and also a good range of sporting goods stores.

On the corner of Orchard Rd and Orchard Link is the new Ngee Ann City, a large Takashimaya centre. The architecture is New York art deco and the shopping is

Japanese. Opposite Ngee Ann City, the Paragon and the Promenade are up-market shopping centres with many designer boutiques. Further along and much more down market is Lucky Plaza. It is a bustling, hustling place with dozens of shops crammed together. It is good for cheap clothes, bags and shoes, but bargain hard and shake off the touts and pesky tailors. Opposite Lucky Plaza is Wisma Atria, which has an Isetan department store, boutiques and a small fascinating aquarium wrapped around the basement lift well.

On the corner of Scotts and Orchard Rds is Tang's, one of Singapore's oldest, establishment department stores. Scotts Rd is becoming the preferred shopping area for Japanese visitors and this is noticeable in the newly extended Shaw Centre with its large Isetan department shore and Kinokuniya bookshop. Also on Scotts Rd, the Scotts Shopping Centre has plenty of boutiques and an excellent food court in the basement. The Far East Plaza is a big centre with electronics and a bit of everything.

At the top of Orchard Rd the Far East Shopping Centre has some sporting stores that are good for golfing needs and bicycles. The Forum Galleria is dominated by Toys 'R' Us, and other children's gear specialists are in the same centre.

Tanglin Rd is quieter, and the main shopping centre is the Tanglin Shopping Centre, which has the best selection of expensive Asian arts and antiques. Well worth a browse and some refined bargaining if you want to buy.

Colonial District (map 3)

In the colonial district, Raffles City is architecturally one of the most impressive shopping centres, though it doesn't have a large range of shops. Sogo department store is here. Nearby, Marina Square does have a huge array of shops in a massive complex which includes three hotels and plenty of restaurants. Raffles Hotel has a shopping area, and as you would expect it is fairly up-market with designer clothes and the like. Nearby on Beach Rd, Shaw Towers is more down-to-earth and good for cheaper clothes.

On Bencoolen St, Sim Lim Square is renowned for its electronic goods and computers, as is Sim Lim Tower across Rochor Canal Rd. These centres do have a good selection of audio and video gear, but they are popular with tourists and so the first asking price is often higher than elsewhere.

Other possibilities in the colonial district are the Albert Complex and Fou Lu Shou Complex, and on

Chinatown Point Shopping Centre (RN)

Selegie Rd you'll find a variety of shops in the Paradiz Centre and Parklane Shopping Mall.

Chinatown (map 2)

Chinatown is a popular shopping area with more local flavour. The People's Park Complex and the People's Park Centre are good places to shop. They form a large complex with plenty of electronics, clothing and department stores. The electronics are only as cheap as you make them. The Chinatown Complex has an interesting market for everyday goods and cheap shops.

Chinatown Point specialises in craft shops and the quiet Riverwalk Galleria has some more arts and crafts stores. Pagoda St and Trengganu St have some craft/souvenir shops.

Other Areas

Little India (map 4) has lots of oddities, and the Serangoon Plaza on Serangoon Rd has two department stores with electrical and everyday goods at honest prices. Arab St (map 5) is good for textiles, basketware and South-East Asian crafts.

East of the city is Parkway Parade (map 8) on Marine Parade Rd, a large, general shopping centre that is popular with beachgoers – park at the shopping centre and take the underground walkway to East Coast Park.

The tourist office produces *Your Guide to Good Bargains in the Suburbs*, an excellent booklet that is good for exploring different areas of Singapore. It includes housing estate areas, where the shopping is good for cheaper clothes and household items and bargaining is the exception rather than the rule. Try Ang Mo Kio, Bedok, Clementi, Toa Payoh, Geylang etc – all easily reached by the MRT.

Shopping Complexes

Some of the shopping centres in Singapore include:

Albert Complex
    60 Albert St
Blanco Court
    585 North Bridge Rd
Centrepoint
    176-184 Orchard Rd
Cuppage Centre
    55 Cuppage Rd
Far East Plaza
    14 Scotts Rd
Forum Galleria
    583 Orchard Rd
Funan Centre
    109 North Bridge Rd
High Street Centre
    1 North Bridge Rd
International Building
    300 Orchard Rd
Liang Court Complex
    177 River Valley Rd
Liat Towers
    541 Orchard Rd
Marina Square
    6 Raffles Blvd

Meridien Shopping Centre
   100 Orchard Rd
Orchard Plaza
   150 Orchard Rd
Orchard Point
   160 Orchard Rd
Paragon
   290 Orchard Rd
Parkway Parade
   80 Marine Parade Rd
Peninsula Plaza
   111 North Bridge Rd
People's Park Centre
   101 Upper Cross St
People's Park Complex
   Eu Tong Sen St
Plaza Singapura
   68 Orchard Rd
Promenade
   300 Orchard Rd
Raffles City
   250 North Bridge Rd
Scotts
   6 Scotts Rd
Serangoon
   320 Serangoon Rd
Shaw Centre
   1 Scotts Rd
Sim Lim Tower
   10 Jalan Besar
South Bridge Centre
   95 South Bridge Rd
Specialists' Centre
   277 Orchard Rd
Tanglin
   19 Tanglin Rd
Wisma Atria
   435 Orchard Rd

Department Stores

There is also a wide variety of department stores offering
both their own brand goods and other items, generally
at fixed prices – ideal if you've had enough of bargaining. They include shops like C K Tang, Isetan, Metro or
Yaohan, all with branches along Orchard Rd. Some of
the department stores in Singapore include:

C K Tang
   320 Orchard Rd
Daimaru
   Liang Court, 177 River Valley Rd

Galeries Lafayette
    Liat Towers, 541 Orchard Rd
Isetan
    Wisma Atria, 435 Orchard Rd
John Little
    Specialists' Centre, 277 Orchard Rd
Metro
    Lucky Plaza, 304 Orchard Rd
    Royal Holiday Inn, 25 Scotts Rd
    Marina Square, Raffles Blvd
Robinsons
    Centrepoint, Orchard Rd
St Michael of Marks & Spencer
    Centrepoint, Orchard Rd
Tokyu
    Marina Square, Raffles Blvd
Yaohan
    Plaza Singapura, Orchard Rd
    80 Marine Parade Rd

WHAT TO BUY

From clothes irons to luggage and from oriental rugs to
model aeroplanes, Singapore's shops have whatever
you want. Singapore is even a good place to shop for
medical needs – spectacles are cheap, and for that matter
so is dental work. Lefties can try the Left-Handed Shop
in the Far East Shopping Plaza on Orchard Rd. The
following information, only a sample of Singapore's
shopping possibilities, suggests places to start looking.

Arts, Crafts & Antiques

Singapore has no shortage of arts and antiques, mostly
Chinese but also from all over Asia. When buying
antiques, ask for a certificate of antiquity, which is
required in many countries to avoid paying customs
duty. A good guide is *Antiques, Arts & Crafts in Singapore*
by Ann Jones.

Tanglin Shopping Centre (map 6) is one of the easiest
places to find arts and antiques. Check out Antiques of
the Orient which has a fascinating collection of antiquarian
books, maps and prints. Marina Square (map 3) also
has some expensive shops specialising in oriental arts.
In the Holland Road Shopping Centre in Holland
Village, dozens of shops sell everything from cloisonné
ware to Korean chests.

Also good for antiques and furniture is the Watten
Rise district, well out along Bukit Timah Rd, where
you'll find large shops like Tomlinson Antique at 32-34
Watten Rise and Shang Gift & Decor at 24 Watten Rise.

Fans, Chinatown (CT)

Upper Paya Lebar Rd, well to the north-east of the city centre, has a number of antique shops including Mansion Antique House at No 107 and Just Anthony at No 379.

Riverwalk Galleria (map 2) has a number of art galleries and shops selling Chinese pottery and antiques on the 4th floor. On the 1st floor are a number of jewellery and jade shops. The Singapore Handicraft Centre in Chinatown Point has mostly Chinese lacquerware, pottery, jewellery etc, but there are some Indonesian and other Asian crafts as well.

Arab St (map 5) is a good place for South-East Asian crafts such as caneware, batik and leather goods. In Chinatown (map 2) around Terengganu and Pagoda Sts are shops selling goods ranging from trinkets and souvenirs, basketware, fans and silk dressing gowns, to more expensive curios and antique pottery.

Cameras & Film

Cameras are available throughout the city. Camera equipment is not such a bargain these days as camera prices are often as heavily discounted in the West as in Singapore or Hong Kong.

When buying film, bargain for lower prices if you're buying in bulk – 10 films cost less than 10 times one film. Developing is cheap all over Singapore, eg a roll of print film costs about S$2 for developing and 20c to 40c per print. Developing and mounting for a 36-exposure slide film costs around S$12. Kodachrome slide film has to be sent to Australia for developing and can take up to a week, but other slide film takes about a day, or there are one-hour express services. Fuji has a laboratory in Singapore.

Clothes & Shoes

Clothes and shoes – imported, locally made and made to measure – are widely available but Singapore is not as cheap as most other Asian countries. Indonesia, Thailand and Hong Kong are much cheaper, and Malaysia is also cheaper for clothes. Singapore is good for top brands and designer labels,and you can be sure of the authenticity and quality. Shoes and brand-name sneakers (Reeboks, Nike, Adidas) are a good buy.

Many of the department stores have reasonably priced clothes; Nison in the People's Park Complex has cheap clothes. Lucky Plaza on Orchard Rd is a good centre for cheap clothes and shoes, but bargain hard for everything and avoid the badgering tailors. The Peninsula Shopping Centre is good for men's shoes.

Wisma Atria, Orchard C&E and OG Department Store are good places on Orchard Rd (map 6) for clothes. Park Mall on Penang Rd has a number of international designer clothes companies. There are plenty of expensive boutiques selling designer labels: try the Promenade Shopping Centre and Paragon Shopping Centre.

Computers

Computer systems and laptops are a good buy, though for US-made or Japanese-made name-brand hardware, prices are good but not necessarily as low as in the countries of origin. Be wary of the cheap, no-name brands, mostly from Taiwan, that you won't be able to get support for back home. Computer components and accessories that are made in Singapore, such as hard disks, are very competitively priced as are blank diskettes and accessories. Singapore is enforcing international copyright laws, so the cheap software and software manuals are not so openly on display as in other Asian countries; however, 'Asian editions' are readily available. The top floors of Sim Lim Square (map 3), on the corner of Bencoolen St and Rochor Canal Rd, is the best place for computers in Singapore. The 5th and 6th floors of the Funan Centre (map 3) on North Bridge Rd is another major computer centre.

Electronic Goods

TVs, CDs, VCRs, CBs – you name it, all the latest hi-tech
audio-visual equipment is available all over Singapore
at very competitive prices. With such a range to choose
from, it's difficult to know what to buy; it pays to do a
little research into makes and models before you arrive
in Singapore. Make sure your guarantees are world-
wide, your receipts are properly dated and stamped,
and your goods are compatible with electricity supplies
and systems in your country of origin.

There are two main types of TV system used: PAL in
Australia and much of Europe, and NTSC in the USA
and Japan – video recorders must be compatible to the
system you use.

Sim Lim Square, on the corner of Bencoolen St and
Rochor Canal Rd, has a concentrated range of electronics
shops, and Sim Lim Tower, nearby on Jalan Besar, has
everything from cassette players to capacitors, but be
wary and be prepared to bargain hard. Plaza Singapura
on Orchard Rd also has a number of shops selling electronic goods, but really you can buy electronic goods
everywhere in Singapore.

Jewellery

Gold shops abound in Singapore. Gold jewellery is sold
according to weight, and quite often the design and
work is thrown in for next to nothing. Gold is often 22
to 24 carat and you should always retain a receipt
showing weight and carat. Gold shops are all over town,
but you'll find a concentration in Little India (map 4) and
People's Park Complex in Chinatown (map 2).

Singapore is a good place to buy pearls and gemstones
but you really need to know the market. Jade is a Chinese
favourite and expensive. In general, the lighter in colour
the more expensive it is. Beware of imitation jade and
don't pay too much for cheap jade, such as the dark
Indian jade. Examine solid jade pieces for flaws, as these
may be potential crack lines.

Musical Instruments

Guitars, keyboards, flutes, drums, electronic instru-
ments, recording equipment etc are all good buys,
though not necessarily as cheap as the country of origin.
Good shops to try include: Swee Lee Company, No 03-09
Plaza Singapura, 68 Orchard Rd (map 6) and City Music,
No 02-12 Peace Centre, 1 Sophia Rd, on the corner of
Selegie Rd (map 3). Yamaha has a number of show-

rooms, including one on the 7th floor of Plaza Singapura in Orchard Rd. If you want to lug around a piano, Singapore Piano Company is also in the Plaza Singapura.

The cheap pirated tapes are things of the past but legitimate tapes, records and CDs are reasonably priced.

Sporting Goods

Almost every shopping centre in Singapore has a sports store offering brand-name equipment and sportswear at good prices. Most of the department stores also have well-stocked sports sections. For general sports stores, try the Far East Shopping Centre and Plaza Singapura on Orchard Rd (map 6). Lucky Plaza on Orchard Rd also has sports shops including diving shops.

For brand-name bicycles and components, try Soon Watt & Co, 418 Changi Rd, or Kian Hong, 313 Tanjong Katong Rd. For equestrian gear go to Connoisseurs in the Shaw Centre on Scotts Rd.

Excursions

Singapore is only a stone's throw from its two larger neighbours, Malaysia and Indonesia. Both can be visited in less than an hour from Singapore, and on weekends and holidays Singaporeans flee the lion city in search of fun and sun. The beach resorts and towns of southern Malaysia are just across the Causeway, while Indonesia's Riau Archipelago includes Batam and Bintan islands, which have well-developed tourist facilities.

Travel agents in Singapore offer a host of package tours, and the competition is fierce. Tours are reasonably priced and offer an easy way to explore attractions in Malaysia or Indonesia if your time is limited. Look in the *Straits Times* for advertised tours.

Some examples of cheap tours from Singapore, including transport and accommodation, are:

Desaru
    two days for S$110
Melaka
    one day for S$40, two days for S$70
Tioman Island
    three days, including air fare, for S$310
Penang
    three days, including air fare, for S$320, S$130 by bus
Batam Island
    one day for S$45, two days for S$90
Bali
    four days for S$650
Lake Toba
    five days for S$470

Travel in Malaysia is covered in detail in Lonely Planet's *Malaysia, Singapore & Brunei – a travel survival kit*, while *Indonesia – a travel survival kit* and *Bali & Lombok – a travel survival kit* cover the world's largest archipelago. Lonely Planet's *Indonesian phrasebook* may also come in useful.

MALAYSIA

Just across the Causeway, Malaysia has a host of attractions, many of which can be visited on day trips from Singapore. Johor Bahru is almost a suburb of Singapore, and the seaside village of Kukup, the waterfalls at Kota Tinggi and the beach resort of Desaru are easily reached from Singapore.

If you have a couple of days or more to spare, then further afield is the historic town of Melaka and the beautiful islands off the east coast of Malaysia, of which Tioman Island is the largest and most popular.

Heading further inland and to the north are the hill resorts of Fraser's Hill and Cameron Highlands, which can be reached via Malaysia's thriving capital, Kuala Lumpur. Further to the north, on the west coast of Peninsular Malaysia, are the popular islands of Penang and Langkawi. The east coast has a string of good beaches, and Kota Bharu in the very north is a centre for Malay culture. Over on Borneo, Sabah and Sarawak are adventure destinations where you can explore the mountains and jungle, and experience unique wildlife.

For more details and other destinations, contact the Malaysian Tourism Promotion Board (☎ 532 6351) on the ground floor of the Ocean Building, Collyer Quay in Singapore. It is open Monday to Friday from 9 am to 4.45 pm and Saturday from 9 am to 12.30 pm.

Most visitors to Malaysia do not require a visa; you will usually be given a one or two-month entry permit on arrival. Crossing the Causeway to Malaysia is straightforward and clearing immigration and customs normally only takes a few minutes. The Malaysian dollar (or ringgit) is a stable currency and exchange rates are: S$1 = RM1.58 and US$1 = RM2.55.

Johor Bahru

Capital of the Malaysian state of Johor which comprises the entire southern tip of the peninsula, Johor Bahru is the southern gateway to Peninsular Malaysia. Connected to Singapore by the 1038-metre-long Causeway, JB (as it is known) inevitably suffers as a poor relation to its more glamorous neighbour, yet its lively chaos is an interesting contrast to Singapore's order.

JB is a popular place with Singaporeans looking for shopping bargains and cheap petrol, although it is an offence to leave Singapore with less than three-quarters of a tank of fuel! Johor Bahru did have a name as a mild 'sin city' attracting Singaporeans looking for nightlife, though recent clean-ups have closed the nightclubs, at least for a while.

Things to See The **Istana Besar**, overlooking the Straits of Johor, is the main palace of the Johor royal family. It was built in the Victorian style by anglophile Sultan Abu Bakar in 1866. The palace is now a museum full of the sultan's possessions, furniture and hunting trophies. There are some superb pieces. The palace is open daily from 9 am to 6 pm (no entry after 5 pm) and a guide accompanies you. Entrance for foreigners is a hefty US$7 per person, payable in ringgit; Malaysians and students pay RM5. It's well worth a visit.

The **Abu Bakar Mosque** on Jalan Abu Bakar was built from 1892 to 1900. The large mosque can accommodate 2000 people and overlooks the Straits of Johor.

With a 32-metre-high tower that serves as a city landmark, **Istana Bukit Serene** is the actual residence of the Sultan of Johor but it is not open to the public.

Another city landmark is the 64-metre-high square tower of the imposing **State Secretariat Building** on Bukit Timbalan, overlooking the city centre.

Places to Stay Few visitors stay in JB but there are plenty of hotels. Budget travellers head for the friendly *Footloose Homestay* (☎ 07-242881) at 4H Jalan Ismail, about 10 minutes' walk from the bus station, just off Jalan Gertak Merah. There's one double room for RM24, or just six dorm beds for RM12 per person, all including breakfast. The *Hotel Chuan Seng Baru*, at 35 Jalan Meldrum, is a very basic Chinese cheapie which costs RM20/25 for a single/double.

The *Hotel JB* (☎ 07-234788) at 80A Jalan Wong Ah Fook is at the bottom of the mid-range and has good singles/doubles from RM33.60. Also good value is the *Top Hotel* (☎ 07-244755) at 12 Jalan Meldrum. Rooms with air-con and attached bath cost RM38/44. The relatively new *Causeway Inn* (☎ 07-248811) is at 6A Jalan Meldrum. All rooms have air-con, TV and attached bath. Some also have good views across the Straits of Johor. Singles cost from RM66 to RM104, doubles from RM75 to RM113, including taxes.

There's no shortage of top-end places in JB. The *Tropical Inn* (☎ 07-247888) at 15 Jalan Gereja has 160 rooms from RM92/105. The hotel has a restaurant and coffee house as well as a bar and health centre, but no swimming pool.

The *Holiday Inn* (☎ 07-323800) is a couple of km north of the centre in Century Gardens on Jalan Dato Sulaiman. Rooms cost from RM180/200. There is a swimming pool, health club, restaurant and 24-hour coffee lounge.

The shiny new 500-room *Puteri Pan Pacific Hotel* (☎ 07-236622), in the centre of town and easy to spot, has an impressive range of features including swimming pool, fitness centre, business centre and four restaurants. Rooms start at RM270/300 and head up.

Places to Eat JB is an interesting change of venue for the favourite Singaporean pastime – eating. The seafood is excellent and slightly cheaper than Singapore; the beer is also cheaper.

For cheap Muslim food, try the *Restoran Medina* on the corner of Jalan Meldrum and Jalan Siew Niam. They serve excellent murtabak and curries. There's also a food centre opposite the railway station on Jalan Tun Abdu Razak. In the evening, there's a fairly active *pasar malam* (night market) outside the Hindu temple on Jalan Wong Ah Fook, and another near the Komtar Building between Jalan Wong Ah Fook and Jalan Tun Abdul Razak.

Jaws 5 on Jalan Skudai is outdoors, serves excellent seafood and sometimes has live music. It faces the sea, a couple of km from the Causeway.

All the major hotels have their own restaurants. The coffee shop in the *Holiday Inn* is open 24 hours and serves reasonably priced local and Western dishes.

Getting There & Away See the Getting There & Away chapter for full details on getting to Johor Bahru by bus, train and taxi from Singapore. From JB to Singapore there are regular buses (SBS bus No 170) for RM1. A taxi will cost RM35 any time of the day or night.

There are buses from Johor Bahru to Kota Tinggi (RM2), Melaka (RM10), Mersing (RM8) and Kuala Lumpur (RM17). From the JB taxi station, regular shared taxis go to Kota Tinggi (RM4), Melaka (RM25), Mersing (RM12) and Kuala Lumpur (RM38).

Car-rental companies with offices in Johor Bahru include: Avis (☎ 07-24 4824), Budget (☎ 07-24 3951), Hertz (☎ 07-23 7520) and National (☎ 07-37 0088).

Kukup

About 40 km south-west from Johor Bahru on the Straits of Melaka is the fishing village of Kukup. It is famous throughout Malaysia and Singapore for its seafood, especially prawns, and open-air restaurants, most of which are built on stilts over the water.

Getting There & Away Kukup is less than two hours by car from Singapore, or it can be reached by bus from Johor Bahru.

Johor Bahru to Melaka

Ayer Hitam is a popular rest stop for buses, taxis and motorists, so there are lots of small restaurants.

Kampung Macap, south of Ayer Hitam, is well known for its Aw Pottery works.

Batu Pahat is a riverine town famed for its Chinese cuisine, although it also has a minor reputation as a 'sin city' for jaded Singaporeans. Accommodation can be hard to find here on weekends.

Muar, north-west of Batu Pahat, is a centre of traditional Malay culture, including ghazal music and the Kuda Kepang (prancing horse) dances.

Mt Ophir (Gunung Ledang in Malay), north of Muar, has a series of waterfalls and pools for swimming.

Melaka

Melaka (Malacca), Malaysia's most historically interesting city, has been through some dramatic events over the years. The complete series of European incursions in Malaysia – Portuguese, Dutch and English – were played out here.

Under the Melaka sultanates, the city was a wealthy centre of trade with China, India, Siam and Indonesia due to its strategic position on the Straits of Melaka. Admiral Cheng Ho, an envoy of the Ming emperor, visited Melaka in 1409 to establish relations. In 1511, Alfonso d'Albuquerque launched an assault on the city and the sultan fled to Johor. Melaka's trade continued to thrive, but the period of Portuguese strength in the East was a short one.

As Dutch influence grew and Batavia (modern-day Jakarta) became the principal port of the region, Melaka declined. Finally, the Dutch attacked the city and in 1641 it passed into their hands after a siege lasting eight months.

During the Napoleonic wars, the British took over administration of the Dutch colonies. In 1824, Melaka was permanently ceded by the Dutch to the British in exchange for the Sumatran port of Bencoolen.

Under the British, Melaka once more flourished as a trading centre, although it was soon superseded by the growing commercial importance of Singapore.

Today, it's a sleepy backwater town and no longer of any major commercial influence. It's a place of intriguing Chinese streets and antique shops, old Chinese temples and cemeteries, and nostalgic reminders of the now-departed European colonial powers.

Things to See The **Stadthuys**, built between 1641 and 1660, is the most imposing relic of the Dutch period and the oldest Dutch building in the East. Other interesting buildings around the main square include the **GPO**, the old clock tower and the bright red **Christ Church**. The pink bricks were brought out from Zeeland, and old Dutch tombstones are laid in the floor.

Bukit St Paul (St Paul's Hill) rises up above the Stadthuys, and on top of it stand the ruins of **St Paul's Church**. Built by the Portuguese in 1571, it was regularly visited by Francis Xavier; the saint's body was buried here before being transferred to Goa in India. The church fell into disuse after the Dutch takeover and has been in ruins for 150 years.

All that is left of the old Portuguese fortress is the main gate to A'Famosa, the **Porta de Santiago**. Sound and light shows are held here each evening at 8.15 pm (in Malay) and at 10 pm (in English). Entry to the Porta de Santiago is free, but the sound and light show is RM5.

The **Proclamation of Independence Hall**, in a typical Dutch house dating from 1660, is a small museum displaying events leading up to independence in 1957.

The **Cultural Museum**, or Muzium Budaya, on the same side of St Paul's Hill as the Porta de Santiago and Independence Hall, is a wooden replica of a Melaka sultan's palace. Admission to this interesting museum is RM1.50.

The **Baba-Nonya Heritage Museum**, 48-50 Jalan Tun Tan Cheng Lock, is a traditional 19th-century Peranakan (Straits-born Chinese) townhouse. It is owned by a Baba family who conduct tours of the house, which has typical Peranakan furniture and artefacts. The museum (☎ 06-23 1273) is open from 10 am to 12.30 pm and from 2 to 4.30 pm. Admission is RM7.

Old Melaka is a fascinating area to wander around. Although Melaka has long lost its importance as a port, ancient-looking junks still sail up the river and moor at the banks. You may still find some of the treasures of the East in the antique shops scattered along Jalan Hang Jebat. There is a whole assortment of interesting shops and the odd mosque and Chinese or Hindu temple squeezed into this intriguing old street. The **Sri Pogyatha Vinoyagar Moorthi Temple**, dating from 1781, and the Sumatran-style **Kampung Kling Mosque** are both in this area.

Some other interesting churches, temples and mosques include: **St Peter's Church**, built in 1710; the fascinating **Cheng Hoon Teng Temple** on Jalan Tokong, the oldest Chinese temple in Malaysia; and the **Masjid Tengkera**, where you'll find the tomb of Sultan Hussein of Johor who, in 1819, signed over the island of Singapore to Stamford Raffles.

In the mid-1400s, the Sultan of Melaka wed the Ming emperor's daughter to seal relations between the two countries, and their residence was on **Bukit China** (China Hill). It has been a Chinese area ever since and, together with two adjoining hills, forms a huge Chinese graveyard. At the foot of Bukit China is the **Sam Po Kong Temple** and nearby is the **Hang Li Poh Well**.

A few km beyond the fort is **Medan Portuguese**, or Portuguese Square, an area where many people of Portuguese and Malay descent live. The main points of interest here are the restaurants and cultural shows on Saturday nights at 8 pm.

Although the British demolished most of Fort Santiago, they left the small Dutch **Fort of St John** untouched; it is on a hilltop to the east of town. **Tanjung Kling** and, a little further out, **Pantai Kundor**, are the main beaches in the area but they have become increasingly polluted. There are some budget accommodation places at these beaches. On a clear day, you can see Sumatra from Tanjung Kling – it's only about 50 km away. The small island of **Pulau Besar**, a little south of Melaka, is a popular weekend joy ride. Boats operate from Umbai near Melaka.

The tourist centre runs daily **riverboat tours** of Melaka which leave from the quay behind the tourist centre. The trip takes 45 minutes and costs RM6 per person (minimum six people); departures are at 10 and 11 am, noon, 2, 3 and 4.30 pm.

Major **festivals** in Melaka include the Good Friday and Easter Sunday processions at St Peter's and, at the same church, a feast during June in honour of the patron saint of fishers.

Places to Stay Melaka has a wide range of accommodation from travellers' hostels to international-standard hotels.

Melaka has quite a number of traveller-oriented guest houses. Most of them are in the area known as Taman Melaka Raya, the reclaimed land just south of Jalan Merdeka. The standard price is RM6 for a dorm bed and RM12/16 for singles/doubles. Try the popular *Travellers' Lodge* at 214B, the long-running *Trilogy Guest House* (☎ 06-245319) at 223B, *Amy Home Stay* at 244B or *Robin's Nest Guest House* at 247B. On the main thoroughfare in this area is the *Malacca Town Holiday Lodge* (☎ 06-248830) at 148B. Away from Taman Melaka Raya there are a number of other guest houses dotted around. The pick of them is probably the popular *Eastern Heritage Guest House* (☎ 06-233026) at 8 Jalan Bukit China. The *Paradise Hostel* (☎ 06230821) at 4 Jalan Tengkera is close to the historical Chinatown.

Jonkers Melaka Restoran, Melaka (TW)

Of the many cheap hotels, some of the better ones are: *Ng Fook* (☎ 06-22 8055) at 154 Jalan Bunga Raya, and next door, the *Hong Kong Hotel*. The cheapest hotel is the slightly shabby *Central Hotel* (☎ 06-22 2984) at 31 Jalan Bendahara. For a little bit more, the rambling old *Majestic Hotel* (☎ 06-22 2367) at 188 Jalan Bunga Raya has atmosphere though it could do with a scrub.

The *May Chiang Hotel* (☎ 06-22 2101) at 52 Jalan Munshi Abdullah is good value in the middle range of hotels and costs RM35/40 with air-con and bath. Other places in this price range include the *Plaza Inn* (☎ 06-24 0888) at 2 Jalan Munshi Abdullah with rooms from RM90. The *Visma Hotel* (☎ 06-238799) is close to the bridge and Jalan Munshi Abdullah, at 111 Jalan Kampung Hulu. All rooms are air-con and have attached bath. It's a good clean place and rooms cost RM42, or there are family rooms for RM80.

On Jalan Bendahara, the *Malacca Renaissance Hotel* (☎ 06-24 8888) charges from RM250 per night. Facilities include a swimming pool, tennis and squash courts, and disco. The *City Bayview Hotel* (☎ 06-23 9888), also on Jalan Bendahara, has singles/doubles from RM220 to RM420. Not quite as luxurious is the *Emperor Hotel* (☎ 06-238989), in the same area at 123 Jalan Munshi Abdullah. The room rate is RM200 for the cheapest rooms up to RM530 for executive suites.

Places to Eat Melaka has no shortage of places to eat. On Jalan Taman, on what used to be the waterfront, the permanent stalls serve all the usual food-centre special-ities. Try the *Bunga Raya Restaurant* at No 40 which has excellent steamed crabs.

On Jalan Laksamana, right in the centre of town, the *Restaurant Kim Swee Huat* at No 38 is a cheap restaurant that is good for Chinese food and Western breakfasts.

At the *Melaka Pandan Restoran*, behind the tourist office, you can eat outdoors under umbrellas. It is a popular watering hole with locals and visitors alike.

In the heart of the old town on Jalan Hang Jebat, the *Jonkers Melaka Restoran* is in a traditional Peranakan house and serves both Western and Nonya dishes. The set menu of four Nonya dishes for RM16 is a good deal. The restaurant is open daily from 10 am to 7 pm.

At Medan Portugis (Portuguese Square), you can sample Malay-Portuguese cuisine at tables facing the sea. They serve excellent seafood, and for around RM20 per person you can eat very well. Just outside the square is a Malay-Portuguese restaurant, the *San Pedro*. The food is similar to what you find in the square but the atmosphere is more intimate and the prices higher.

Getting There & Away Melaka is 216 km north-west from Johor Bahru. Melaka can be visited as a day trip from Singapore if you have your own car, but it takes at least three hours if you drive like a maniac, more like four or five hours if there are hold-ups. By bus, it takes nearly six hours, so a visit to Melaka really requires two days. Buses from Singapore can be booked at the Laven-

Christ Church, Melaka (TW)

der St Malaysia bus station. You can fly to or from Melaka to Singapore (RM110, S$110) or Ipoh (RM125) with Pelangi Air (☎ 06-351175) on their thrice weekly services.

Melaka-Singapore Express buses leave hourly from 8 am to 6 pm from the express bus stand and the fare is RM11. The trip takes around 5½ hours and you should book in advance at the office at the bus station.

The following car-rental companies have offices in Melaka:

Avis
    124 Jalan Bendahara (☎ 06-2469918)
Hertz
    2 Quayside Rd (☎ 06-228862)

Getting Around A bicycle rickshaw is the ideal way of getting around compact and slow-moving Melaka. By the hour they should cost about RM10, or RM3 for any one-way trip within the town, but you'll have to bargain.

Kota Tinggi

The small town of Kota Tinggi is 64 km north-east from Singapore on the road to Mersing. The waterfalls, 15 km north-west of the town, cascade down through a series of pools which are ideal for a cooling dip. Entry to the falls is RM1.

At the falls, the *Waterfall Chalet* (☎ 07-241957) has run-down self-contained chalets for RM40 per night, but new chalets are being built. Weekend bookings are heavy. There is also a camping area, or the town has cheap hotels.

About 30 km down the Johor River from Kota Tinggi is Johor Lama, the seat of the sultan between 1547 and 1587.

Getting There & Away From Singapore, it is a 1½-hour drive to Kota Tinggi. Regular buses (No 41, RM2) and taxis (RM4) go from Johor Bahru to Kota Tinggi. Take bus No 43 from Kota Tinggi to the waterfalls.

Desaru

Desaru, on a 20-km stretch of beach at Tanjung Penawar, is 88 km east of Johor Bahru. This beach resort area, also reached via Kota Tinggi, is a popular weekend escape for Singaporeans, though there are better beaches in Malaysia.

The *Desaru View Hotel* (☎ 07-821221) has rooms from S$190 up to S$600 for suites; and *Desaru Holiday Resort* (☎ 07-821240) has so-so chalets from RM31/62 to RM200, or a bed in the 21-bed dorm costs RM12.

The camping ground costs RM5 per person in tents, or RM10.50 in dorms. The only restaurants are at the big hotels.

At Batu Layar, 16 km south of Desaru, the *Batu Layar Beach Resort* (☎ 07-821835) is a new place with garishly painted A-frame chalets from RM65, more on weekends.

Getting There & Away Buses (RM3.50) and taxis operate from Kota Tinggi. A popular way for Singaporeans to reach Desaru is to take the ferry to Belungkur from North Changi for S$4, and from there a taxi to Desaru costs RM30.

Mersing

Mersing is a small, picturesque fishing village on the east coast of Peninsular Malaysia and the departure point for the beautiful islands lying just off this coast in the South China Sea. The river bustles with fishing boats and there's plenty to see.

Mersing has a number of hotels. *Sheikh Tourist Agency* (☎ 07-793767), 1B Jalan Abu Bakar, is the budget travellers' place with dorm beds for RM5. The *Hotel Embassy* (☎ 07-791301) is one of the best cheap hotels with rooms from RM16 to RM27. The *Mersing Merlin Inn* (☎ 07-791312) is fully air-conditioned and has a swimming pool; singles/doubles are RM92/103.

Getting There & Away Mersing is about 150 km north-east of Singapore, and it takes four hours to reach by car. You can catch buses directly from Singapore for S$11.10 or from Johor Bahru for RM8. Express buses from Mersing to Singapore are often full. A shared taxi from Mersing to Johor Bahru costs RM12 per person.

Tioman Island

The largest and most spectacular of the east coast islands, Tioman Island has beautiful beaches, clear water and coral for snorkelling or diving enthusiasts. Its major attraction, however, has to be the contrasts and diversity it offers – high mountains and dense jungle are only a short walk away from the coast.

Pulau Tioman is the most popular destination on the east coast and it can get quite crowded at peak times, particularly in July and August. Tioman has a host of cheap accommodation at the popular backpackers' beaches of Air Batang, Salang, Juara and Tekek. Accommodation is mostly in very simple huts, longhouse rooms or more comfortable chalets. Expect to pay at least RM10 for a hut, and up to RM30 for a chalet.

The *Berjaya Imperial Island Resort* (☎ 09- 44 5445) is the only international-class hotel on the island. Rooms cost from RM245 to RM500 and there is a very impressive range of facilities: a beautiful golf course, tennis, horse riding, jet-skis, scuba diving, etc.

A number of smaller islands near Tioman also have superb beaches and accommodation, these include: Rawa, Sibu, Babi Besar and Tengah.

Getting There & Away

Air Silk Air and Pelangi Air have daily flights to/from Singapore for RM132 (S$99). Pelangi also flies daily to Kuala Lumpur (four daily, RM125), and to Kuantan (daily, RM77). Berjaya is another small feeder airline with daily flights to KL for the same price. The booking office for all air tickets is in the Berjaya Imperial Resort.

Boat A whole flotilla of boats make the 56-km trip from Mersing to Tioman. Air-conditioned fast boats take about 1½ hours and cost RM25 one way, and moderate boats take three hours and cost RM20.

There's a daily high-speed catamaran service between Singapore and Tioman. It departs Singapore daily at 7.50 am, and from the Berjaya Resort jetty at 1.30 pm. The trip takes 4½ hours and costs RM142. Bookings can be made at the desk in the lobby of the Berjaya Imperial Island Resort. In Singapore the office for bookings is Resort Cruises Pty Ltd (☎ 02-2784677), 02-03, 337 Telok Blangah Rd.

INDONESIA – RIAU ARCHIPELAGO

Indonesia is a fascinating collection of islands and cultures. If you have a few days to spare and the money for air fares, you can make a number of short tours from Singapore. You can arrange a trip independently or there are dozens of packages available from Singaporean travel agents.

Some easily reached highlights of Indonesia are: Lake Toba and Bukittinggi in Sumatra; Jakarta, Yogyakarta and Borobudur in Java; and, of course, Bali. For day trips, there are the islands of the Riau Archipelago, which cover an area of over 170,000 sq km, curving south-east from Sumatra to Kalimantan and north to Malaysia.

Tanjung Pinang on Bintan Island is the main town in the archipelago, though Batam Island is now the centre of all activity. Singapore investors are pouring millions of dollars into the islands, and the Indonesian and Singaporean governments are developing the area as a special economic zone that will support a variety of industries. Batam gets most of the investment and now is the centre for transport in and out of Riau.

Both islands can be visited as a day trip from Singapore, and there is a wide variety of accommodation. Batam is a duty free port, and used to attract Singaporean day trippers stocking up on duty free goods, until the government woke up and made duty free allowances subject to being away from Singapore for 48 hours. As such Batam attracts mainly Indonesian tourists. It provides a taste of Indonesia, though not a particularly memorable one. Bintan has a little more of interest, though there are much fewer ferries and you may have to spend the night there. To see the best of Indonesia, you must travel further afield.

Most nationalities – including citizens of the USA, Canada, Australia, New Zealand, UK, Ireland, Netherlands and most other European countries – do not require a visa to Indonesia for a visit of up to two months. Entry must be at specified ports – Sekupang on Batam Island and Tanjung Pinang on Bintan Island are visa free entry ports – otherwise a visa must be obtained. The Indonesian monetary unit is the rupiah (rp). Indonesian exchange rates are: S$1 = 1350 rp, US$1 = 2150 rp.

For more information, contact the Indonesia Tourist Promotion Office (☎ 534 2837), 15-07 Ocean Building, 10 Collyer Quay, Singapore. It is open Monday to Friday from 9 am to 5 pm (closed for lunch from 1 to 2 pm) and on Saturday from 10 am to 1 pm.

Batam Island

Batam is being heavily developed to become a virtual industrial suburb of Singapore. Already, there are resorts on the north coast and there will soon be factories, warehouses and even a huge reservoir to supply water to the nearby city state. Meanwhile, there's a distinct frontier town atmosphere to the place, with high prices, ugly construction sites and no reason to pause longer than you have to.

Sekupang is the arrival port and, after you clear immigration, there are counters for money exchange, taxis and hotels. **Nagoya**, the main town, looks and feels like some sort of gold-rush place, complete with bars and prostitutes. It's sometimes referred to as Batu Ampar. **Kabil** is the tiny port from where boats cross to Tanjung Uban and Tanjung Pinang on Bintan. **Batu Besar** is a small fishing village on the east coast from which the airport takes its name. **Nongsa** is the centre for the Singapore beach resort hotels on the north-east corner of the island.

Singapore dollars are easier to spend than Indonesian rupiah on Batam. There's a money-exchange counter at the Sekupang ferry building and a bank outside which will probably be closed. You can change money in Nagoya. There's an efficient phone office on Jalan Teuku Umar, out of town towards the cluster of cheap hotels.

Places to Stay There is no pressing reason to stay on Batam but if you must there are a variety of places in Nagoya and a number of beach resorts on the north-east coast at Nongsa.

There are no accommodation bargains in Nagoya. About a km out of town at Blok C, Jalan Teuku Umar, there's a line-up of utterly rock-bottom *losmen* for 15,000 rp. The town centre has plenty of hotels. Try the *Horisona Hotel* (☎ 45 7111) at Blok E, Kompleks Lumbung Rezeki, with rooms from S$50 and up. The pick of the bunch is probably the pleasant *Bukit Nagoya Hotel* (☎ 52871) at Jalan Sultan Abdul Rahman 1 with rooms without bath at S$30 or more expensive rooms from S$40 to S$70.

The beach resorts around Nongsa are mainly for visitors from Singapore. The fancy *Batam View* and *Turi Beach Resort* both cost from about US$100 a night for a double. Many agents in Singapore have packages to these resorts. They are of a good standard, and though the beaches are passable, there is nothing to see outside of the resorts. The *Nongsa Beach Cottages* are plain, cost from S$80 and include breakfast.

Places to Eat The best eating in Nagoya is found at the night food stalls which are set up along Jalan Raja Ali Haji or at the big, raucous and noisy *Pujasera Nagoya* food centre. There are some good nasi padang places like *Mak Ateh Nasi Padang*.

There are a number of waterfront seafood places dotted around the coast of the island, particularly around the Singapore resorts at Nongsa. They include *Setia Budi* and *Sederhana* near the Nongsa Beach Cottages and *Selera Wisata* at Batu Besar.

Getting There & Away See the Getting There & Away chapter for details of the ferries from Singapore.

To/From Elsewhere in Indonesia There are a variety of flights from Bintan's Batu Besar Airport to other places in Indonesia. Typical fares include Jakarta 178,000 rp, Pekanbaru 89,100 rp, Medan 172,100 rp, Padang 117,100 rp, Pontianak 151,200 rp and Balikpapan 304,100 rp. There are flights with SMAC and PT Deraya Air Taxi to Dabo on Singkep Island. Batam's airport terminal is a scruffy and stuffy little place.

It is possible to continue straight on from Batam to Bintan by ferry. From Kabil, the tiny port on the southeast coast, an assortment of boats shuttle across.

Batam has ferries to the western islands of the Riau Archipelago, from where other boats go to the Sumatran mainland. There are direct boats to Sumatra. A daily speedboat goes to Pekanbaru at 10.30 am and costs 35,000 rp. Other speedboats (40,000 rp, four hours) go to Tembilahan (via Kuala Gaung, Perigi Raja and Sapat) at 10.30 am on Mondays, Wednesdays and Fridays. On Tuesdays, Thursdays and Saturdays, boats go to Kuala Tungkal for 50,000 rp and take six hours. From Kuala Tungkal buses go to Jambi. The other alternative is to go via Selat Panjang, and a number of boats go from Batam, and then from Selat Panjang to Pekanbaru.

Getting Around There is a hard-to-find bus service from Sekupang to Nagoya for 600 rp but otherwise the only transport around Batam is taxi, and you have to bargain hard. Between Sekupang and Nagoya or between Nagoya and Kabil, you should be able to get a shared taxi at around 1500 to 2000 rp per person, otherwise pay 5000 rp for the whole taxi. From Nagoya to the airport should be a bit less. Don't believe cards showing 'official' fares.

Bintan Island

Bintan is larger than Batam and much more interesting. Singapore development is, at present, on a much lower key on Bintan but a mega-resort is on the drawing boards for the north coast.

For visitors, the island has three areas of interest – the town of Tanjung Pinang and nearby Penyenget Island; the relatively untouched beaches along the east coast; and Tanjung Pinang's useful role as a departure point for ships bound to other parts of the country.

Raya Sultan Riau Mosque,
Penyenget Island, Indonesia (RN)

Tanjung Pinang Tanjung Pinang is the biggest town
in the Riau Archipelago and there is a constant stream
of boats arriving and departing. These vary from large
freighters to tiny sampans. An old and quite picturesque
wooden section of the town juts out over the sea on stilts
but there are also some lush parks and gardens on dry
land.

The town is famed for its two red-light villages – Batu
Duabelas and Batu Enambelas – no prizes for guessing
that they are respectively 12 (*duabelas*) km and 16
(*enambelas*) km out of town.

The piers and market are colourful places to explore.
There is a **Chinese temple** right in town. Not far from
the city centre is the small **Riau Kandil Museum** with
its curious collection of old bits and pieces, some dating
from the Riau Kingdom.

Tiny **Penyenget Island** is in the harbour across from
Tanjung Pinang. It was once capital of the kingdom and

the whole place is steeped in history. It is littered with reminders of its past and there is an interesting mosque.

Beaches Bintan's beaches are relatively untouched, apart from the inevitable overlay of bottles and other driftplastic. There's a fine 30-km-long beach strip along the east coast, although getting there can be a problem. **Pantai Trikora** is the main east coast beach with some accommodation. Snorkelling is fine most of the year except during the November to March monsoon period.

Places to Stay In Tanjung Pinang, at the end of Lorong Bintan II, which runs off Jalan Bintan in the centre of town, is the very popular *Bong's Homestay* at No 20. A bed costs 3000 rp, includes breakfast and the friendly Mr and Mrs Bong make this a great place to stay. Next door, at No 22, *Johnny's Homestay* is a good overflow.

The *Hotel Surya* (☎ 21811/293) on Jalan Bintan is a good average losmen with singles/doubles at 11,500/15,000 rp or 17,500 rp with bath. Around the corner on Jalan Yusuf Khahar, the *Penginapan Sondang* is very bare, basic and costs from 10,000 to 12,500 rp.

There's a string of mid-range places on Jalan Yusuf Khahar including the simple but modern *Sampurna Inn* where rooms cost from 15,000 rp with fan or from 25,000 to 45,000 rp with air-con.

At the Km 38 marker, the flashier *Trikora Country Club* at Pantai Trikora has singles from S$50 to S$70 and doubles from S$60 to S$80.

Places to Eat Tanjung Pinang has a superb night market with a tantalising array of food stalls offering delicious food at bargain prices. A meal typically costs 1800 to 2500 rp. It sets up in the bus & taxi station on Jalan Teuku Umar. More night-time food stalls can be found at the Jalan Pos and Lorong Merdeka intersection.

During the day, there are several pleasant cafes with outdoor eating areas in front of the stadium (Kaca Puri) on Jalan Teuku Umar. Try *Flipper* or *Sunkist*.

Getting There & Away See the Getting There & Away chapter on getting to Bintan from Singapore.

To/From Java & Sumatra Bintan's airport is much smaller than Batam's, there are fewer flights and they operate with smaller aircraft. The Jakarta flight (177,450 rp with Sempati and 198,500 rp with Merpati) is often booked up a week ahead. In that case, the easiest alternative is to backtrack to Batam. You can easily get from Tanjung Pinang to Kabil by ferry and on to the airport by taxi in less than two hours. Despite modern phone connections Garuda charge 5000 rp to make a flight booking for Bintan and they need a day to do it!

For the journey from Tanjung Pinang to Pekanbaru in Sumatra see Singapore to Sumatra via the Riau in the Sumatra Getting There & Away section.

Boats also operate west to Tanjung Balai (16,500 rp) and south to Dabo, Singkep Island (15,500 rp).

Pelni has resumed its service through Tanjung Pinang with the ship KM *Lawit*. Ekonomi class (the old deck class) costs 32,000 rp to Jakarta and 31,000 rp to Belawan (Medan). Sailings are from Kijang, the port at the south-eastern corner of the island.

Getting Around Buses to other parts of Bintan, including Tanjung Uban for the cheap boat to Kabil, operate from the bus & taxi station on Jalan Teuku Umar. The Tanjung Uban bus costs 3000 rp and takes two hours. The Kijang bus costs about 1100 rp.

Public motorbikes, known as *ojeks*, are the favourite form of local transport. You can recognise them by the yellow construction worker helmets worn by their riders. Around town a ride costs about 250 rp. There are also some local *oplets* around town, they also cost from 250 rp.

You can rent motorbikes from PT Info Travel on the main wharf for 25,000 rp a day. Other places may be cheaper, particularly by the day rather than 24 hours.

Index

239

Maps

MAP LEGEND

BOUNDARIES

— · — · · .... International   — · · — .... Regional

SYMBOLS

✈	.... Airport	♀ ⊥	.... Mosque, Temple
◓	.... Bus Station	▲	.... Mountain
⋏	.... Camping Area	⊖	.... MRT Station
✝ ✝	...... Church, Cathedral	Ⓟ	.... Parking
✚	.... Hospital	✉	.... Post Office
i	...... Tourist Information	⊶	.... Railway Station

ROUTES

═══	.... City Street	┼┼┼┼┼┼	.... Railway
━━━	.... Major Road	⊣⊢⊣⊢	.... Cable Car
───	.... Minor Road	─ ─ ─	.... Bicycle Path
▰▱▰	.... Subway	....	.... Walking Tour
─ ─ ─	.... Ferry Route		

HYDRPGRAPHIC FEATURE

| ⌒ | .... River, Creek | ⌒ | .... Coastline |
| ⬭ | .... Lake | ⌒ | .... Waterfall |

OTHER FEATURES

▢	.... Park, Garden	▢	.... Place to Shop
⊞	.... Cemetery	▢ ■	.... Place to Stay
▨	.... Pedestrian Street, Mall	▢ ▼	.... Place to Eat
▢	.... Urban Area	▢	.... Building

Note: not all symbols displayed above appear in this book

MAP 2

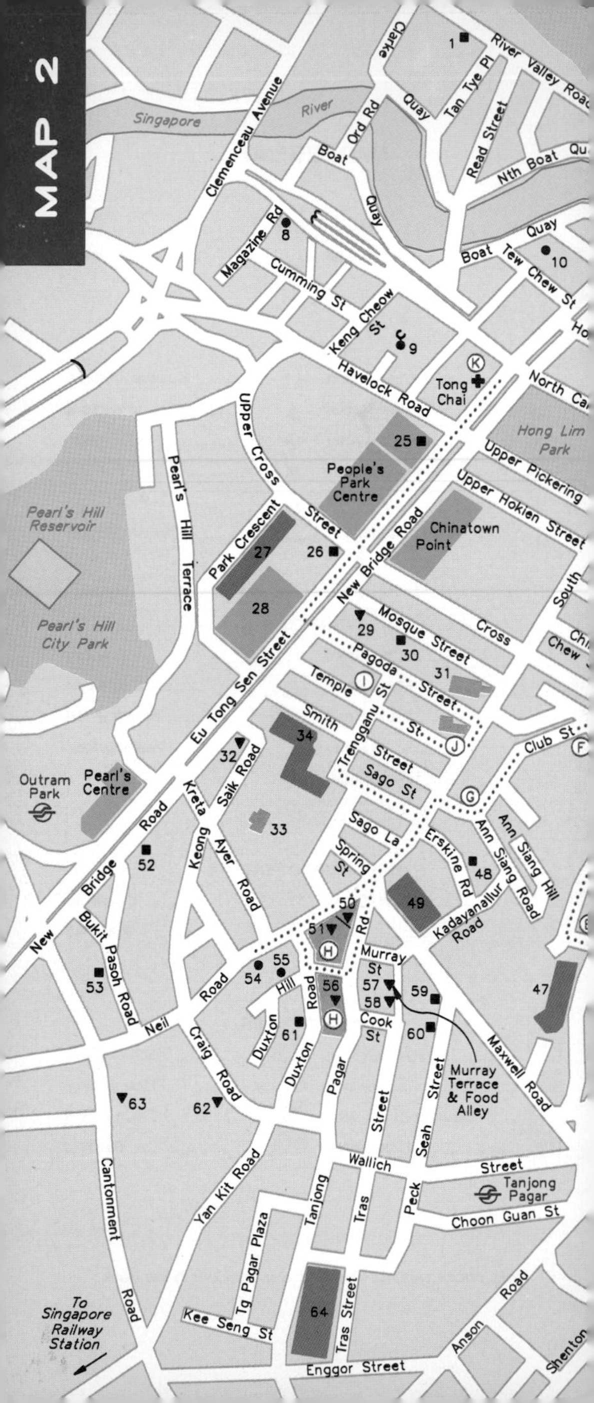

Singapore River

River Valley Road
Tan Tye Pl
Clarke Quay
1
Ord Rd
Read Street
Boat Quay
Nth Boat Qu
Clemenceau Avenue
Magazine Rd
8
Cumming St
Keng Cheow St
9
Boat Quay
Tew Chew St
10
Ho

Havelock Road
Tong Chai
K
North Ca

Upper Cross Street
Pearl's Hill Terrace
Hong Lim Park
Upper Pickering
25
People's Park Centre
Upper Hokien Street
Park Crescent
27
26
Chinatown Point
Pearl's Hill Reservoir
28
New Bridge Road
Cross
South
Chi
Chew
Pearl's Hill City Park
Eu Tong Sen Street
29
Mosque Street
30
31
Temple St
Pagoda Street
J
Smith
Trengganu St
Street
Club St
F
34
32
Sago St
G
33
Sago La
Ann Siang Hill
Outram Park
Pearl's Centre
Kreta Ayer Road
Keong Saik Road
Spring St
Erskine Rd
Ann Siang Road
48
Kadayanallur Road
49
New Bridge Road
50
51
52
Bukit Pasoh Road
55
54
H
Murray St
57
58
59
60
47
53
Neil Road
56
H
Craig Road
61
Cook St
Duxton Hill
Duxton
Murray Terrace & Food Alley
Maxwell Road
63
62
Tanjong Pagar
Yan Kit Road
Pagar
Street
Peck Seah Street
Tras Street
Wallich Street
Tanjong Pagar
Choon Guan St
Cantonment Road
To Singapore Railway Station
Kee Seng St
Tg Pagar Plaza
64
Tras Street
Enggor Street
Anson Road
Shenton

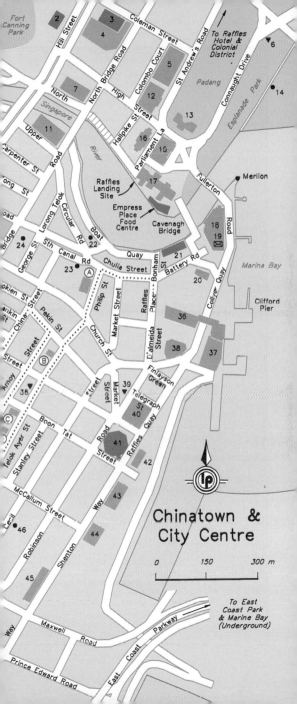

Chinatown & City Centre

0   150   300 m

Map labels:

Fort Canning Park

Hill Street
Coleman Street
St Andrew's Road
To Raffles Hotel & Colonial District
Connaught Drive
Padang
Esplanade Park

North Bridge Road
Colombo Court
High Street
North
Singapore
Upper
Carpenter St
ong St
oad
bridge
George St
Sth Canal Rd
Chulia Street
Pekin St
okien St
ankin
St
Amoy
Street
Hokien St
China Street
Boon Tat
Stanley Street
McCallum Street
Cecil
Robinson
Way
Maxwell
Road
Prince Edward Road
East Coast Parkway

Parliament La
Halpike St
Parliament St
Raffles Landing Site
Empress Place Food Centre
Cavenagh Bridge
Fullerton
Merlion
Quay
Bonham St
Battery Rd
Collyer Quay
Marina Bay
Clifford Pier
Raffles Place
Market Street
Church St
Philip St
D'almeida Street
Finlayson Green
Telegraph St
Raffles Quay
Shenton Way
Road
Lorong Telok
Circular Rd
Boat Quay
River
Leng
To East Coast Park & Marine Bay (Underground)

Numbered locations: 2, 3, 4, 5, 6, 7, 11, 12, 13, 14, 15, 16, 17, 18, 19, 20, 21, 22, 23, 24, 35, 36, 37, 38, 39, 40, 41, 42, 43, 44, 45, 46

A, B, C

MAP 2
CHINATOWN & CITY CENTRE

■ PLACES TO STAY

1 New Otani Hotel
3 Peninsula Hotel
25 Furama Hotel
26 Great Southern Hotel
30 Dragon Cityview Hotel
48 Inn of the Sixth Happiness
52 Chinatown Guest House
53 Majestic Hotel
59 New Asia Hotel
60 Air View Hotel
61 Duxton Hotel
64 Amara Hotel

▼ PLACES TO EAT

2 Hill Street Food Centre
6 Satay Club
21 Boat Quay Food Centre
27 People's Park Food Centre
29 Tai Tong Hoi Kee Coffee Shop
32 Tiong Shan Eating House
34 Chinatown Complex
 – Market & Food Place
35 Nasi William Restaurant
39 Movenpick Restaurant
41 Lau Pa Sat (Telok Ayer Centre)
42 Telok Ayer Transit Centre
47 Amoy St Food Centre
49 Maxwell Food Centre
50 Jinrikisha Station
51 Tea Chapter
56 Goldleaf Restaurant
57 Moti Mahal Restaurant
58 Beng Hiang Restaurant
62 Siamese Fins
63 Hillman Restaurant

OTHER

4 Funan Centre
5 City Hall
7 High Street Centre
8 Tan Si Chong Su Temple
9 Melaka Mosque
10 Ellenborough Street Market
11 Riverwalk Galleria
12 Supreme Court
13 Singapore Cricket Club
14 Queen Elizabeth Walk

Bird Cages (TW)

Colonial District

0   75   150 m

MAP 3
COLONIAL DISTRICT

■ PLACES TO STAY

4 New 7th Storey Hotel
5 New Backpackers Lodge
6 Willy's 2 Guest House
7 Das Travellers' Inn
8 Lee Travellers' Club &
  Willy's Guest House
9 Lido Hotel
10 Raffles Home Stay
11 Ah Chew Hotel
12 South-East Asia Hotel
14 Goh's Homestay & Hawaii Hostel
16 Why Not Homestay
17 Sun Sun Hotel
22 Hotel Bencoolen
23 Lee Travellers' Club,
   Peony Mansions & Latin House
25 San Wah Hotel
26 Bencoolen House
27 Strand Hotel
28 Bayview Inn
30 Allson Hotel
31 Victoria Hotel
35 Shang Onn Hotel
38 Metropole Hotel
39 Marina Mandarin Hotel
40 Westin Plaza Hotel
41 Westin Stamford Hotel
42 Carlton Hotel
44 YMCA
45 YWCA Hostel
48 Mayfair City Hotel
54 Peninsula Hotel
55 Excelsior Hotel
70 New Otani Hotel

▼ PLACES TO EAT

2 Fatty's Wing Seong Restaurant
15 Sahib Restaurant
29 Regency Palace
33 Swee Kee Restaurant
34 Loo Tien Food Centre
36 Tropical Makan Palace Food Stalls
37 Yet Con Restaurant
51 Third Man
52 Satay Club
56 Hill Street Food Centre
62 Food Centre
63 Empress Place Food Centre

Supreme Court (AR)

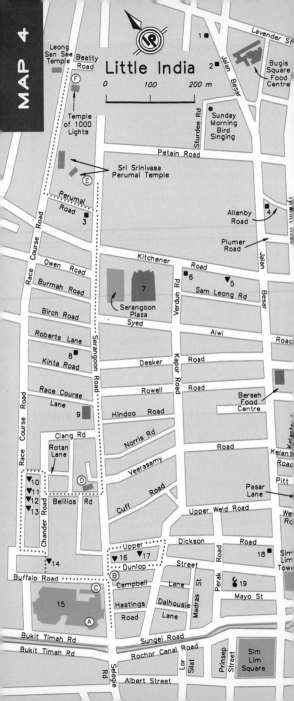

MAP 4
LITTLE INDIA

■ PLACES TO STAY

1 Palace Hotel
2 Kam Leng Hotel
3 Friendly Rest House
4 International Hotel
6 Tai Hoe Hotel
7 New Park Hotel
8 Nan Yong Hotel
9 Broadway Hotel
18 Boon Wah Boarding House

▼ PLACES TO EAT

5 Fut Sai Kai Coffee Shop
  & Restaurant
10 Muthu's Curry Restaurant
11 Nur Jehan Restaurant
12 Delhi Restaurant
13 Banana Leaf Apolo Restaurant
14 Chakra Restaurant & Food Stalls
15 Zhujiao Centre
16 Komala Vilas Restaurant
17 Madras New Woodlands Cafe

OTHER

19 Abdul Gaffoor Mosque

Ⓐ WALKING TOUR

A Zhujiao Centre
B Spice Shops
C Jewellers
D Veerama Kali Amman Temple
E Sri Srinivasa Perumal Temple
F Temple of 1000 Lights

Sri Krishnan Temple (RN)

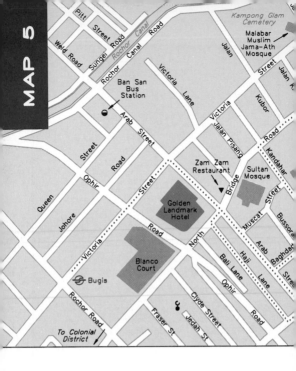

MAP 5

Caneware, Arab Street (PT)

Arab Street

0   100   200 m

Assorted Goods, Arab Street

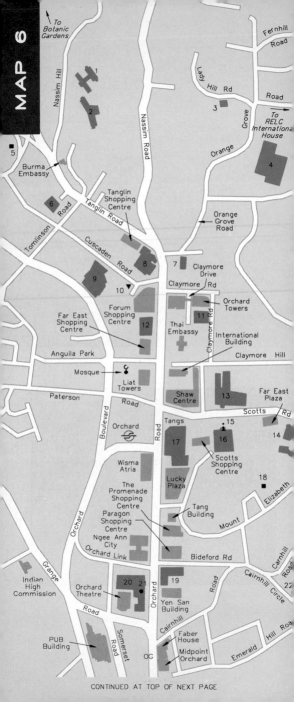

MAP 6

To Botanic Gardens

Fernhill Road

Nassim Hill

Lady Hill Rd

Road

3

Grove

To RELC International House

Orange

4

5

Burma Embassy

Nassim Road

6

Tomlinson Road

Tanglin Road

Tanglin Shopping Centre

Orange Grove Road

Cuscaden Road

8

7

Claymore Drive

Claymore Rd

Orchard Towers

9

10

Far East Shopping Centre

Forum Shopping Centre

12

11

Thai Embassy

International Building

Claymore Rd

Claymore Hill

Anguila Park

Mosque

Liat Towers

Paterson Road

Boulevard

Orchard Road

Shaw Centre

13

Far East Plaza

Scotts

Rd

14

Tangs

15

16

17

Wisma Atria

Lucky Plaza

Scotts Shopping Centre

18

Elizabeth

The Promenade Shopping Centre

Paragon Shopping Centre

Ngee Ann City

Orchard Link

Tang Building

Mount

Bideford Rd

Cairnhill Circle

Cairnhill

Grange

Indian High Commission

Orchard Theatre

20 21

19

Yen San Building

Road

Cairnhill

Hill Road

Emerald

Road

Orchard

PUB Building

Somerset Road

Faber House

Midpoint Orchard

OG

CONTINUED AT TOP OF NEXT PAGE

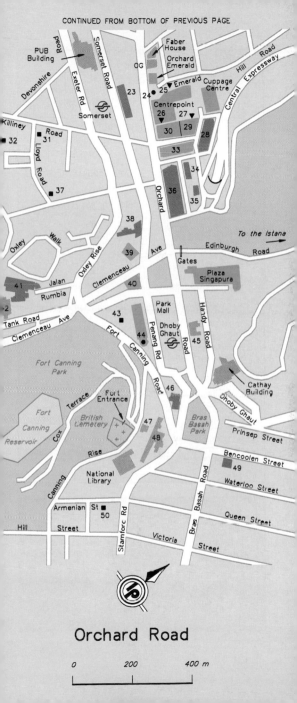

Orchard Road

0   200   400 m

MAP 6
ORCHARD ROAD

■ PLACES TO STAY

1 Hotel Premier
2 ANA Hotel
3 Ladyhill Hotel
4 Shangri-La Hotel
5 Omni Marco Polo Hotel
6 Regent Hotel
7 Orchard Hotel
8 Orchard Parade Hotel
9 Boulevard Hotel
11 Hotel Negara
12 Hilton International Hotel
13 Royal Holiday Inn Crowne Plaza
14 Goodwood Park Hotel
16 Hyatt Regency Hotel
17 Dynasty Hotel
18 York Hotel
19 Crown Prince Hotel
20 Mandarin Hotel
22 Cairnhill Hotel
23 Hotel Phoenix
28 Holiday Inn Park View
31 Mario-Ville Boarding House
32 Mitre Hotel
34 Hotel Grand Central
35 Supreme Hotel
36 Le Meridien Hotel
37 Lloyd's Inn
38 Cockpit Hotel
41 Imperial Hotel
43 YWCA
46 YMCA
49 Bayview Inn
50 Mayfair City Hotel

▼ PLACES TO EAT

10 Hard Rock Cafe
25 Azizas Restaurant
26 Saxophone Bar & Grill
27 Cuppage Thai Food Restaurant

OTHER

15 STPB Tourist Office
21 Singapore Airlines
24 Peranakan Place
29 Cuppage Plaza
30 Orchard Point
33 Orchard Plaza
39 House of Tan Yeok Nee
40 Singapore Shopping Centre
42 Chettiar Hindu Temple
44 Supreme House
45 MacDonald House
47 Drama Centre
48 National Museum & Art Gallery

Souvenirs, Chinatown (RN)

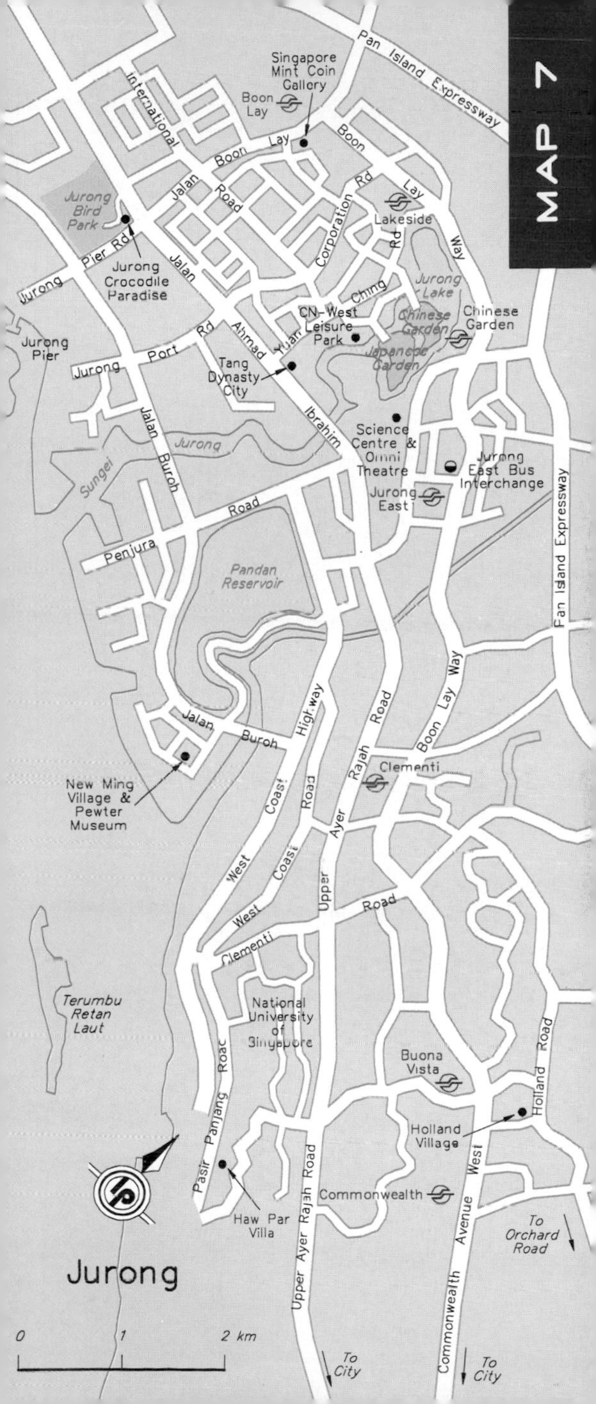

MAP 7

Pan Island Expressway

Singapore
Mint Coin
Gallery

Boon
Lay

Boon

Lay
Way

International

Jalan

Boon

Lay

Road

Corporation

Rd

Lakeside

Jalan

Pier Rd

Jurong
Bird
Park

Ching

Jurong
Lake

Chinese
Garden

Jurong

Jurong
Crocodile
Paradise

Jalan

Ahmad

Jalan

CN-West
Leisure
Park

Chinese
Garden

Jurong
Pier

Jurong

Port

Rd

Tang
Dynasty
City

Ibrahim

Japanese
Garden

Jalan

Jurong

Rd

Science
Centre &
Omni
Theatre

Jurong
East Bus
Interchange

Sungei

Jalan Buroh

Road

Jurong
East

Jurong

Penjura

Pandan
Reservoir

Pan Island Expressway

Jalan

Buroh

Highway

Road

Boon Lay Way

New Ming
Village &
Pewter
Museum

Coast

Rajah

Clementi

West

Coast

Road

Ayer

West

Clementi

Road

Upper

Terumbu
Retan
Laut

National
University
of
Singapore

Buona
Vista

Holland

Road

Pasir

Panjang

Road

Upper

Ayer

Rajah

Road

Holland
Village

Haw Par
Villa

Commonwealth

Avenue

West

Commonwealth

To
Orchard
Road

Jurong

0   1   2 km

To
City

To
City

MAP 8

Tanah Merah

Bedok Road

Upper Changi Road

Bedok South Road

New Upper Changi Road

Bedok

Bedok South Avenue

Coast Road

Upper East Coast Road

Siglap Road

Siglap Canal

Kembangan

Telok Kurau Road

Paya Lebar Way

Eunos

Still Road

1 ▶

2 ▶

3 ●

4 ■

Joo Chiat Road

Tanjong Katong Road

6 ●

5 ●

7 ▲

8 ▲

9 ▲

10 ▲

11 ▲
12 ●
13 ▲

East Coast Road

Marine Parade Road

14 ■

19 ●

Amber Rd

15 ◀

Haig Road

Mountbatten Road

Meyer Road

16 ■

17 ●

18 ●

20 ●

East Coast Park

East Coast Parkway

East Coast Parkway

21 ▶

22 ●
23 ▶

24 ▲

Jetty

East Coast Lagoon

Straits of Singapore

Paya Lebar

Aljunied

Sims Avenue

Geylang Road

Guillemard Road

Old Airport Road

Geylang River

East Coast

0   0.5   1.0 km

MAP 8
EAST COAST

■ PLACES TO STAY

4   Lion City Hotel
14 Sea View Hotel, Paramount Hotel
16 Duke Hotel
24 East Coast Campsite

▼ PLACES TO EAT

1   Makan House
2   Geylang Serai Market
6   Guan Hoe Soon Coffee Shop
8   Hok Tong Hin Restaurant
9   Katong Bakery & Confectionary
10 Haadyai Beefball Restaurant
11 Peranakan Inn & Lounge
13 House of Sundanese Food
21 UDMC Seafood Centre
23 Food Stalls

OTHER

3   Malay Cultural Village
5   Hollywood Theatre
7   Senpaga Vinayagar Temple
12 Katong Antique House
15 Sri Guru Nanak Sat Sangh Sabha
17 Singapore Crocodilarium
18 Big Splash
19 Parkway Parade Shopping Centre
20 East Coast Recreation Centre
22 East Coast Sailing Centre

Temple Roof (PT)

MAP 9

Sentosa Island

MAP 9

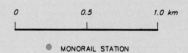

● MONORAIL STATION

Eu Tong Sen Street (RN)

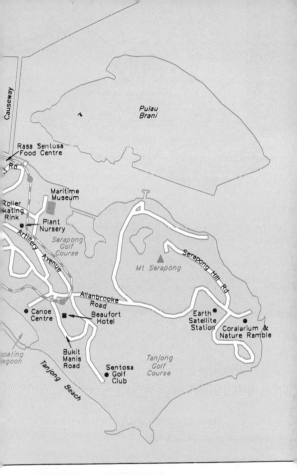

Pulau
Brani

Rasa Sentosa
Food Centre

Rd

Roller
Skating
Rink

Maritime
Museum

Plant
Nursery

Serapong
Golf
Course

Mt Serapong

Serapong Hill Rd

Artillery Avenue

Attanbrooke
Road

Canoe
Centre

Beaufort
Hotel

Earth
Satellite
Station

Coralarium &
Nature Ramble

Causeway

oating
agoon

Bukit
Manis
Road

Tanjong Beach

Sentosa
Golf
Club

Tanjong
Golf
Course

Masks, Chinatown (RN)

MAP 10

To Kuala
Lumpur
(75 km)

Segamat

MELAKA

Muar

Pulau
Rupat

Batu
Paha

STRAITS

OF

MELAKA

Pulau
Bengkalis

INDONESIA

Pulau
Padang

Pulau
Rangsang

Around
Singapore

Pulau
Tebingtiggi

0   25   50 km

Jonkers Melaka Restoran, Melaka (TW)

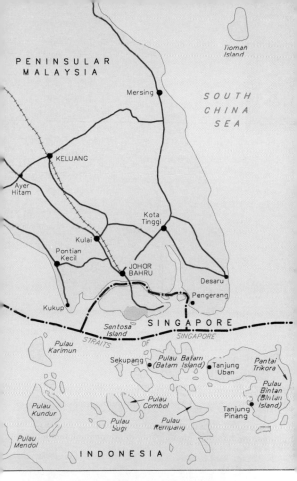

Haw Par Villa (TW)

MAP 11

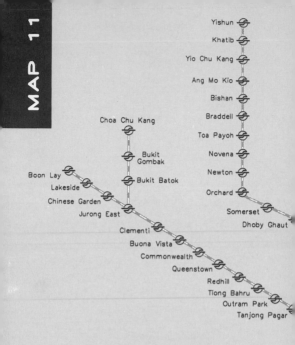

Yishun
Khatib
Yio Chu Kang
Ang Mo Kio
Bishan
Braddell
Toa Payoh
Novena
Newton
Orchard
Somerset
Dhoby Ghaut

Choa Chu Kang
Bukit Gombak
Bukit Batok

Boon Lay
Lakeside
Chinese Garden
Jurong East
Clementi
Buona Vista
Commonwealth
Queenstown
Redhill
Tiong Bahru
Outram Park
Tanjong Pagar

Sri Vadapathira Kaliamman Temple (AR)

Singapore MRT

- Pasir Ris
- Tampines
- Simei
- Tanah Merah
- Bedok
- Kembangan
- Eunos
- Paya Lebar
- Aljunied
- Kallang
- Lavender
- Bugis
- City Hall (Interchange)
- Raffles Place (Interchange)
- Marina Bay

Merlion (PT)

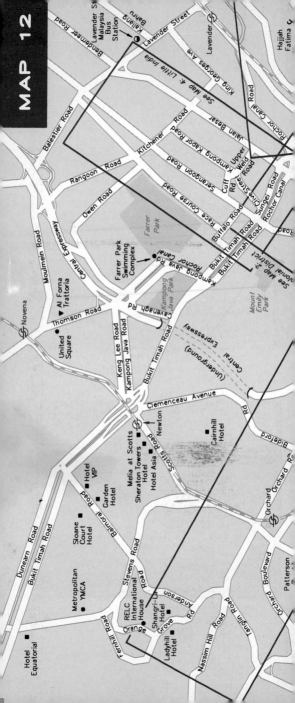

MAP 12

Bendemeer Road
Balestier Road
Lavender St
Malaysia
Bus Station
Lavender Street
Kallang Bahru
Lavender
King Georges Ave
Hajjah
Fatima
See Map 4: Little India
Kitchener Road
Jalan Besar
Serangoon Road
Kampong Kapor Road
Gulf
Rd
Upper
Weld
Weld Rd
Syed Alwi Road
Sungei Road
Rochor Canal Rd
Rochor Canal
Rangoon Road
Race Course Road
Buffalo Road
Owen Road
Farrer
Park
Moulmein Road
Central Expressway
Farrer Park
Swimming
Complex
Kampong Java Rd
Rochor Canal
Kampong Java Park
Bukit Timah Road
Bukit Timah Road
See Map 2:
Colonial District
Mount
Emily
Park
▼ Al Forna
Trattoria
Novena
Thomson Road
Cavenagh Rd
Kampong Java Rd
● United
Square
Keng Lee Road
Kampong Java Road
Bukit Timah Road
Central Expressway
(Underground)
Clemenceau Avenue
Bideford Rd
Newton
● Cairnhill
Hotel
Rd
Orchard Rd
Orchard
■ Hotel
VIP
Melia at Scotts
Sheraton Towers
Hotel
Scotts Rd
Hotel Asia
Peony Rd
Balmoral Rd
■ Garden
Hotel
Dunearn
Road
Bukit Timah Road
Sloane
Court
Hotel
Stevens Road
■ Metropolitan
YMCA
RELC
International
House
Orange
Fernhill Road
■ Shangri-La
Hotel
Grove
Anderson
Rd
Tanglin Road
Orchard Boulevard
Patterson
■ Hotel
Equatorial
■ Ladyhill
Hotel
Nassim Hill Road